SUPERMAN IS JEWISH?

How Comic Book Superheroes
Came to Serve Truth, Justice, and
the Jewish-American Way

HARRY BROD

Free Press

New York London Toronto Sydney New Delhi

*f*P

Free Press
An Imprint of Simon & Schuster, Inc.
1230 Avenue of the Americas
New York, NY 10020

Copyright © 2012 by Harry Brod

First Free Press trade paperback edition January 2016

FREE PRESS and colophon are trademarks of Simon & Schuster, Inc.

For information about special discounts for bulk purchases,
please contact Simon & Schuster Special Sales at 1-866-506-1949 or
business@simonandschuster.com.

The Simon & Schuster Speakers Bureau can bring authors to your
live event. For more information or to book an event, contact the
Simon & Schuster Speakers Bureau at 1-866-248-3049 or
visit our website at www.simonspeakers.com.

Book design by Ellen R. Sasahara

Manufactured in the United States of America

1 3 5 7 9 10 8 6 4 2

The Library of Congress has cataloged the hardcover edition as follows:

Brod, Harry, 1951–
Superman is Jewish? : how comic book superheroes came to serve
truth, justice, and the Jewish-American way / Harry Brod.
p. cm.
1. Comic books, strips, etc.—United States—History and criticism.
2. Superheroes. 3. Jewish cartoonists. 4. Jews—United States—
Intellectual life. I. Title.
PN6725.B75 2012
741.5'973089924—dc23
2012012187

ISBN 978-1-4165-9530-4
ISBN 978-1-4165-9531-1 (pbk)
ISBN 978-1-4165-9845-9 (ebook)

To the owners of Prince and Ginny
and
An die Nachgeborenen
(to the generations to follow)

"Jews created comic books, as best I can tell. Two Jews created Superman. Another created Batman. And a certain Jacob Kurtzberg, who renamed himself Jack Kirby . . . well, don't get me started."

Frank Miller

Eisner/Miller: A One-on-One Interview Conducted by Charles Brownstein, "Introduction"

CONTENTS

CONTENTS

ILLUSTRATIONS

PREFACE

Two roads led to this book.

The longer road reaches all the way back to my childhood love for comic books. As a kid I learned to read from comic books, or at least to improve my reading skills. I remember the first time my parents drove me home from summer camp at age seven. My mother saw me reading a comic in the backseat of the car and asked me what I was doing.

"Reading," I replied brusquely, eager to get back to the story and peeved at being interrupted by such an obvious question.

"You mean you're looking at the pictures."

"No, I'm reading," I insisted, and again buried my head in the comic book.

She had me read aloud to prove it, and made sure my father, in the driver's seat, was listening too.

As I progressed through elementary school I regularly walked the two blocks to the corner luncheonette where I bought my comics from the rack on the wall. I had usually finished one by the time I reached home. (Who says multitasking is new? I could walk and read at the same time.) Somewhere in those years I unwittingly revealed at school what we would now call my comics geekdom. When our teacher had us play Hangman to reinforce our spelling lessons, I wanted to show off what I'd learned from *Superman* comics. I put up the word *invulnerable* to stump my classmates.

The first book that I specifically remember pulling off the bookstore shelf to buy—or rather, to ask my mother to buy for me—is Jules Feiffer's *The Great Comic Book Heroes*.[1] I figure I was around thirteen at the time, and I was amazed that right there, sitting on a shelf near the checkout counter in the Doubleday store on Fifth Avenue in Manhattan, was an actual book about comic books. It was an oversize book, no less, so large that it stood out conspicuously from the other books on the shelf. The Doubleday people seemed unembarrassed openly displaying a book on comic books in their esteemed establishment. Feiffer's way of thinking about comic book superheroes entered my consciousness at such a young age that it became an integral part of how I think about the subject. As far as I'm concerned, his essay in that book remains the greatest thing ever written about comic book superheroes.

Comic books were junk, he said. People need junk, so it's perfectly legitimate to enjoy this junk. Get over it. It was a kind of intellectual jujitsu move. Go with the force of your opponent's attack and turn it against them. If you don't understand the great satisfaction junk brings to people's lives, then that's your deficiency, not mine. When I first read it I was at an age where it was still sort of okay socially to read comics, but you knew that sooner or later you'd be put down for it and you'd need to defend yourself. As I saw it, Feiffer provided an unassailable defense. I could keep to myself the fact that I didn't actually think comics were junk, and adopt this impenetrable public posture. Kind of like the false front I'd keep up when I watched scary movies. I would surreptitiously lower my glasses down my nose, then tilt my head forward and look up at the screen over the rims. I couldn't see a thing up there on the screen, but nobody could catch me looking away.

Feiffer also gave me a model for what I've tried to do in this book: that is to think and write about the comics superheroes who've been my friends for so long in a way that keeps the faith with both my childhood and adult selves. When I start to write about how these stories affected "the reader," I think back to how they affected *me*. And of course I try as best I can not to overgeneralize from my personal idiosyncratic reactions—my memories are just one source of information, to be balanced and augmented by other sources. Nonetheless, they are a valid research resource, and shouldn't be ignored.

It took me quite a while to consider my childhood memories a research resource. When I began my academic career, the study of popular culture wasn't yet as established a field as it is today. Studying culture then meant either studying everyday life (in an anthropological or sociological sense) or studying the "high" culture of "serious" art—music, literature, philosophy, etc. It took the passage of enough time for a body of analytical writing about popular culture to reach a certain critical mass before I started to consider moving my own scholarly pursuits in this direction.

All of us academics have taken part in conversations where, upon meeting other academics, we dutifully inquire about their areas of interest. "What are you working on?" we ask, and we make sure to talk about that topic just long enough not to appear rude. But you should see how faces light up when I say I'm writing about comic books. Especially among guys, eyes that are otherwise fixed in a dull glaze suddenly spark to life: *You mean we're going to get to talk about* comic books *now? Really?* And before I know it, I'm hearing about who their favorite superheroes were, and maybe they still have some of those issues—they hear that some of them are supposed to be valuable now—and on and on.

So why can't we come out of those closets in which we've packed away our pleasures along with those boxes of back issues of *Superboy* and *Spider-Man*? Why can't we have fun writing about comics, even as we make serious points? Part of the problem is the nature of what's become standard style for academic prose. Years ago Stanislav Andreski's book *Social Sciences as Sorcery* explained that much of the social sciences consisted of restating the obvious so as to make it obscure, noting their "pretentious and nebulous verbosity."[2] Unfortunately, that's true of too much of current academic scholarship in general. Extraordinary theoretical sophistication and specialized technical vocabulary are employed to say things that could be easily said without activating all that machinery. When applied to comic books, such pedantry is more than just disappointing. As scholars we're supposed to remain faithful to our source material; if we take the comic out of comic books, we end up falsifying the data. I understand the need to demonstrate the legitimacy of a new field by sounding like the other grown-ups, especially in this case, where we must overcome "the continuing and widespread prejudice that comics are a simplistic and juvenile medium," as it's described in the inaugural editorial of a recently launched academic journal devoted to the study of comics and graphic 'novels.[3] And there is much of great value in this scholarship. But if we're so busy proving that comics should be taken seriously that we forget to appreciate and communicate that they're also fun, we are throwing out the baby with the bathwater.

Pete Seeger once said, when speaking of the songs Woody Guthrie wrote for children: "Any damn fool can get complicated. It takes genius to attain simplicity."[4] We can understand that comics aren't necessarily simplistic, but they're still simplified. Following Seeger's lead means understanding that achieving their simplicity often requires inspired creativity and highly sophisticated techniques worthy of serious examination. Comics art necessarily remains close to the art forms of cartoon and caricature, and these are simplified forms. They're intended to bring smiles to the faces of their viewers precisely by virtue of their simplicity. Every creative form has its limitations, and struggling against those limitations is often precisely what lifts a work out of the pack and elevates it to greatness. That should indeed be appreciated. But the form's intrinsic limits are still there. Let's not forget that in comics we're talking about characters who speak in balloons and who acquire speed lines trailing behind them when they move quickly. Do you really mean to tell me there's nothing inherently comic in all this, that it's not intended to still appeal to the child in us, even when it may also be dealing with serious matters of great note? "Philosophy begins in wonder," said Aristotle, and we should not let our theorizing about comics blind us to the childlike wonderment of it all. Our task here is to unite our simple enchantment with comics with our adult appreciation of how that enchantment was produced.

As a kid I read *Superman* with the same science-fiction mind-set with which he was created. His powers had to make the same kind of scientific sense to me that they did to his initial creators. By the time I arrived on the scene, what had started as Superman's power of leaping over tall buildings had long since escalated into his flying powers that we now take for granted. While I would have understood the leaping, this flying thing perplexed me. I kept puzzling away at it, until I thought I had it figured out in my young mind. While the more stereotypical comic fanboy obsessions were about comparative power—who could beat up who—I was more concerned with puzzling out how each of these superheroes' powers worked, with analytically taking each one apart. It's my childhood version of what motivates this book, trying to figure out from the inside what really makes the whole thing work. Here, then, presented for your reading pleasure and revealed for the first time ever, is my boyhood explanation of how Superman flew. I'm still proud of it.

It seemed to me he must fly like a jet. That meant he took in air up front, and somehow sent it out through the back. I figured he must do that through the pores in his skin. In humans they excrete sweat, and do so involuntarily. But Kryptonians must be wired differently. Superman didn't sweat (well, we sure never saw him sweat), so it made sense that in the Kryptonian body the pores might excrete air instead, and could be brought under voluntary control, like breathing.

So full throttle meant mouth wide-open, and low cruising speed meant breathing through the nose. We knew he had super breath, so sucking in sufficient quantities of air would pose no problem.

So there's my childhood theory of how Superman flew, in all its glowing creativity and boyhood thoroughness, my own personal contribution to the Superman lore, revealed here for the very first time anywhere. Super flying was really a variation of super sweating. Having thus thought it all through to my satisfaction, I could now go back to enjoying *Superman,* in good conscience and full confidence that I wasn't giving up my rational mind to do so, good science-fiction fan that I was.

Comics didn't just fuel what scientific interests I had. I attribute much of my motivation to become a philosopher by profession to my early reading of science-fiction and comic books. The world need not be as it was. There were alternative possibilities, reached not by fantasy but by rational extension of the world we knew. "What if . . ." became a guiding question for me, and wanting to think that through became second nature.

The second road leading to this book was the one that led me to write specifically about the Jewish aspects of comics. I'd known for a long time that many of the writers and artists behind comics were Jews. At first that knowledge was simply a matter of a kind of ethnic pride. But then my scholarly work led me to explore issues of gender, race, and class, especially in the emerging field of men's studies, or masculinity studies. I became aware of how societies are dominated by certain mainstream ideals of how men should be, "hegemonic" masculinity, in the theoretical terminology that was developed to talk about this. Part of the way that domination works is that even groups of men who don't fit the dominant model, who are marginalized by their race, ethnicity, class, sexual orientation, physical appearance, or ability, and other subordinate categories, still measure themselves by that dominant model. So it isn't just other groups oppressing them that judged such men to be not "real" men; they themselves internalize those standards too. Now I had new things to think about. The Jewish men who created supermen were men who were themselves seen as not measuring up to the standards of what real men were supposed to be. They—we—were seen as bookworms, timid, not athletic, and all the other stereotypes about Jewish men. Hmm. Less-than-real men creating supermen. Now that sounded interesting. And worth looking into further.

So now you know the kind of background that eventually leads to a book like this. Welcome to my worlds. Up, up, and away!

INTRODUCTION

S uperman is Jewish?
A surprising question, one that takes a certain amount of chutzpah to even raise. To add even a bit more chutzpah, this book considers questions about the Jewishness of more superheroes than just Superman, and offers answers that will surprise many.

You mean Spider-Man is Jewish too? Well, actually, yes, but in a very different way than Superman is. And, as we'll see, the shift between them reflects the evolution of Jewish life in America itself in the generation between the two, the generation that gets us from World War II and the "Golden Age" of comics to the 1960s and the "Silver Age" of comics. The historical turning points of those tumultuous years and others, like the powerful 1950s crusade against comics for supposedly causing juvenile delinquency, turn out to be central to our story because these events, and their great impact on American Jews, appear on comic book pages themselves, and behind the scenes in their production. For it turns out that the history of Jews and comic book superheroes, that very American invention, is the history of Jews and America, particularly the history of Jewish assimilation into the mainstream of American culture.

There's even more to this history. We'll see how the story of Jews and comics in America actually starts back in Europe, in literary and artistic traditions that inform the stories the pioneer Jews told, and illustrated, to create comic book superheroes. Here we'll find a mystical legend from the Old Country transmuted to emerge in the new world as a foundational inspiration for modern superheroes. We'll see that these superheroes owe their origins to an American science-fiction tradition that has surprising connections to Jewish modes of thought.

And throughout, we'll come to understand that in many surprising ways the bad guys superheroes fight against are, in the final analysis, those people who have oppressed the Jewish people for centuries.

We'll also pursue our story further than just superheroes, looking at some more fully realized and sophisticated portrayals of Jewish life in graphic novels both in the U.S. and abroad. We'll see how two giants of the comics industry came to create wonderful graphic novels illuminating important Jewish topics. We'll take a voyage to discover some treasures that are relatively unknown in the U.S., traveling to France to discover Jewish aspects in amazingly creative stories of dungeons, vampires, and a rabbi's cat, and to Israel to see the extraordinary recent flourishing of creativity in Israeli graphic novels, and the first full-length "animated documentary" of international cinema that evolved from it. Finally, we'll spend some time with two Pulitzer Prize–winning books, one a Jewish comic book and the other a novel about the Jewish guys who created comic book superheroes.

To return to my opening question about Superman being Jewish, it's said that Jews typically answer a question with another question, so here's my answer to that opening question: What on Earth or on Krypton would it even mean to say that Superman is Jewish? For that matter, what does it mean to place any creative work within the tradition of a certain people? What do people really mean when they say that a particular novel, play, painting, etc. is Jewish, or African-American, or whatever? One approach to the question of what makes something Jewish is biographical, based on the identities of the creators. It seems this is what many people assume I mean when I say that Superman is Jewish. Oh yes, they say, they had heard that he was created by Jewish guys. Framed this way, anything created by a Jew is Jewish, just as anything by an African-American would be part of African-American culture, etc.

Well, this definition certainly has clarity going for it, which is a point in its favor. But it brings with it its own set of problems. For one, it's pretty restrictive. Jazz and the blues are recognized as African-American art forms. But does this mean that whites can't play in these genres? Tell that to John Mayall or Eric Clapton. Does it mean that African-

American clarinetist Don Byron's klezmer music isn't really klezmer because he's not Jewish? (I defy anyone to tell me that an album titled *The Music of Mickey Katz* isn't Jewish music.) And this definition has problems going in the other direction too. Not only does this assume that Jewish art can only be created by Jews, it also assumes that everything created by Jews is Jewish. But can't Jews ever step outside of their Jewish identity? Let's say (getting totally hypothetical here) that my true passion is painting pastoral landscapes of the cornfields near my office at the University of Northern Iowa. Could we really claim these as necessarily Jewish paintings? Can't Jews create some works that really aren't Jewish? And what about cases where we're not sure who created a work of art? Would that mean we therefore can't say anything about how it might embody a certain tradition? This approach is just too simplistic.

A different approach to deciding whether a work is Jewish is to look for explicit Jewish references in the piece, typically characters identified as Jewish or references to Jewish religious practices, perhaps the use of Yiddish or Hebrew phrases, etc. This is the approach taken by Jack Dann in two edited volumes, *Wandering Stars: An Anthology of Jewish Fantasy & Science Fiction* and *More Wandering Stars: An Anthology of Outstanding Stories of Jewish Fantasy and Science Fiction*.[1] These short stories provide a good range of examples of such explicitly Jewish tales: Many of these stories simply transport to outer space common themes in Jewish literature. For example, some adapt tales of a golem or dybbuk, mythological Jewish figures, while others use new settings to raise the old question, Who is a Jew? which is often a contentious issue here on Earth. These stories play off Jewish traditions of Talmudic disputation, which encourages thoughtful debate, so when two camps argue it out when nonhuman aliens who have been inspired by some far-wandering Jew seek to be recognized as Jews, we get familiar divisions between more inclusive versus more restrictive tendencies. One group argues that the people of Israel must obviously be people, so the idea of alien Jews is unacceptable, indeed offensive. The other side responds with classic Jewish fidelity to the text: Show me where it's written that Jews can't have, say, short gray tentacles jutting out of small bodies that look like wrinkled brown pillows, instead of human torsos, arms, and legs? Since such a proof text obviously can't be found, the universalist sentiment wins the day, and the new Jews are accepted as members of the tribe.[2] Explicit Jewish references such as these certainly provide legitimate reasons for flagging a story as Jewish. But even this doesn't get us far enough. It doesn't get us to what's implicit, below the surface. And as is true in many areas, what lies below the surface is often of much greater significance than what's readily visible up top. So let's dig deeper into the question of what might make Superman Jewish.

It seems to me that a reasonable answer to the question of what makes a work of art Jewish would take something from both of these approaches, but would also reject much of each. To reasonably claim a work as belonging to a particular tradition—Jewish, in this case—we should be primarily looking at the work itself, not its creators. Firstly, one should be able to see that Jewish themes or ideas are central to the work. These themes need not be explicitly named as Jewish within the work; they simply need to be present. It may therefore require some analysis of the work, conducted against a background of some knowledge of Jewish traditions, before the work becomes visible as Jewish. Secondly, one should be able to see some line of transmission by which the creators could plausibly have come into contact with these Jewish elements, accounting for the possibility of their presence in the work. If the creators are in fact Jewish, that makes this task easier, but it doesn't exclude non-Jews from creating work that could be counted as part of a Jewish tradition. Looking at it this way saves us from the twin dangers of claiming either too much or too little for Jewish traditions, on the one hand being blind to what's there versus on the other hand imagining what isn't really there. The first content-based criterion implies that not everything created by Jews should be counted as part of Jewish tradition, and that seems right to me. The second modified biographical criterion serves as a check against granting everyone a blanket license to just read whatever they wish into a work without offering any plausible account of how the meaning they're attributing to the work could possibly have gotten in there.

Here's an example, from a very different kind of work, which may help clarify what I mean when I say that the ethnic identity of the people doing the work does not by itself determine the ethnic nature of the work. In the earlier decades of the twentieth century there was a stereotypical image in U.S. cities of the Irish cop out on the beat. There was indeed a high proportion of Irishmen in the police forces at that time, caused in large part by how the timing of waves of immigrants from Ireland meshed with an expansion of urban police forces. But the large presence of the Irish policemen didn't by itself make policing Irish.

This biographical background only gets you as far as saying that these were cops doing their jobs, who happened to be Irish. One could only reasonably see this as Irish policing if it turned out that there was something in how they went about their policing that was in some way distinctively Irish. Now, I don't know enough about either policing or the Irish to know if this was so or not. The Irish cop had a reputation for both toughness and tenderness, meted out to individuals as he saw fit by his own standards. One could consider whether this might have its roots in the Irish experience, perhaps in a certain relationship to authority or in an allegiance to local neighborhood identities. If this image of the Irish cop were more than a stereotype, if it accurately captured some social realities, understanding that it of course didn't apply to all Irish cops but would have been valid only as a sort of sociological generalization, then one could indeed legitimately speak of Irish policing in our urban centers at this time. But to be clear, it's not just the presence of Irish police that would make this policing Irish. It would be the visibility of the Irish influence in the activity itself, coupled with an explanation of how it got there.

For me, it's not enough to pick any random tangential detail and blow it up out of proportion to make a claim that a story is Jewish. You can't legitimately claim, as the author of one book on Jewish aspects of comic book superheroes does, that Spider-Man is Jewish because there's a story about King David once being saved by a spider who hid him from enemy soldiers by spinning a web across the entrance of a cave.[3] By that logic, *Charlotte's Web* is a Jewish story too, but it's hard to see how a story about a pig could be kosher.

Let's look more closely at these criteria. Suppose, for example, that we find a story in which a superhero from an alien race becomes romantically involved with a human, and is getting grief about it from others of his kind. Well, yes, that's similar to what many Jews have experienced from their families when the question of intermarriage comes up, but that's not enough in itself for this to be called a Jewish story. There are simply too many other cultures where you'd find the same dynamic of intragroup solidarity coupled with a suspicion of outsiders. If it's just a question of us versus them, that doesn't get us any further than the Montagues and Capulets of *Romeo and Juliet* or the Jets and Sharks of the updated musical version of that tale, *West Side Story*. But if the tale lets us know that the objections to the romance with the outsider come from a group who have been historically persecuted by the very group to which the beloved belongs, then we're getting closer to its being a Jewish story. And if we know that the creators of the tale have come under the influence of Jewish culture, either because they're Jewish themselves or because they've been significantly exposed to Jewish culture, then I'm prepared to lend a sympathetic ear to someone who makes the case that this should be understood as a Jewish story. And if, furthermore, it turns out that this history of persecution in this fictional story has been accompanied by negative stereotypes that are undeniably similar to the stereotypes we find in the actual history of anti-Semitism, then you'll find me fully ready to sign on the dotted line of an affirmation that this is indeed a Jewish story.

One final example, involving an iconic American character who is not explicitly identified as Jewish, will help to further clarify the nature of this book. I turn our attention to what is often regarded as the classic play of the American theater, Arthur Miller's *Death of a Salesman*. Published discussions of whether Willy Loman is really Jewish, as is his creator, can now fill a fairly lengthy bookshelf.

The play opened on Broadway in 1949, and the Yiddish theater production opened in Brooklyn in 1951. George Ross, who reviewed that production for *Commentary*, the magazine published by the American Jewish Committee, makes his opinion clear in the title of his review:

"*Death of a Salesman* in the Original."[4] Ross's thesis is that *Toyt fun a Salesman* (the Yiddish title) "is really the original, and the Broadway production was merely—Arthur Miller's translation into English."[5]

Ross offers many example of how in the Yiddish translation one more poignantly becomes aware of Willy Loman as

> a Jewish salesman in America striving proudly and defensively to hold together his scattered family and himself, wandering all the cities . . . trying desperately to be "known," "liked," accepted, and incidentally "not laughed at" . . . Recall also Willy's exaggerated Americanism and his excessive attachment to his father through his older brother; his intense preoccupation with American sports and American gadgets, the "well-advertised refrigerator"; his unhappy dependence on the pinochle-playing Charley and Charley's *yeshiva bocher* son, Bernard.[6] [The "yeshiva bocher" is a student in a religious school, here used semi-pejoratively for an overly studious one.]

He even gives examples of Miller's specific language, claiming that it is "in the English version as if Miller were thinking in Yiddish and unconsciously translating." For example, Linda's "impassioned 'attention must be paid,' while not at all unlikely in English, is not so embedded in the language and so frighteningly strong as 'gib achtung'."[7] And to Ross's example of how the original English is really an unconscious translation of a more original Yiddish I would add another: Since when does a supposedly all-American guy sitting in a restaurant call another man's attention to an attractive woman entering the establishment by referring to her as "strudel"?

When the direct question was put to him of whether he intentionally made Willy Loman Jewish, as it was on a number of occasions, Miller replied that he wasn't thinking of him that way consciously. But he nonetheless did not dismiss such an interpretation, and indeed sanctioned it. Witness this exchange during a question-and-answer session:

Audience Member: In an essay by fellow playwright David
Mamet about *Death of a Salesman,* he wrote: "The greatest
American play, arguably, is the story of a Jew told by a Jew
and cast in 'universal' terms. Willy Loman is a Jew in a Jewish industry. But he is never identified as such. His story is
never avowed as a Jewish story, and so a great contribution
to Jewish-American history is lost. It's lost to culture as a
whole, and, more importantly, it's lost to the Jews, its rightful
owners." I wonder how you feel about that?

Arthur Miller: Well, he got it, so it couldn't have been lost.
I mean, what more could anyone want?[8]

Note that nobody here is trying to reduce *Death of a Salesman* to being
merely a Jewish story. We still fully acknowledge and value its univer-
sality. To claim it as Jewish is to add a layer of understanding, not to
pigeonhole it away from the mainstream.

The notion of Miller's "unconscious translation" from Yiddish to
English or Jewish to Gentile context seems to me very useful in explaining how Superman is rooted in the Jewishness of his creators. It's not
that they consciously set out to create a Jewish superhero. Creativity
doesn't work that way; so much of it takes place at the unconscious
level. Contexts and backgrounds seep into creative work in much more
subtle ways.

Jews as a people lost a precious bridge to their history in the Holocaust, and many of the traditions and characteristics of Jewish culture
have been lost, either in their entirety, or in being recognized as Jewish.
It is the aim of this book to see to it that the stories of Superman and
other comic book superheroes not be similarly lost as they are assimilated into mainstream culture. This is an exercise in reclamation.

So that's what this book is about. Maybe this is the time to also say
something about what it is not about. First, I'm not attempting to
deliver a Who's Who of Jews in comics. While we will indeed at times

focus on key individuals, this book fundamentally isn't a chronicle of the Jews in comics, it's a story of the influence of Judaism and Jewishness on comics. (Judaism is a religion, Jewishness is an affiliated culture). Second, this pursues Jewish aspects of the history of comic book superheroes—it doesn't pretend to be a comprehensive account covering all other aspects of the history of the field. I also want to say that when I discuss the fantasized cartoon violence of the comic book superheroes created by these Jewish men, this should not be equated with actual violence. The approach I take here, which valorizes the ways Jewish men expressed a fight against anti-Semitism through their fantasy comic book creations, is not the same as endorsing the use of violence. Barbara Breitman articulates the distinction in her analysis of psychological dimensions of Jewish men and violence: "Owning the capacity to do violence must not be misconstrued as *being* violent."[9] I'm situating the meaning of good guys beating up bad guys in the context of a Jewish people with a history of anti-Semitic violence practiced against them. I imagine that endorsing a "beat 'em up" approach to solving issues has a very different meaning for those coming from a dominant culture, and analyzing that meaning is beyond the scope of this book. In mainstream U.S. culture the problematic aspects of superhero violence were not addressed by the medium itself until the maturation of the post–Vietnam War and post-Watergate generation, first emerging most strikingly in Alan Moore and Dave Gibbons' *Watchmen* and Frank Miller's *Batman: The Dark Knight Returns*. As we'll see later, in Israel it similarly took the maturing of a generation of artists who grew up with the occupation to express their concerns about societal violence in the form of graphic novels.

I hope the above orients the reader to how I'm approaching the question of Jews and comics in this book. The question of the Jewish influence on comic book superheroes did indeed first enter my mind because I knew about the Jewishness of the creators. But as I was writing this book I kept asking myself, "Do I see something in the work itself that would lead me to look for a Jewish influence in its creation even if I didn't know in advance of the Jewish presence behind the scenes?" As I say in the first chapter, the Jewishness of his creators explains how Superman got to be Jewish, but what I mean by his Jewishness is in the character himself.

There are many ways of being Jewish and many ways of being a superhero, so it shouldn't be surprising that there are many ways in which Jewishness can emerge in comics and graphic novels. Sometimes it's submerged and sometimes explicit; sometimes it's humorous and sometimes serious; sometimes it's in response to specific historical events and sometimes it's a reflection of ancient ideas. Sometimes it's in the story and sometimes in the art; sometimes it's claimed by the artists and writers and sometimes it's disavowed. But if you know what to look for, it's always interesting, and sometimes quite pleasantly surprising.

Throughout I am trying to present a new way of seeing the Jewish dimensions in Superman, in comic book superheroes more broadly, and in the graphic novels I discuss. If I'm successful, readers of this book should come to see and appreciate these characters and works with greater insight, and perhaps understand a bit more about the patterns of Jewish life reflected in the adventures of these characters, and about how the people of the book became the people of the comic book.

Superman is Jewish?

From Dave Sim's *Judenhass* (German for "Jew Hatred"):

Every creative person should consider doing a work addressing the Shoah [Holocaust] . . . this is nowhere truer than here in the comic-book field which was created, developed and built primarily by Jews. . . . But for geographic happenstance and the grace of God, any one of these ordinary men [at Auschwitz] could have just as easily been . . .

. . . JACK KIRBY OR JOE SIMON: THE CO-CREATORS OF CAPTAIN AMERICA; JERRY SIEGEL OR JOE SHUSTER, THE CO-CREATORS OF SUPERMAN; BOB KANE, THE CREATOR OF BATMAN...OR STAN LEE, THE CO-CREATOR OF SPIDER-MAN... OR WILL EISNER...OR COUNTLESS OTHERS

JOE SIMON

JACK KIRBY

STAN LEE

JOE SHUSTER

WILL EISNER

JERRY SIEGEL

BOB KANE

MAX GAINES

SHELDON MAYER

Dave Sim, Jewish comic book creators.

1

SUPERMAN AS SUPERMENTSH *

How the Ultimate Alien Became
the Iconic All-American

S uperman is one of the most well-known fictional figures in the
world. We all know who he is. Or at least we think we do. In the
timeless words of the 1950s TV series, he's "a strange visitor from
another planet who came to Earth with powers and abilities far beyond
those of mortal men." But those who are used to the current scope of
Superman's powers—where he's capable of performing such feats as
flying into a blazing sun, freezing a lake with his super breath or lifting
mountains—may be surprised to learn that in his original comic book
incarnation his powers were much less expansive: "He could hurdle
skyscrapers, leap an eighth of a mile, raise tremendous weights, run
faster than a streamline engine, and nothing less than a bursting shell
could penetrate his skin."**[1]

For those reading comics in 1938, Superman was much more than

---

* *Mentsh* is Yiddish for "human being," usually used to mean an ethical person, as in,
"You're a real mentsh for taking care of me when I was sick."

** This last was illustrated by a puzzled doctor in white holding Superman's arm and
exclaiming, "What th—? This is the sixth hypodermic needle I've broken on your skin!"
while Superman grins mischievously and says, "Try again, Doc!"

just a new super character. He inaugurated the entire genre of comic book superheroes. Prior to this, heroes of adventure comic strips or books had been detectives, cops, cowboys, pirates, magicians, soldiers, etc. No one had seen a costumed figure with superpowers before.

At the time, "comics" meant the comic strips found in newspapers. Comic books, to the extent they existed at all, were mostly just reprints of the newspaper strips bound together. But all that changed when magazine distributor and publisher Jack Liebowitz was looking for a lead player for a different type of comic book that would feature stories that appeared first in this bound form.

These new comic books were part of a new fusion of words and pictures that was in the air in the 1930s. "Talking pictures" (instead of silent films) had just appeared, with *The Jazz Singer* premiering in 1927. *Steamboat Willie,* Disney's first cartoon featuring Mickey Mouse, came out the next year, and was the first animated short film with a sound track that was entirely synchronized. *Life* magazine, with its new and distinctive brand of photojournalism, premiered in 1936, and was a great success—appearing in *Life* became synonymous with having made it into the American cultural mainstream. Advertising was taking off, with ever more elaborate illustrations in magazines and roadside billboards.

In that context, comic books are clearly the runt of the litter. The comics industry came out of the streets of Lower Manhattan, mostly from Jews and Italians who were one step away from the immigrant experience and two steps away from social respectability.[2] Poor Jews from immigrant backgrounds ended up finding their way into this ragged end of publishing, what we might call rag, or *shmate,* publishing, since the Yiddish word *shmate* has the same dual meaning as the English word *rag,* meaning, literally, a throwaway piece of cloth and, by extension, a junky, throwaway publication. Businessmen like Liebowitz and Harry Donnenfeld, who came to be behind Superman's publication, also published girlie magazines and pulp fiction with names like *Spicy Detective Stories.* And more than a few of them had mob connections.

As Al Jaffee, later of *Mad* magazine fame, put it, "We couldn't get into newspaper strips or advertising; ad agencies wouldn't hire a Jew.

2

One of the reasons we Jews drifted into the comic-book business is that most of the comic-book publishers were Jewish. So there was no discrimination there."[3]

Comics historians offer other theories linking the predominance of Jews in the early comics industry to the Jewish attraction to communicative media more generally. Gerald Jones notes that of all the immigrant cultures of the period, the Jews were the most literate population. Trina Robbins attributes Jewish communicative skills to the need to be able to talk yourself out of getting beaten up. Journalist Jay Schwartz writes of the founding generation of comics creators: "They came from homes where Yiddish was shouted across the dining room table, along with at least one other language. That—plus English lessons outside the home and Hebrew to boot—made for multilingual youngsters keen on the Sock! Zoom! Bam! power of language."[4]

These Jewish comic book creators forged a road into American culture in much the same way the Jewish immigrants who became the founding moguls of the American film industry did, with Lower Manhattan as their Hollywood. Motion pictures came out of cheap nickelodeon and peep show entertainments whose primary audience was single men, mostly working class, and largely immigrants. A good deal of the content was pretty lurid for its time—not unlike the girlie magazines or the pulps. It was primarily the Jewish entrepreneurs who became the movie moguls—men like Adolph Zukor, William Fox, Carl Laemmle, and Samuel Goldwyn—who had a vision of the greater commercial possibilities if it could be transformed into more socially acceptable mass family entertainment.[5] Likewise with the comics. Personally marginalized out of the mainstream by their foreign backgrounds, the publishers and artists created an alternate, idealized version of America, with larger-than-life idols soaring above the audiences below on the movie screen, on the comics page, and above all in their imaginations. Their strategy of assimilation by idealization worked. As audiences accepted the idealized images these Jews created, these new cultural icons became the vehicles through which these marginalized Jews were able to enter the cultural mainstream. Shut out of the centers of American culture, they created new cultural forms to bring America to them.[6]

In this period of the birth of comic books, the team of Jerry Siegel as writer and Joe Shuster as artist had been working together on trying to create successful comic strips since they met at Glenville High School in Cleveland, a school with a large Jewish population, reflecting the surrounding neighborhood. Now twenty-three, they'd had earlier success placing some strips, most notably one chronicling the adventures of their character Slam Bradley, who, as his name suggests, was a tough slugger of a detective, as well as others including *Federal Men, Henri Duval, Radio Squad, Spy,* and *Dr. Mystic: The Occult Detective.*[7] The strip they were peddling now was just too different from what any newspaper was running to find any takers. But it turned out to be just the thing for this new idea of a comic book with new stories.

Among their new hero's powers, the notion of being impervious to bullets had a powerful personal dimension for Jerry Siegel. Jerry's father, Mitchell (originally Mikhel Segalovich of Lithuania), had worked as a sign painter for a time, and encouraged his son's artistic interests. But eventually Mitchell had to give up his more artistic side for the more secure living of running a secondhand-clothing store. Mitchell Siegel died as a result of a nighttime robbery at his store, although stories vary as to whether his death was caused directly by the bullets that were fired or as a result of a heart attack brought on by the event. Whatever the actual facts, the story that many in the family were told and believed was that he was murdered and died from a gunshot wound. Siegel never spoke about it publicly, but the earliest version of Superman that we know about appeared shortly thereafter, illustrated with a drawing of Superman swooping in to stop an armed robbery.[8]

Joe Shuster's father, meanwhile, had arrived in Toronto from Rotterdam, the Netherlands, where the family had had a cinema and hotel. In Toronto he found work as a movie theater projectionist. The family then moved to Cleveland when Joe was nine. Of the two, Jerry was the more outgoing and assertive, while Joe was more shy and retiring. Both were physically small, and uninterested in physically rough competitive sports. Joe was severely nearsighted, and tried to make up for being physically slight by getting into the bodybuilding fad that was popular at the time. They met while working on their school newspaper, *The Torch*. But the school paper wasn't enough for them, and they became active in the new world of the mimeographed and then mailed pages that came to be called the "fanzines" of the science-fiction pulp magazines. Through this they first met other science-fiction fans, some of them later becoming men who would play major roles in the early comics field.

It was in one sense natural to find Jews making illustrated books. The biblical admonition against making graven images or idols had caused a lack of much of a real visual arts tradition among European Jews. In contrast to literature and music, the visual arts were relatively underdeveloped. One of the few outlets for Jewish visual artists was the illustrated book, which was deemed kosher in the culture of the people of the book. This art had thrived particularly in illustrating the Passover Haggadah, the book that guides the service at the celebratory, highly ritualized Passover meal. The Haggadah, what I'll call in this context the first "graphic novel," tells a story in both words and pictures, so that those sitting at the table who are too young to read can follow along. The story is the tale of Moses, sent off in a small vessel by his parents to save him from the death and destruction facing his people. He is then raised among people to whom he really is an alien, but who do not suspect his secret identity, and he grows up to become a liberator and champion of the oppressed, with the aid of miraculous superpowers displayed in some truly memorable action scenes. Sound at all familiar?

Who knows what lurked in the memories of young Jerry Siegel and Joe Shuster when they created their tale of immigrant refugee baby Kal-El's arrival on Earth? Can it really be coincidental that Kal-El's original Kryptonian name spoken with a Hebrew pronunciation sounds like the Hebrew words for "all is God" or "all for God"? Is it just chance that he is sent from an old world, Krypton, that is about to explode, to a new one, Earth (which could readily be seen as standing for Europe, on the verge of self-destruction, and America, with its promise of new life, especially in those 1930s)? And is the name of his home planet really a secret invitation to decode Superman's encrypted secret identity as a crypto-Jew (Jews who, since the days of the Spanish Inquisition, have publicly given up their faith to escape persecution, but who remain Jews in their private lives and personal allegiance)?

Traditional comics lore gives the major credit for Siegel and Shuster's finally securing publication for *Superman* to an ex-schoolteacher named Maxwell Charles Ginsberg, who changed his name to Gaines when he went into business as a salesman peddling cheap goods in various and sundry enterprises because Gaines sounded better than Ginsberg, meaning it sounded less Jewish. Among other things, Gaines became a comics packager and producer, obtaining material from writers and artists and selling it to publishers. He had Siegel and Shuster's submission of their *Superman* strip, but it was editor Sheldon (Shelly) Mayer, himself even younger than Siegel and Shuster, who saw its potential and selected it.[9]

The boys had mixed feelings when they received the offer. After multiple rejections, they were pleased that this work was finally being accepted. But they were disappointed that it was appearing in a mere comic book, not being placed with a syndicate for newspaper distribution, the holy grail for aspiring artists like themselves, because that was how you acquired both artistic recognition and financial reward. To fit the new format, Siegel and Shuster literally cut up the strips they had drawn for the newspapers and pasted their work into the page format of the new comic book. The comics page format was so new then that when the layout departed from the linear strip format to even a small degree, some artists inserted arrows leading from one panel to the next or even numbered the panels because they didn't think the reader would be able to follow the sequence.[10] If you scan the sequence of those panels today you'll find they still embody the rhythm of a strip: four panels per day, with the fourth stopping at the best mini-cliffhanger they could muster. Then restart at that point the next day, count four, stop. The rhythm broke on Sundays, when there was more space. But then it was back to the same rhythm. Repeat until done.

Siegel and Shuster worked frantically on a tight deadline, cutting and pasting their strips into a book. And so in June 1938 the cover of the first issue of *Action Comics* came to feature a man wearing a blue costume with a red and yellow emblem on his chest and a red cape flowing behind him, heaving a car over his head and smashing it into a hillside. Thus was the world introduced to the adventures of Superman.

But Superman was far more than this superpowered character. Once inside the comic book, the reader discovered another, less heroic character, Superman's alter ego, Clark Kent, a mild-mannered and timid reporter. And here is the question that brings us to the heart of our examination of these Jewish men and the comic book superheroes they created: Why? What in the logic of the story or, as we shall come to see, in the psyches of its creators, motivated the introduction of the Clark Kent role?

In contrast to most of the other costumed superheroes who were to follow in Superman's wake, in the Superman saga it is the superman who is real, and the alter ego, Clark Kent, who is fictitious. Think for a moment of other familiar superheroes: Batman, for example, also has a secret identity, Bruce Wayne, who is a real person who existed long before the costumed Batman came into being. Likewise for Spider-Man and Peter Parker. Superman is the inverse of what would later become that standard model. Especially when one considers the nerdy nature of Clark Kent's personality, one has to ask, Why on Earth would Superman want to perpetrate this masquerade?

The answer is that the psychology of Siegel and Shuster's imaginary world only worked if, at the same time that we the readers knew who Superman really was, we also knew that in the world of the story people saw him only as Clark—a timid, socially inept, physically weak, clumsy, sexually ineffectual quasi intellectual who wore glasses and apparently owned only one blue suit. In other words, the classic Jewish *nebbish* (roughly: "nerd"). But little did they know! Jewish men had only to tear off their clothes and glasses to reveal the surging superman underneath, physique fully revealed by those skintight blue leotards, and flaunted by that billowing cape. Listen to Jerry Siegel describe his early inspirations:

As a high school student, I thought that someday I might become a newspaper reporter and I had crushes on several attractive girls who either didn't know I existed or didn't care I existed. It occurred to me: What if I was real terrific? What if I had something special going for me, like jumping over buildings or throwing cars around or something like that? Then maybe they would notice me.[11]

But why does Superman want Lois Lane to fall in love with his false self, nebbish Clark, rather than with who he really is, a Superman? Renowned Jewish cartoonist Jules Feiffer had an answer. Feiffer writes that this is Superman's joke on the rest of us.[12] Superman sees "mortal men" as the world sees Clark, which is essentially how the anti-Semitic world sees Jewish men. His wish for Lois to fall in love with Clark is then the revenge of the Jewish nerd for the world's anti-Semitism. I would add that it also reflects the same verdict on humanity found in Shakespeare's *A Midsummer-Night's Dream,* wherein faerie King Oberon shows his contempt for, and power over, Queen Titania by having her fall in love with an ass, Bottom. The Superman–Lois Lane–Clark Kent triad conveys the same message that the Oberon-Titania-Bottom relationship does, delivered in the play by chief faerie Puck: "Lord, what fools these mortals be!" So say Shakespeare, Siegel, Shuster, and Superman.

The reference to Jules Feiffer above is from his 1965 book *The Great Comic Book Heroes,* the first book on the subject. Feiffer, a longtime cartoonist for the *Village Voice* and other publications, is an appropriate commentator not only on account of his affinity for comics but also because he has deep insight into the psychology of human nature, in particular the childishness of much adult behavior.[13] It is worth quoting from Feiffer's essay "The Minsk Theory of Krypton," written about Jerry Siegel in 1996 for the annual issue of the *New York Times Magazine* in which prominent figures write about other prominent figures who have passed away in the previous year.

There he was, a first-generation Jewish boy of Russian stock, planted in the Midwest during the birth of native American fascism, the rise of anti-Semitism, the radio broadcasts of Father Coughlin. . . . Superman was the ultimate assimilationist fantasy. . . . Jerry Siegel's accomplishment was to chronicle the smart Jewish boy's American dream. . . . It wasn't Krypton that Superman really came from; it was the planet Minsk or Lodz or Vilna or Warsaw.[14]

It is hard to resist—too hard for me, in fact—quoting Zeddy Lawrence here: "It may not be true in all cases, but it's a pretty good rule of thumb. If the word 'man' appears at the end of someone's name you can draw one of two conclusions: a) they're Jewish, as in Goldman, Feldman, or Lipman; or b) they're a superhero, as in Superman, Batman, or Spider-Man."[15]

Superman is "the hero from Ellis Island, personified as an (undocumented) alien who had been naturalized by the ultimate American couple, Eben and Sarah Kent."[16] Immigrant refugee baby Kal-El had been sent to Earth by his parents when they, along with his entire culture, were annihilated in the great holocaust of the destruction of his home planet, populated by what were said to be "highly evolved inhabitants."[17] In the context of the time, his story echoes that of the "Kindertransports" of Europe, via which Jewish children were evacuated to safe countries to escape the Nazis, leaving their parents behind.[18]

Set adrift in a very advanced version of a basket of bulrushes, Kal-El undertook a journey recalling that of Moses, adrift on the Nile. The change from his native Kryptonian name Kal-El to the adoptive and adaptive Clark Kent (like the change of Siegel's family name, and those of millions of Jews, at Ellis Island), and his later movement from the small town of Smallville to the big city of Metropolis, mirrored Jewish immigration patterns. American Jews and American superheroes share an urban environment—how would we know of Superman's powers if he didn't have those tall buildings to leap over in a single bound? From what looming shadows would Batman emerge, and from where would

Spider-Man swing on his webbing were they not citizens of the cities? The plains and prairies were okay for cowboys, and pirates could sail the open seas, but the natural habitat of the superheroes created by urban Jews is the streets of the cities.

The ridiculed personality that Clark Kent sheds when he casts off his street clothes is a gendered stereotype of Jewish inferiority. Superman exists to counter the notion that strength or manliness and Jewishness are incompatible. One example: In the movie *Outbreak*, Dustin Hoffman plays a military doctor who saves humanity from a deadly virus. During the filming, when Hoffman complained about being uncomfortable in the biohazard suit he had to wear, director Arnold Kopelson told him that was the price of being turned into an action-adventure hero. Hoffman's immediate response was, "There's no such thing as a Jewish action-adventure hero."[19] Though said humorously, this reflects a deeply held stereotype defining Jewish men as non-heroic, weak, overly intellectual, and effeminate, a stereotype from which Jewish men, as well as women, have long suffered. These conceptions have been used as weapons against Jewish men and culture for many centuries. Writer Arthur Koestler was a member of a Jewish fraternity, a *Burschenshaft*, in Vienna in the early part of the twentieth century. He wrote that its members felt they needed to prove that "Jews could hold their own in dueling, brawling, drinking, and singing, just like other people. According to the laws of inferiority and overcompensation, they were soon . . . becoming the most feared and aggressive swordsmen at the University."[20]

It is the combination of Superman's invincibleness and the nebbish-like characterization of Clark Kent that makes Superman such a Jewish character. The two contrasting types are deeply ingrained in Jewish culture. In Eastern Europe, the ideal of Jewish masculinity emphasized brain not brawn, scholarly rather than athletic abilities and pursuits. From this emerged one stereotype of Jewish culture, a people dedicated to education but detached from physical labor—the guy you'd hire to do your accounting but not to fix your car. In the Old Country of Eastern Europe, the gentle ideal of Jewish masculinity came into being in the same breath as its opposing counterpart. In his book *Unheroic*

Conduct: The Rise of Heterosexuality and the Invention of the Jewish Man, Daniel Boyarin writes of how this idea of "a gentle, timid, and studious male" (*Edelkayt* in Yiddish) gave rise within Jewish culture to its counterimage: "Jewish society needed an image against which to define itself and produced the 'goy'—the hypermale—as its countertype, as a reverse of its social norm."[21] The goy came to be understood as the Gentile male. Thus the counterintuitiveness of thinking of Superman as Jewish, the very way we resist the thought, is precisely the point. Clark's Jewish-seeming nerdiness and Superman's non-Jewish-seeming hypermasculinity are two sides of the same coin, the accentuated Jewish male stereotype and its exaggerated stereotypical counterpart.

Siegel and Shuster's intuitive stroke of genius was to combine the superman and the super nerd into a single character, and let the result play itself out in the media of American mass culture. It is the polarization of the Superman/Clark Kent personas, the fusion into one character of these two extremes, the superhero and the super nebbish, that distinguished Superman from other figures in the superhero genre.

The choice to make Superman so nearly invincible also relates compellingly to Jewish history, in ways that reveal themselves if we contrast Superman and Batman. Unlike most other superheroes, Batman actually has no superpowers. Rather, Bruce Wayne, Batman's secret identity, witnesses his parents being killed in a robbery in the streets of Gotham City when he is a small child. Vowing to avenge their deaths, he strengthens his mind and body with the aim of becoming a great crime fighter, and takes on the identity of Batman as a symbol to strike fear into the hearts of criminals. Again we turn to Jules Feiffer to capture the difference between the two, particularly as it relates to his own Jewish psyche:

> Superman's superiority lay in the offense, Batman's lay in the rebound. . . . The Batman school preferred a vulnerable hero to an invulnerable one; preferred a hero who was able to take punishment and triumph in the end to a hero who took comparatively little punishment. . . . My own observations led me to believe that the only triumph most people eked out of adversity

was to manage to stay alive as it swept by. With me, I didn't think it would be any different. I preferred to play it safe and be Superman.[22]

Having been persecuted for millennia, the Jews needed a hero who was really above the fray. Their experience told them that if you had to engage in combat with adversity on a level playing field you'd probably lose. To feel safe required having overwhelming superiority on your side. Hence, Superman.

While Jews were at the heart of the comics publishing industry, their creations were certainly not all Jewish. Again, a contrast between Superman and Batman makes this essential point clear. Batman was created by Bob Kane and Bill Finger. Both were Jews, but that does not make Batman Jewish.* In fact, Batman's secret identity, that of Bruce Wayne, makes him practically a villain in Jewish iconography. Years ago I happened to be in the Harvard University Library when they had an exhibit of historical Haggadoth. Many of them were opened to the page that illustrates the four sons of the Passover Seder with their characteristic questions: the wise, the wicked, the foolish, and the one unable to ask. In older Haggadoth, the wicked son was most often depicted as a soldier, but as one moved into the modern period another motif emerged: Over and over again, the wicked son was depicted as whatever the image of the non-Jewish wealthy playboy was in that time and place—in other words, the Bruce Waynes of their day. While Clark Kent worked for a living and was even a writer—a good Jewish boy, in other words—Bruce Wayne was a Jewish parent's ultimate assimilationist nightmare. If shorn of their superhero identities, Clark could

---

* Robert Kahn legally changed his name to Kane when he turned eighteen in 1934. His contract stipulated that he be given sole credit as Batman's creator, leading one comics insider to suggest that the industry name an annual award in Bill Finger's honor to be given to the most underrecognized contributor to comics. That way every year the industry could give somebody the Finger. (And there is now indeed a Bill Finger Award for writing in comics, often given to someone who has been underrecognized).

easily be imagined as Jewish, but Bruce was definitely a WASP, literally to the manor born.

While Batman pursued his personal vendetta, Superman was a "champion of the helpless and oppressed."[23] In his first full-length adventure, Superman saves an innocent man from a lynch mob, finds the real murderer, rescues a woman from her wife-beating husband, saves Lois Lane from a hoodlum, exposes a corrupt U.S. senator and a munitions manufacturer, and halts the South American war they have engineered. The villains in those early stories were very much whom you'd expect a progressive urban reformer or crusading reporter to go after. Superman didn't just beat up commonplace hoodlums; his adventures typically had him exposing corrupt politicians, thwarting the schemes of exploitive landlords and wealthy businessmen, and generally fighting for the little guy. This is a mundane list by the standards of what we now expect superheroes to face, but the idea that costumed superheroes fight against costumed, maniacal villains originated in Batman comics, in the character of the Joker. If one distinguishes crimes against persons from crimes against property, Superman was more likely to be rescuing persons or saving humanity while Batman was more likely to be foiling thefts of jewels from people who moved in Bruce Wayne's elite circles.

Superman's values would have been recognized at the time of his debut as very much those of a New Dealer. The Jewish-American, Yiddish-English joke of Siegel and Shuster's generation was that Jews believed in three "worlds": *die velt* ("this world"), *yenne velt* ("the other world"), and Roosevelt. That generation recognized in the New Deal what they saw as traditional Jewish ethical values, and Superman's costume was cut from that same cloth. Superman and Batman defined the poles of the comic book superhero universe. Superman was a sky god, Batman a creature of the night; Superman motivated by his high ideals, Batman driven by his inner demons; the super cop versus the vigilante, justice dispensed with a lofty glow from above versus vengeance delivered in the dark. True, each character was tempered in the direction of the other—Batman had his own strict moral code, and Superman too, at least originally, operated outside the law and showed a mischievous "bad boy" streak, enjoying taunting authority and flaunting his powers, scaring people out of their wits by threatening to drop them from the heights if they didn't cooperate with his plans—but the two were nonetheless marked by clearly distinct sensibilities.

Despite their differences, DC paired Superman and Batman in a series of adventures in the early days, for obvious marketing purposes. In the 1980s writer Frank Miller reinvented Batman, returning him to the darker roots of the original 1939 conception of the character. Here he got the Superman-Batman relationship right. Even when united against common enemies, the alien immigrant and the native scion of wealth "would never have been friends."[24]

Miller's retelling not only made Batman darker but also more firmly cemented Superman in place as Batman's antithesis, as the representative of the establishment, removing any last vestiges of his earlier slightly scampish and outsider status. Since then, Superman has been increasingly whitewashed, and his mischievous streak erased. The steady and persistent sanitizing amounts to a de-Jewification,[25] and Superman's ascension to sainthood brought with it an even more miraculous transformation in Clark Kent, moving him from sideshow performer to center-ring star. As we have seen, in Siegel and Schuster's conception it was clear that the real man in the story was the superman, and the puny human called Clark Kent was a complete fabrication. But in the 1990s and the first decade of this century, episodes were published that made it seem like Clark was the real person and Superman a costumed identity he assumed. His heroic persona and values appeared to be rooted not so much in his Kryptonian heritage as in the values imparted to him by his adoptive parents and their family farm home in Smallville. DC even created a heroic lineage for the Kent family, whom it turns out had met and aided Harriet Tubman in freeing slaves, and were even originally brought to their farm in Kansas by ancestor Silas Kent as part of the pre–Civil War antislavery struggle.[26] This was all part of the process of wrapping Superman ever more tightly in the American flag.

One can see the different ways of relating to heroic idols when students discuss the stories they encounter in the Hebrew and Christian Bibles, what Christians call the Old and New Testaments. Christian students are accustomed to reading biblical figures as saints, and they typically want to interpret Hebrew Bible/Old Testament characters in this same way, seeing whatever they did as somehow morally exemplary. But Jews typically don't regard biblical figures this way. Indeed, upper-class Englishman Duff Cooper famously quipped that most of the stories of King David must be true, for no people would ever invent such a deeply flawed figure to be their national hero.[27] The Book of *Genesis*, for example, is an extended tale of a multigenerational, highly dysfunctional family, complete with the crimes they commit against each other, including murder, rape, incest, lying, and stealing. And that's not to mention what they do to others! Treating Superman's biography as the life of a saint, as the life of a squeaky-clean do-gooder, sacrifices the original Jewish sensibility that created a more human hero to a Christian sensibility of saintliness. (There's actually a name for the whole genre of such sanitized biographies—"hagiography"—and it's a profoundly non-Jewish approach to life).

With each wrapping of the flag, the Superman/Clark Kent character moved up a level in what medieval Christian thinkers called the Great Chain of Being, the hierarchical order of the cosmos. Over the years, as Superman's powers increased so that he came to achieve near divinity, Clark became more humanized, even allowed to be heroic in his own right, gaining greater humanity. Over the long term a Pinocchio-like transformation turned Clark from a wooden figure of ridicule into a "real boy." (I *really* want to invent the word *Pinocchic* at this point, but I just don't think that will fly.)

Turning Clark into the foundational figure in the story as well as an adventure hero in his own right is central to both of his recent TV incarnations, in *Lois and Clark: The New Adventures of Superman* and *Smallville*. The latter series deals with his teen years and has Clark gradually growing into his powers. But the first page of Siegel and Shuster's Superman origin story shows the super baby still in diapers while smilingly holding up heavy furniture in one hand, those around him "astounded at his feats of strength."[28] The complications of how his identity was kept secret for all those years given such displays were never addressed. Siegel and Shuster lived in a pre-Internet world, and they seemed to assume that when someone arrived in the big Metropolis from the rural world of small-town life, they really could be swallowed up by the anonymity of the city and leave their earlier origins entirely behind them. Another classic immigrant's wishful fantasy.

While later writers came to address the problem extensively, Siegel and Shuster weren't much bothered at all by all the obvious difficulties in Superman's maintaining his secret identity. Here's an interesting take on the disguise by one of Superman's later editors, E. Nelson Bridwell:

> It may surprise the sophisticate of today that she [Lois Lane] took so long to penetrate the simple disguise of a pair of glasses. But in a day when people accepted the old chestnut about the girl whose attractions are never noticed until she is seen without her glasses, Superman's camouflage worked.[29]

Note that Dorothy Parker's line that men seldom make passes at girls who wear glasses specifically applies to women, so to the extent this works for Clark it also marks him as feminized, as less than a "real man."

In recent years there have been some ingenious explanations of how he's been able to keep his secret. It turns out that in public appearances Superman is vibrating in place at super speed, so in any photo of him his facial features appear blurred. Then he also changes his body language (posture, gait) as well as his voice when he switches from Clark to Superman, some of this under the tutelage of a book on acting given to him by Ma Kent. The voice-changing trick isn't new but dates back to the old radio show, which gave birth to much of the Superman lore. The audience learned to visualize Superman taking flight when they heard the now iconic phrase "Up, up, and away" accompanied by a "whoosh" sound effect, as the show came up with many ways to verbally communicate what could be shown visually in other media.

Superman was played on radio by actor Bud Collyer, who became known to a later generation on TV as the host of game shows *To Tell the Truth* and *Beat the Clock*. One listener reports:

As Kent, Collyer always sounded as if the blue tights beneath his red shorts beneath his gray flannel trousers were too snug. When at last he found a convenient phone booth and he could cry, "Off with these clothes—this looks like a job for [*Sigh*] Superman!" the voice dropped an octave in relief.[30]

By the time we reached the 2006 *Superman Returns* film that brought Superman back to the big screen after a long hiatus, Superman's de-Jewification had proceeded so far that he was not only the ultimate all-American, he was even being claimed as a Christ figure. Another nice Jewish boy was being resurrected as a Christian god. The Warner Brothers/DC Comics publicity machine launched a two-pronged campaign before the film's release, one aimed at the usual action-adventure crowd, and the other aimed at conservative Evangelical Christians and flying under the general cultural radar, specifically positioning *Superman Returns* as the next Christian blockbuster, hoping to cash in on the trend following *The Passion of the Christ* and *The Chronicles of Narnia*.

In addition to basic plot elements, verbal and visual cues to see Superman as Jesus appear throughout the film, ranging from repetition of the film's guiding mantra that "the father becomes the son and the son becomes the father," to Superman in countless Christlike poses, to him receiving a piercing stab wound that replicates Jesus's wound on the cross.*

Superman's voyage from Krypton to Earth was originally a tale of an infant's rescue from his world, which was about to perish in a great conflagration. This film reverses that Jewish contrast between Krypton and Earth. Now we hear his father telling Kal-El that he sent his "only son" to Earth to save *us*, rather than the other way around. This is language right out of the Gospel of John, including a declaration that these humans "lack the light to show the way."

---

*The *Smallville* TV series has been just as explicit in its Christ imagery. The most memorable image from the show's opening episode, used prominently in its advance publicity, showed Clark in a clear crucifixion pose, suffering and hung up on a scarecrow pole in a cornfield.

That Jewish understanding of Krypton as the Old World (Europe about to self-destruct) and Earth as the New World (America with its promise of new life) is replaced in this film by Christian coding of Krypton as a lost Paradise (in all its crystalline purity) and Earth as the scene of life after the Fall, or even worse—his fall to Earth has never before been depicted as such a hellish voyage. I suppose it's just a coincidence that his mother here is played by an actress named (Eva Marie!) Saint, and that his earthly father is absent from the scene.*

However you track Superman's path, it's been a long journey: from Krypton to Earth, from immigrant refugee to adopted iconic son, from Cleveland to Hollywood, from pencil to pixel, from Jewish ideals to Christian symbolism. We'll shortly meet Superman's supernatural ancestor in Jewish lore, the golem, a powerful figure made of clay, humanlike in shape but large and devoid of speech, who was said to have been brought to life by a ritual involving writing the Hebrew word *emeth*, "truth," on either its forehead or a piece of paper (versions differ). It is returned to inanimate clay by erasing the first letter, leaving *meth*, "corpse." The golem was thus animated by truth to serve the cause of justice. These two principles of truth and justice were in fact originally the principles Superman was said to uphold; "the American way" was added by the radio show in the wartime 1940s.[31] The line from the golem to Superman is thus the path through which all the other comic book superheroes who were to follow came to serve truth, justice, and the Jewish-American way. In the rest of this book we will follow this path.

So the next time someone tells you to look at Superman as a Christ figure, tell them that for the real meaning of Superman they need to look elsewhere. Look, up in the sky! It's a man! It's a Jew! It's Supermentsh!

---

* His Earth parents, Jonathan and Martha Kent, carried the conspicuously more Hebraic names Eben and Sarah in the first Superman novel, published in 1942, *The Adventures of Superman*, by George Lowther, a scriptwriter for the Superman and other radio shows, as well as later for TV.

As to the further adventures of Joe Shuster and Jerry Siegel personally, they enjoyed a degree of fame as Superman's creators for some years, but reaped little financial reward. When they accepted the initial offer to publish *Superman*, they sold all their rights to their character for $130, at the time the going rate of $10 per page for that first story. This came to haunt them (and a whole bunch of other people too) for the rest of their lives. A long campaign to get Siegel and Shuster compensation for Superman, led by some leading figures in the comics industry, finally got some positive results decades later. It was nowhere near enough money to make up for the fortune they had lost, but at least since 1976 every Superman story once again says "Superman created by Jerry Siegel and Joe Shuster," a credit line that had been absent since 1948, when a first lawsuit failed to restore their rights.[32] The impetus to reach a deal at that time was the corporation's fear of negative publicity spoiling the pending launch of the new *Superman* movie franchise. As of this writing, litigation reopened by Siegel's heirs over the Superman rights continues. There is in place, however, a ruling establishing their rights to Superboy, the judge in that case having ruled that even if DC owned the Superman rights, in establishing this new character of Superboy based on Superman they had overstepped what they were entitled to do without permission from Siegel and Shuster.[33]

Siegel and Shuster created another short-lived hero in the late '40s, Funnyman, an actual clown of a hero, who appeared in only a few comic books and strips.[34] Siegel returned to writing *Superman* for a time in the '50s, and went on to write other characters. Joe Shuster fell on much harder times, his eyesight starting to fail even back in the heyday, and eventually had very little money. In 2009, comics historian Craig Yoe published *Secret Identity: The Fetish Art of Superman's Co-creator Joe Shuster*.[35] It reprints Shuster's pornographic illustrations from a 1950s "Nights of Horror" series of cheap S&M paperbacks. Though the work is anonymous, Shuster's style is unmistakable; even though it's fairly mild by today's standards, there's no denying that to all appearances that's a skimpy-lingerie-clad Lois Lane whipping Clark Kent. Some have turned this discovery into speculation on secret fetishistic desires of Shuster, and how that might be seen in the comics, but there's really a much simpler explanation. Shuster would have known publishers of pornography from the days when comics publishing began, back when it was the same people who were publishing girlie magazines for the men and comics for the boys. It's likely one of them threw some work his way when he needed the money.

If one is looking for a more fulfilling turn in the later story of Siegel and Shuster, here's one. Early on, they hired a model, Joanne Kovacs, to pose for Lois Lane. Here's how Tom De Haven tells the story:

> Siegel and Shuster, who must have been around twenty years old at the time, each still living at home and neither gainfully employed, had gone and hired a model. . . . Jerry would come over whenever Joanne Kovacs was at the Shuster apartment, to keep an eye on his, you know, creation. The three hit it off . . . and remained friends, staying in touch even after Joanne moved away.
>
> Years later, they met again in New York City—at a cartoonists' convention in the Plaza Hotel—and Jerry . . . asked Joanne for a date. They married in 1948. They were still married when Jerry died in 1996.[36]

If you want to think of this as Superman having married Lois Lane in real life, go ahead, enjoy. I do.

2

FLIGHTS OF JEWISH IMAGINATION

From the Old Country to Tales
of a Better Tomorrow

efore Joe Shuster drew Superman, the only artist drawing
Jews flying through the air was Marc Chagall. But his weren't
in heroic poses. They were fiddlers way above the roof, lovers
embracing, men praying, women working, figures fantastically drawn
but nonetheless engaged in daily rather than fantasized life.

Chagall is today the most famous member of the Jewish modern art
movement in Russia that flourished in the early years of the Russian
Revolution. In the twentieth century, Jews were drawn to movements
that identified them as modern in their outlook not only in the arts but
also in social and political life. In their orientation toward the future,
modernist movements promised a decisive break with the past. For Jews
coming from a long history of persecution, embedded in that break was
the promise of deliverance from anti-Semitism, a promise that echoed
Judaism's messianic nature. The new world to come was going to be a
just world, a world liberated from oppression. The same conjunction of
forward-looking art and ideology that we see in the progressivism of the
artistic movements around Chagall in the old world is also evident in
the genesis of the superheroes in the new world. In this chapter we will
probe the old-world Jewish roots of comic book superheroes.

21

To better understand the powerful pull that modernity and its promise to leave a tragic past behind had on Jews, we first need to understand the persecutions that endured for millennia. European anti-Semitism has religious, economic, and political roots, which arose in successive time periods. As we turn to explore these, I should stress that the brief overview of the history of anti-Semitism that follows is most decidedly not a history of Judaism. It is the actions of the perpetrators that pose the fundamental problems that need to be studied, not the actions of the victims, and thus a history of anti-Semitism is much more a history of Christians than of Jews.

The religious roots of Christian anti-Semitism begin at a well-known juncture. The young rebellious rabbi Jesus of Nazareth gained a following for his teachings in the outlying Roman province of Judea, for which the Roman authorities crucified him. Shortly before these events, that good Jew John the Baptist had been wandering in the same countryside, telling his fellow Jews to prepare the way for the coming of the Lord. After Jesus's passing, the vast majority of Jews basically went about their business as before. Some were aware of the challenges the young rabbi had posed to their own traditions, as well as to the Romans, but these weren't all that different from other challenges in the past. Looking around at the world after Jesus had come and gone, the vast majority saw that nothing had fundamentally changed.

But a small number among them disagreed vehemently. As these folks saw it, the Lord had indeed come (and then gone again) in the person of Jesus. To them, the ancient Jewish prophecies had been fulfilled, and these were indeed the times of messianic deliverance spoken of in their revered texts. So this group set off to convert others to their point of view. They managed to convert a small number, but the preponderance of Jews remained unconvinced.

Proselytizing became easier as Paul's view was accepted, that one could simply bypass these recalcitrant Jews and preach the good news about Jesus to non-Jews. These Gentiles already knew about Judaism because it was a part of the culture of the time, and they had to be shown that these Jesus followers weren't really just plain old Jews with some new twist. The new task was therefore to show how Christians were not only different, but different in a way that was better. This meant extolling the virtues of the new Christianity, which at that time meant not so much its distinctive theological elements, but its distinctive way of life. After all, much of what is today regarded as distinctive of Christian theology was actually common to a number of widely held belief systems. A god who was incarnated in a human body? What, you never heard of a pharaoh or Caesar? A god who was resurrected? Go brush up your Egyptian mythology. As for the performance of miracles, well that was really minor-league stuff given all the stories of magicians and sorcerers that were commonplace at the time. No, it was what they were being told about the Christians themselves, more than about Christianity, that attracted people. Here was a group of people whose religion told them to practice certain virtues, things like charity toward each other and the pursuit of peace. And they were forming themselves into communities intended to actually put these ideals into practice.[1]

The unfortunate flip side of this was that distancing Christianity from Judaism entailed not only praising Christians, but also denigrating Jews. To bring into greater relief the practices of Christian charity and peacefulness, one told contrasting stories of Jewish acquisitiveness and aggressiveness. To emphasize that Christians practiced liberating virtues of the heart, one told stories of Jewish servile obedience to the law. This mythology of Jewish character defects became more pernicious as time passed.

I don't want to make it sound like the animus toward Jews was all intentionally developed as Christian propaganda. Anyone who knows anything about families will recognize the psychodynamics of a son trying to emerge from his father's shadow, just as this religion of the Son struggled to gain independence from the religion of the Father. Early Christians felt not simply rejected by Jews, but betrayed by them. If Christianity was the fulfillment of the promise of Judaism, other Jews should have been the most likely to embrace Jesus, and were in effect betraying their own traditions by *not* doing so.

Intentional or not, the list of negative qualities attributed to Jews grew over the years until, by the time we reach the medieval period, tales of the infamous "blood libel" spread throughout Europe. This widely believed myth told of secret Jewish rituals that involved the slaughter of Christian children in order to obtain the blood of innocents for arcane and evil purposes, including the supposed baking of this blood into the bread of Passover, matzoh. Jews were tried, convicted, and executed on this charge throughout Europe, often without any legal formalities.

The Black Plague and other plagues of the fourteenth and fifteenth centuries that decimated Europe also fueled anti-Semitism. Jews suffered proportionately fewer deaths, for which modern scholars offer various explanations: The isolation of Jews from the general population inhibited the spread of disease; and the Jewish dietary rules of keeping kosher (*kashrut*), which mandated more frequent washing of dishes and hands, separation of meat from dairy, and not eating often-tainted pork, turned out to be hygienically sound practices. The general Christian population might have chosen to see Jewish lives being spared as a sign that the Jews were a "chosen" or favored people, but instead went in the opposite direction: This was a clear sign that the Jews were in league with the devil.

The period of transition from the medieval to the modern period saw the rise of the second root of anti-Semitism: an economic rather than religious basis. During this period, Jews were restricted in many ways that made making a living difficult. Most professions were controlled by guilds, and only guild members could work in the profession, whether butcher, baker, or candlestick maker. Memberships were reserved for Christians. Further, Jews could not own land or work for the state, and were prohibited from military service. About the only fields generally left open for Jews were trade and finance; thus Jews became the traveling merchants of Europe, and Hebrew became a language of international commerce.

The precapitalist agricultural economy of medieval Europe was a pre-market economy, meaning that the basic structure of society was such that goods and services were more likely to pass from one person to another through exchange than through monetary purchase. In such circumstances, people would most likely borrow money only when some disaster struck. Under these conditions it was considered unethical to profit from the misfortune of another, so it was unethical to charge anything more than minimal interest on money lent, and often any interest at all was seen as being immoral. The Catholic Church condemned what it considered to be the sin of usury.

Jewish ethics and law, while they prohibited charging excessive or exploitive interest rates, had nothing against the charging of interest. In the world of finance and commerce, one borrowed money in the normal course of business to try to make more money. Money lending did not have the association with misfortune or anything being abnormal that it had in the Christian economy, and there was nothing wrong with the moneylender getting a reasonable share of the profits from a venture. As the capitalist marketplace developed, Christian traders and entrepreneurs lagged behind, trying to adjust to the new realities, and Jewish moneylenders increasingly became seen as a necessary evil. From this collision between an older Christian agricultural ethic and new economic realities came the widespread proliferation of the negative stereotypes regarding Jews and money that are still the common currency of anti-Semitism.

To these religious and economic roots, the modern era added a political foundation for anti-Semitism. The modern political era begins with the French Revolution. To the extent that it was ideologically driven, the revolutionaries drew their inspiration from the philosophy of the Enlightenment, whose principles included ideas about limited government rather than absolute monarchy, popular sovereignty, the abolition of special privileges of birth, and individual liberty, especially in the forms of free trade and religious liberty. These Enlightenment ideas were welcomed by certain segments of the population, especially the educated elites of the rising merchant classes. It was they who had become the de facto new rulers in place of the old aristocratic regime that was overthrown by the revolution, and the new state was structured to benefit them.

The critical idea of separation between church and state was not born in the French Revolution—remember that other revolution across the Atlantic—but it took a more extreme form in France, and it was in that form that it was spread through Europe by the conquests of Napoleon's armies. Most Enlightenment thinkers saw religion as a form of ignorant superstition. It was they who, looking back, popularized viewing the medieval period as the "Dark Ages," in contrast to the new enlightened era to which they were helping to give birth. Nativism, populism, even patriotism came to be identified with a defense of traditional religion, meaning Christianity, against those who had colluded to separate church and state: the merchant classes, the educated, the foreigners. To tie it all together into one neat package, the most visible beneficiaries of this new separation of church and state were the Jews. It was the Jews to whom previously closed doors were now opened, the Jews who were now competitors with Christians in areas of life and work from which they'd previously been excluded. All those who were displaced and disaffected by the political and economic changes brought on by modernity now found a chief culprit and a common enemy in the Jews, and antimodernism became inextricably intertwined with anti-Semitism.

Then, as the nations of Europe developed nationalist ideologies in the nineteenth century, the Jews were again excluded. These ideologies defined a nation or a people as united by common language, common land, and common culture, the latter often including, if not a common religion in the strict sense, then at least religious commonalities. By these criteria the Jews just didn't fit into the map of Europe being carved out by national identities. They had no land in Europe to call their own. The Hebrews as well as the Romani and Sinti, the "Gypsies," were the nomadic peoples of Europe, which is a principal reason why in the twentieth century the Gypsies were the other ethnic group targeted by the Nazis for extermination. They were seen as not only without a homeland but in principle incapable of having one.

As the Nazis were coming to power in Germany during the Depression, they developed an ideology that exploited the multiple components of anti-Semitism by developing narratives such that whatever your underlying political ideology, the Jews could be scapegoated for Germany's problems. If you were coming from a populist stance that blamed bankers and financiers, they drew on economically based anti-Semitism to say that everyone knew that Jews were the primary exploiters. If you were coming from the right and saw the left as troublemakers, they invoked politically based anti-Semitism to remind you that Marx was a Jew, and everyone knew that Jews were communist internationalists. This bled easily into the idea that Jews were alien nomads, not real Germans, which tied nationalist ideology more fervently to anti-Semitism.. Conspiracy theories that Jews run the world through a secret cabal that unites Jewish capitalists and communists are still a staple of the paranoid right.

The final culmination of all this came when the Nazis added their own vehemence and brand of racially based anti-Semitism.[2] Aided by new classificatory and evolutionary theories in the biological sciences, the difference between Jew and Aryan was proclaimed to exist in the domain of biology rather than ideology. In Nazi thought the Jews were a race, not a religious group; it was a question of the impure blood, not the mistaken beliefs of this inferior race. In his landmark work on the Holocaust, *The Destruction of the European Jews,* historian Raul Hilberg summarized the progression of the stages of anti-Semitism that culminated in the Holocaust by saying that the messages delivered to Jews through the ages could be succinctly stated in this way: "You shall not live among us as Jews. [Hence conversion.] You shall not live among us. [Therefore expulsion, exclusion, and ghettoization.] You shall not live. [Finally, annihilation.]"[3]

In a course I taught not long ago, I one day announced to my students that over the weekend I had seen a new and culturally very significant movie: *Borat* (subtitle: *Cultural Learnings of America for Make Benefit Glorious Nation of Kazakhstan*). After recovering from their surprise that their professor had gone to see and actually enjoyed this low humor film, it turned out that a good number of them knew that Sacha Baron Cohen, the man behind our friend Borat Sagdiyev, was Jewish (and observant at that). I called to their attention that Borat clearly has problems with three specific groups of people: Jews, Gypsies, and homosexuals. Given that we had just finished a unit on the Holocaust, that list should have rung a bell with them; these were the three major groups singled out by the Nazis for persecution, and the popular prejudices on which they drew in their campaigns against these groups are still very much alive.

These different but eventually overlapping sources of the anti-Semitism from which twentieth-century Jews sought to escape brought many Jews to develop different but overlapping allegiances to forward-looking social and political movements. While in its broadest sense modernity refers to the period following the collapse of the feudal system in Europe, politically ushered in by the French Revolution, for which the ideas of the Enlightenment paved the way, in the more limited sense most relevant to our discussion here it refers to the political and cultural movements that initially emerged most strongly in the nineteenth century, where the general trends of modernity became self-consciously embraced and focused to form modernist political and cultural movements or attitudes. In its basic outlook, modernity's secularism promised deliverance from religiously based anti-Semitism; its progressivism and socialism seemed capable of rendering obsolete the economic basis of anti-Semitism, and its cosmopolitanism, internationalism, and universalism could transcend the political and racial foundations of anti-Semitism. It all dovetailed nicely with the messianism embedded in Judaism, and it answered the Jewish psychological need for the hope of a better future.

There are other factors that contribute to widespread Jewish progressivism beyond those discussed here, such as a culture that values education (what other group has made their teachers their highest authorities?), and specifically an education that values independence of mind (as seen in the Talmudic tradition of debate and openness to divergent interpretations), and a certain kind of marginality in which Jews are *in* but not *of* their societies. This gave them access to insights and resources not as readily available to groups pushed even further to the edges of society, while at the same time the still widespread exclusion of Jews leads them to identify with outsider and oppressed groups.

The belief that the modern era would prove better than the past has been for Jews more than just an article of faith; one clings to it with the same tenacity as to a sustaining life preserver thrown to those in danger of drowning in the swelling waves of the high seas; many European Jews came to imbue modernism with near messianic meaning. This also held true in the arts, where modernist aesthetics aligned itself not just with intellectual avant-gardism but with progressive politics. Aspects of a European Jewish modernist art movement fueled by these ideas can be seen as feeding into the genre of comic book art, insomuch as some of this movement's major artists came to focus on a new integration of words and pictures. I turn now to first discuss how this integration was rooted in certain developments in the visual arts. Then, in addition to tracing these Jewish roots of the pictorial dimension of comics, I'll also identify a Jewish old-world source for the words, for the stories of comic book superheroes. This chapter will end with a look at the New World context in which these influences converged.

As I sit writing about Jewish cultural influences reaching from Europe to the United States in the twentieth century, there's a huge gap between me and my subject. I'm not talking about just the passage of time, nor am I talking about the Atlantic divide. I'm talking about the Holocaust. We've lost much of our collective records and memory of Jewish cultural transmission. Jewish history and historical memory were truncated in the middle of the twentieth century, destroyed and forced underground, much as the Jews themselves were. It's not just that we lost the primary sources, whether by that we mean people or documents. It's also that in the destruction of European Jewry all those people and their descendants were lost. A generation's worth of conversations never took place, ranging from countless informal discussions to scholarly investigations in which we might have learned more about what comics creators' Jewishness meant to them, or what they knew of the European Jewish traditions in art and story.

So I'm making some speculative leaps when I connect "high" art to comic books, because I can't trace exactly how old-world techniques and tales made their way to influence artists and writers in the New World, other than to point to traces that crop up here and there. I can't fully follow a chain of evidence that would authoritatively link older Jewish art and stories to adventures in the New World, because that chain was broken. And yet, and yet . . . Ancestry announces its arrival in subtle and surprising ways, and there are many unusual influences of the Jewish art of the old world on the new. For instance, who would have thought that one could trace a direct line from synagogue art to carousels? But that's precisely what is documented in Murray Zimiles's book *Gilded Lions and Jeweled Horses: The Synagogue to the Carousel,* based on an exhibit first displayed at the American Folk Art Museum in New York.[4] The art produced by Jewish wood-carvers for synagogues in Europe often portrayed animals, none more frequently than the lions one often saw above the ark that held the Torah. When they immigrated to the new world, these carvers set up shop and used those same designs to carve carousel animals, developing in New York what came to be called the popular "Coney Island" style of elegantly carved and elaborately decorated lions, horses, and other animals. We even have the names of specific artists and their studios; take, for example, Marcus Charles Illions, whose father had been a horse dealer in Eastern Europe. Seen side by side, the carousel lions unmistakably came from synagogues.[5] As in the story I'm about to tell of Jewish modern art, here too a tradition of Jewish religious art was turned to the secular entertainment of children.

At the center of the modern art movement on which I shall focus stands Vitebsk, a Russian town that in the years of the Russian Revolution became "one of the most influential gateways to the art of the twentieth century."[6] It was there in the town of his birth that Marc Chagall (originally Moisei Shagal) painted his iconic fiddler, and many other things. Much of the work of the artists of the Vitebsk school fused words and pictures. In the language of high art rather than of popular culture, these artists sought to integrate traditional Hebraic calligraphy with modern visual art to create new forms of modern Jewish cultural expression.

To speak of the Vitebsk school of art is to speak not just of a set of ideas or techniques but of an actual school. Vitebsk grew because of a conjunction of geography and industrialization. It was a crossroads, first of major roads and then of major railroad lines. (Its inhabitants came to take pride in the fact that the end-of-the-line railway station in Saint Petersburg was named the Vitebsk Station).[7] It was a place of trade, therefore a place with many Jews, therefore a place with many children who needed education. Fortunately for the growing number of artists in Vitebsk who embraced modernism, these children had parents who were willing to endorse progressive arts movements. If one passed beyond the relatively urbanized center where these activities took place, other parts of the town could easily have doubled for Anatevka, that storied village populated by the great Yiddish writer Sholem Aleichem as the home of Tevye the milkman and his daughters, some of whose stories are told in *Fiddler on the Roof*. It was the sort of place depicted recently in James Sturm's graphic novel *Market Day*, portraying life in the Jewish Old World.[8]

As a boy, Chagall was a student at the Artist Pen's School of Drawing and Painting. The word *Pen* here had nothing to do with an artist's tool; it was the teacher's name, Yehuda Pen (Russified to Yuri Moiseevich Pen), and a simple sign with the school's name on it hung on the front of Pen's home on Gogol Street. After some early training there, Chagall left to receive more formal art education in Saint Petersburg, then spent a few years in Paris before returning to Vitebsk, whose streets and surrounding countryside became the settings for many of his early paintings. In September 1918, Chagall was appointed commissar of fine arts for Vitebsk by the minister of culture (or, if you prefer the more grandiose translation from the Russian, "plenipotentiary on matters of art in Vitebsk Province").[9] His first duty was to chair a committee to decorate Vitebsk on the occasion of the first anniversary of the October 1917 Revolution that had brought the communists to power. After that, he was free to devote time to his own priority for the job, establishing a professional art school and museum. The Vitebsk People's Art School opened in January 1919, and it was here that Chagall was to do most of his formal teaching over the course of his long career. Some of his students were former house painters with whom he'd worked in preparing the city for its celebration of the revolution. The local newspaper carried the story of the opening ceremony:

Comrade Chagall, who formally opened the school, . . . spoke of the fundamental difference between the way the artistic development of the masses was carried out under the old regime and how it is now, under the dictatorship of the proletariat.

31

In the old days art existed only for the benefit of "the happy few." For the working masses, among whom there was so much talent, the doors to the temple of art and science were tightly closed; and if one of their number did happen to gain entry, it was seen as some kind of miracle.[10]

The revolution in the arts that Chagall and his comrades intended to carry out involved changing not just who would be let into the sanctum, but also what would be coming out of it. Their program was to create proletarian art, art for the masses that would go beyond that intended to adorn the homes and halls inhabited by the rich and famous. One direction in which they moved was into set design for theater. This brought fine artists into working relationships with house painters and carpenters, the sort of people Chagall knew locally as collaborators from their jointly painting the town red, so to speak, for the celebration of the revolution. That way, modern design would be seen by the proletariat as part and parcel of their world, as the sets were created by local craftsmen, and used for proletarian theater seen by the masses.

They also moved into book production and illustration, as part of a program to improve literacy among the masses. Like their theater sets, their book illustrations were to be more than mere adornments. Text and illustrations were to come together to produce an integrated whole in their new, modern, and politically progressive aesthetic; they had to function together as equal partners, like artist and craftsperson, with neither subordinate to the other.

Chagall invited many artists to come work and teach at the Vitebsk school. Among them was another Jewish artist he'd originally known from their early years together in Vitebsk, where he was also a student at Pen's school: Lazar Markovich Lissitzky, who would become famous as El Lissitzky. It is in Lissitzky's work that we will find our most striking example of the integration of words and pictures, the best example being his illustrations for a children's song traditionally sung at the end of the Passover seder, *"Had Gadya"* ("An Only Kid" or "One Little Goat").

Lissitzky published his illustrated version of the song in 1919, with each verse as a separate illustration on a separate page, bound together in an innovative wraparound cover. The words are actually in Aramaic, a language close to Hebrew and written in the same alphabet. The song begins by telling us that a father bought a young goat for two zuzim.* With each succeeding verse comes a surprising new turn of events: A cat came to eat the goat, a dog bit the cat, a stick beat the dog, a fire burnt the stick, water came to douse the fire, an ox drank the water, a butcher slaughtered the ox, the angel of death came to slaughter the butcher, and finally "the Holy One came, Blessed be He, and slew the angel of death."[11] Each new verse is sung at a standard speed, immediately followed by all the preceding action recapitulated at a quickening pace, leading to a rousing grand ending that, if done right, leaves the children smiling and just about out of breath. This song comes at the end of the Seder and, Judaism being what it is, has accumulated various learned adult interpretations over the generations, usually being understood as an allegory for various failed attempts to destroy the Jewish people over the long course of history.

Lissitzky blends illustration and text in various ways. On the title page, "Had Gadya" appears on the pages of a large book that a boy is holding open in front of him. But the boy isn't looking into it, he's looking back at a goat that's looking over his shoulder into the book. The goat appears more interested in getting into the book than does the boy, with a sort of smile on its face (as much as a goat can be said to smile). We can't fully see the boy's expression, but he doesn't seem to be as happy about the whole situation as does the goat. The scene depicts just where a boy would be emotionally when his father announces that the time for had gadya, the little goat, has arrived.

On the following pages the words literally frame the action, as they are enclosed within an arch over each illustration. Strengthening the connections between words and pictures, the curves of the arches mirror curves in the illustrations beneath them: mountains, clouds, door-

---

* *Zuzim* is the plural of *zuz*, a small coin worth a quarter of a silver shekel. And how much is a shekel, you may ask? Four zuzim. If you want to know more, go ask someone more learned than I. One estimate, however, has a zuz equal to about a day's wages.

way arches, even the exaggerated curvatures of the backs of animals. Key words are color coded, to visually tie words and pictures together and to provide a reading aid for those still learning to read. Thus, when the cat is colored red the word *cat* appears in red, the ox and the word *ox* are both brown, etc. The only page on which no single word is highlighted is the one illustrating the angel of death slaying the butcher. Here the entire usual color scheme of the lettering is reversed, with white letters on a black background instead of the standard other way around. The block of black echoes the black clothing of the corpse on the ground.

The seeming simplicity of the art made the book not just more appealing to young readers, but was also a conscious attempt to reach back into and modernize Jewish folk art. Lissitzky had earlier been commissioned by the Jewish Historical and Ethnographic Society based in Saint Petersburg to study the synagogues of the Ukraine and bring back drawings of what he found there. In an article he published after his return to Vitebsk he wrote: "Searching for our identity, for the character of our times, we attempted to look into old mirrors and tried to root ourselves in so-called folk art."[12] Such a return to the so-called primitive was a major inspiration for modern art; Picasso, for instance, had found it in African art. These artists argued that this work was not primitive at all, but was rather more directly connected to the spontaneous and the unconscious that they wished to retrieve than to the studied formalistic schools of art against which they were rebelling.

Many of the formal elements of Lissitzky's "Had Gadya" drawings point toward Cubism, with its scattered planes and geometric forms.[13] In the backgrounds, houses are monochrome rectangles topped by differently colored monochrome triangles, mountains are simple parabolas, and circles and semicircles proliferate for waves of water, the sun, or more abstract backgrounds, all in a few simple colors. The geometric forms tie Lissitzky to the Constructivist and Futurist art movements that dominated Russian modern art at the time, including in the Vitebsk school. For them, art was intimately connected to the construction of the future, not just figuratively but literally, as art and architecture were to be closely bound together.

Many of the Jewish artists in these modernist movements found inspiration, and a ready-made font for their geometric modernist interests, in the block forms of Hebrew printed letters. They took advantage of postrevolutionary freedoms to explore this dimension, as prior to the revolution it had been illegal to publish texts using Hebrew or Yiddish words, and many Jewish presses had been forced to close. One finds this very much in evidence throughout Lissitzky's explicitly Jewish work, including *Had Gadya*.[14]

In choosing to illustrate a part of the Passover Haggadah, Lissitzky was aligning himself with a long tradition of the Jewish illustrated book. Traditionally, the two texts of Judaism that were illustrated were the Haggadah and the Book of Esther from the Bible, which is read as part of the celebratory Purim holiday.[15] Purim commemorates how Queen Esther, the Jewish wife of Persian King Ahasuerus, managed to save the Jews from an evil plot to kill them by the king's adviser Haman. When the story is told, children are given noisemakers, which they are told to use vigorously whenever they hear the name of evil Haman, so that his name will be drowned out. It is critical to note that in both the Purim story and the story of Exodus related at Passover, the heroes, Esther and Moses, are not known publically to be Jews. Thus, the religious services that accompany these two holidays share two key qualities: They are aimed primarily at children, and they are stories in which the hero who rescues their people has a Jewish secret identity.

Many other religious traditions have illustrated manuscripts, such as the illuminated manuscripts of medieval Christianity. But these illuminated manuscripts were very different in their origins and usage from the Jewish illustrated texts. The Christian illustrated texts were produced by cloistered monks to be used by the elite. In contrast, Jewish illustrated religious texts are very much a family affair, illustrated books for children that tell a heroic story of people in peril being rescued by a savior with a secret identity. Out of this tradition came a connection between Jews and comic books.

In calling attention to the identities of those heroic figures whose stories are illustrated in these works, we have moved from illustration to story. It is time to pick up this other thread of the story of old-world

Jewish roots of comic book superheroes. Here we turn to Jewish lore, specifically the tales of the golem. The golem was a legendary large and powerful being, humanoid in appearance but not really human. Possessed of great strength, he was said to have been shaped into hulking human form out of clay and animated by secret mystical means, brought into existence as a protector of the Jews in times of peril. Part of the mythology of the Jews, the legend of the golem is a defensive one, unlike the myths of the ancient Greeks, for example, whose powerful gods symbolized empires on the rise. In the midst of centuries of anti-Semitic oppression, the lore of the golem is a mythology of survival, not of conquest.

As with any myth good enough to stay in circulation, the origins of the story are shrouded in a good deal of mystery. It's difficult to accurately trace the legend because many of the tales surrounding golem figures were passed down in an oral storytelling tradition. The term *golem* itself has biblical roots, where it refers to a basic raw material out of which something may be made rather than to any kind of a creature that might be made out of that material. In Psalm 139 human life is said to emerge from "the lowest part of the earth" as an "imperfect substance." *Golami* here is also sometimes translated as "unshaped matter" or "unfinished creation."

References to the golem persist through the centuries, mostly through medieval biblical commentary, for example when the esteemed eleventh-century sage and commentator Rashi relates that the golem was created by combining the hidden letters of God's name revealed in a kabbalistic text composed centuries earlier.[16] Other golem legends spring up around other figures of the Middle Ages, for example the great Spanish poet Solomon Ibn Gabirol, and even the Rabbinic founder of the Hasidic movement, the Baal Shem Tov.[17] But the golem comes to the foreground as a character in stories placed in the sixteenth century, as the clay companion to one of the most renowned Jewish scholars of the medieval period.

These legends surround Rabbi Loew of Prague, the "Maharal," as he came to be known. Loew was a key figure in one of the most important Jewish communities in Europe, and became a critic of many of the problems internal to that community. He spoke out against what he saw as the corruption of the community's leadership, including the rabbinate, and struggled against its tradition of a sophistic kind of engagement with the Talmud that centered around memorization and the argumentation of minutiae, an approach that failed to consider more profound religious questions. He was also a bridge to the Christian governing bodies on which the safety and function of the community as a whole depended. Loew held the position of chief rabbi in Prague for seven years, and he met at least once with Emperor Rudolph II, an event much noted at the time.* He died in 1609, five years after resigning from this most distinguished post

The rabbi's fame, however, has been established and passed down primarily through the legends of the golem rather than through these historical achievements. It's not clear why folk traditions chose him as the historical figure to associate with the legends of the golem, but it seems likely that some kind of conjunction of his reputation as a scholar concerned with the spiritual welfare of the community and his political intercessions of behalf of that community made him an appropriate figure. In the various versions of golem stories the golem is always brought to life by a scholar to protect the Jewish community against external threats, and he always remains dependent on being given his marching orders by his learned creator.

The modern spread of these legends stems most directly from two writers of the early twentieth century, Yudl Rosenberg, a Polish rabbi who emigrated to Canada before World War I, and Chayim Bloch, who took much of Rosenberg's material and went on to become famous as a storyteller. Rosenberg claimed to have found an old manuscript (a common literary device) describing the efforts of Rabbi Leyb or Liva of Prague (Loew) and his golem to avenge and protect themselves against

---

*The precise nature of this meeting is still in dispute, whether it was called by the emperor who desired an interview with one of the most renowned contemporary religious scholars or was requested by the rabbi on behalf of his people to ask for righteous treatment under the crown. Perhaps one topic led to the other; but either way the meeting seemed to have forged a relationship with the imperial elite that persisted—one which would been of great benefit to the Jewish community.

the blood libels. According to Rosenberg, the rabbi, along with two assistants, went to the banks of the Moldau River and molded a clay figure from the damp earth there. They recited a prayer as each circled the inanimate object. After each man completed his rounds, the golem opened his eyes and stood when commanded. The group, now of four, returned to the town in the pre-dawn morning. The most well known versions of the golem's creation have him animated by an inscription on his forehead of the Hebrew word for "truth," *emeth*.

Rosenberg's revival of this legend at a time when his community was in desperate need of it speaks to the powerful relationship in Jewish tradition between narrative and survival.[18] Whether in Rosenberg's version of the story, or those of many other storytellers, the golem had many powers, natural and supernatural, which varied depending on the specific tale. He possessed greater than natural strength. He patrolled the streets at night and could go places forbidden to Jews, an especially important task around Passover when Christian accusations of the blood libel were especially rampant. The golem was said to inspect the contents of any bulky cargo in the neighborhood and make sure that no one was trying to plant false evidence in Jewish homes (often in the form of young, recently dead children). He had special powers of intuition—once he sensed an empty grave where a recently buried child was removed as part of a conspiracy to libel a Jew.[19] If he found anything incriminating he would tie the bearer to his bundle and haul them together to the police station.[20] As Elie Wiesel put it in his retelling of the story, the golem was "not limited by his senses, he could see souls and not just their bodies."[21] In another tale, a rabbi puts a series of papers with lettering that he had dreamed before the golem, and the golem instantaneously arranges the letters correctly, allowing the rabbi to interpret the dream and discover the sin of one of the members of the community.[22] In some tales he even wears an amulet that makes him invisible. The variability of his powers in different stories is anchored by his lack of one ability: the power of speech.

Before the golem can go seek out wrongdoers, the rabbi has to have done enough investigating to give him his orders. The golem's ability to exercise his physical strength and powers is entirely dependent on the rabbi's spiritual strength and knowledge to give him purpose, to give him life, such as it is, and for his ultimate disintegration. The tales about how the Maharal destroys the golem are various. In Rosenberg's version, after the threat of the blood libel is done away with, the rabbi and his two assistants go into the attic of the famed Prague Altneuschul synagogue and redo the ritual of his creation in reverse. In other versions, the golem begins to threaten his creator, who is consequently forced to strip him of his powers by removing the aleph, the first letter of the word inscribed on his forehead, changing *emeth* ("truth") to *meth* ("corpse").

Most of us know a golem story without realizing it. Though many of the tales are dark, some are humorous. One has the rabbi setting the golem to work doing domestic cleanup with a mop and pail, then leaving for the synagogue and forgetting to tell the creature to stop. On his return, he finds the golem still at it, creating a flood with bucket after bucket of water. Goethe later turned the story into a poem, which was set to music by Jewish composer Paul Dukas, and ended up being animated by Walt Disney, replacing the hulking clay golem with Mickey Mouse as "The Sorcerer's Apprentice" in the film *Fantasia*.[23] That scene became so iconic that a live-action version was included in the recent film *The Sorcerer's Apprentice*.

Once one begins to take note, one notices the golem showing up in all sorts of places in the culture: in novels by writers such as Cynthia Ozick (*The Puttermesser Papers*), Pete Hamill (*Snow in August*), Marge Piercy (*He, She and It*), Abraham Rothberg (*The Sword of the Golem*), and Thane Rosenbaum (*The Golems of Gotham*), a film trilogy in contemporary settings by Israeli filmmaker Amos Gitai (*Golem: The Spirit of Exile, Golem: The Petrified Garden,* and *Golem: Birth of a Golem*), a sculpture series by Hungarian artist Thury Levente (*A Golem Story May Be?*), a metaphor to explore the ethics of contemporary biotechnology (Byron L. Sherwin's *Golems Among Us: How a Jewish Legend Can Help Us Navigate the Biotech Century*), a doctoral dissertation on "The Golem as Metaphor for Jewish Women Writers" (in which Simone Naomi Yehuda explores views of women as muted and incomplete), and the song "The Golem" sung by the Kabalas (whose lyrics begin

"In 1580 the city of Prague / A place of mystery doused in fog / The Jewish people—the machine's cog / Were getting slammed just like a pog").

There have been some attempts to turn the golem into a comic book character, none of them particularly successful in the U.S., although he was the hero of a parody series of comics stories in Israel. Marvel published a few issues of *Strange Tales* devoted to a modern incarnation of "The Golem: The Thing That Walks like a Man" in 1974 in which he faced an evil sorcerer named Kaballa. In 1996, independent publisher Hall of Heroes ran a "Power of the Golem" issue. DC recently published a series featuring a revival of the golem in a present-day setting as "the Monolith," and he appears as a character in Image Comics's ongoing series *Proof*, whose characters run the gamut of beings of myth and legend (Bigfoot, Kraken, Chupacabra, fairies, dragons, etc.). In two 1972 stories, Superman battles "the Galactic Golem," created by Lex Luthor, who declares in a scene evoking that of the classic laboratory creation, "Anything that bumbling Victor Frankenstein can do—Lex Luthor can do better."[24] In echoes of the golem stories, the creature's center of power is in its forehead, and when Superman finally defeats the Galactic Golem he turns it into an inert statue.[25] And in a story that has Superman time and space traveling into an alternative reality, his appearance at the World War II Warsaw Ghetto uprising has everyone referring to him as a golem, especially two boys who claim that their drawings invented him, a clear invocation of Siegel and Shuster.[26] (The 1998 story demonstrates the difficulties mainstream comics still had in explicitly dealing with Jewish issues. Though markers of Jewish identity abound—in words, names, events, places—the word *Jew* is entirely absent, replaced by things like references to "target population of the Nazis' hate.")[27]

No matter the specifics, the golem is always portrayed as a hulking brute. So it was probably inevitable that one day there would actually be a story comparing the Hulk to the golem. *The Incredible Hulk* #134, dated December 1970, is titled "Among Us Walks the Golem." In the story, a little girl encounters a peaceful Hulk in the forest of Morvania (a typical generic name comics would use to locate something in some small Eastern European country) and takes him home to her peasant cottage, where she tells her father, Isaac (an iconic Jewish name), that he must be the one he's told her about, the golem. The Hulk eventually plays the role of a powerful, liberating golem, helping overthrow the evil dictator against whom the villagers are fighting.

The scene of an innocent little girl naively befriending a dangerous creature who looms above her will be familiar to anyone who knows the classic James Whale 1931 *Frankenstein* film with Boris Karloff. But fewer will know that that scene and other aspects of that film were deeply influenced by *The Golem*, a 1920 German silent film cowritten and codirected by and starring Paul Wegener. Often cited as an early horror film classic, the film boasts a plot that follows some golem stories in which things end badly for the creature's creator. Presumably that's the version James Sturm had in mind in his graphic novel *The Golem's Mighty Swing*, in which the name is taken by a large and powerful baseball player on a touring Jewish team in the 1920s. Among other things, the story examines racial prejudice and ends with an allusion to the destructive and self-destructive endings of some golem stories, with the narrator saying, "It is no surprise that things got out of hand. That is the nature of a golem."[28]

As the golem roamed in the Jewish imagination, the mainstream tradition was never sure how to handle this nonhuman creature animated by a human. There can be little doubt, however, that he was created as a powerful protector of a long-suffering people. Further, it seems clear that, consciously or not, Siegel and Shuster were drawing on this tradition in bringing Superman to the pages of the comics.

If Jews looked away from the past in hopes of a brighter future free of anti-Semitism, how then did they imagine that future might look? Much of this can be seen in the Jewish impact on science fiction, a genre closely related to comics. While science fiction imagines a future, it's at the same time a commentary on the present, and conscious of history. So, for example, as we moved from the space age to the computer age, the emphasis in science fiction moved from exploring the outskirts of the deep recesses of outer space to exploring the inner pathways of the deep corners of the mind. (Think of *Star Trek* versus *The Matrix*, the former a TV show originally pitched to the network as "*Wagon Train* in space" versus a film trilogy with its vision of the mind as computer and "reality" as a giant computer simulation.)

There is much about the science-fiction genre, including its historical consciousness and the way it looks toward the future, that makes it a natural outlet for the Jewish imagination, in part because the Jews originally gave meaning to history. I mean that in the profoundest sense possible. What we call Western civilization traces its intellectual roots back to its origins in two cultural sources: biblical and classical cultures. Or, as we affectionately nicknamed the course on the two for which I served as a graduate teaching assistant decades ago, "the Jews and the Greeks."

In the classical Greek intellectual tradition, especially for Plato (of whom noted twentieth-century philosopher Alfred North Whitehead famously declared "the safest general characterization of the European philosophical tradition is that it consists of a series of footnotes to Plato"[29]), meaning and truth are to be found in an eternal, unchanging realm existing outside of time, unaffected by mere historical contingencies. For Plato, what is caught in the stream of time is not just changeable but ever changing, and therefore cannot really be known precisely because it is always in the process of coming to be and passing away, and hence does not have the stable essence required to be a true object of knowledge. The highest truths, known by the philosopher, are eternal ideas or forms. For the Greeks, the realm of the gods is a higher realm than that of human history.

It was the Hebrew Bible that introduced to the world the idea of a divine presence that reveals itself in and through human events. Meaning, then, reveals itself through the passage of time; truth unfolds within history. When truth is historical rather than timeless, it takes the form of narrative. That's why the Bible is a book of stories, not a book of divine pronouncements, as I keep on wanting to remind people who justify their beliefs and actions by what they say the Bible says. The stories require interpretation in order to obtain meaning, and they are also always capable of carrying multiple but equally valid interpretations, as the rabbinic tradition has always insisted. That's why Jews are interpreters and commentators as well as storytellers. And storytellers of a particular kind: The Jewish story is a morality tale. Whether a grand novel or just the latest joke, the proper Jewish tale must convey higher meaning.

As befitting a historical people par excellence, Jewish consciousness is consciousness of time. One of the great twentieth-century Jewish theologians, indeed one of the great theologians of any stripe, Abraham Joshua Heschel, famously explained that the Sabbath was how Jews built their cathedrals in time rather than in space:

> While the deities of other peoples were associated with places or things, the God of Israel was the God of events: the Redeemer from slavery, the Revealer of the Torah, manifesting Himself in events of history rather than in things or places.[30]

In modern speculative fiction, Jews generally turn to the genre of science fiction rather than fantasy.[31] When imagining another world, Jewish thought moves to an alternative "when" rather than an alternative "where," forward in time rather than elsewhere in location, to a future yet to come rather than to an enchanted realm currently existing in another location alongside ours.*

Because it features prefigurative glimpses of a time to come, and thus dovetails with Judaism's temporal orientation, as well as because of its rationalist bent, science fiction exerts a powerful pull on the Jewish imagination. There's also a negative reason why Jewish writers tend to gravitate away from the fantasy tradition: its heavy reliance on the imagery of medieval Christendom. As Michael Weingrad puts it:

---

*The dichotomy is not absolute; there are certainly good Jewish fantasy stories and writers. There is the golem, tales of dybbuks, as well as angels and demons (the most famous of Jewish legendary demons is probably Lilith, said to have been Adam's first wife, before Eve, but reclaimed by contemporary Jewish feminists as a maligned figure, a demonized feminist rebel). But these are tales of the occasional ingression of the fantastic and supernatural into our world, not stories of imagined other worlds or alternate realities.

To answer the question of why Jews do not write fantasy, we should begin by acknowledging that the conventional trappings of fantasy, with their feudal atmosphere and rootedness in rural Europe, are not especially welcoming to Jews, who were too often at the wrong end of the medieval sword. Ever since the Crusades, Jews have had good reasons to cast doubt upon the romance of knighthood, and this is an obstacle in a genre that takes medieval chivalry to its imaginative ideal.[32]

This bent toward science fiction is part of the background that gave rise to the world of comic book superheroes, and when they created Superman, Siegel and Shuster were deeply influenced by the early pulp science-fiction magazines that were popular at the time. ("Pulp" because they were printed on such cheap paper.) The iconic way of writing *Superman* uses the same basic design format that Frank R. Paul, known as the father of science-fiction art, used for the cover title art of the magazine *Amazing Stories*.* This immensely popular magazine (which Shuster himself claimed as an influence)[33] was started in 1926 by publisher Hugo Gernsback, a Jew originally from Luxembourg. For his influential role in publishing these pulps, Gernsback is sometimes grouped together with H. G. Wells and Jules Verne as one of the fathers of science fiction.

It's common to trace the history of comic book art through newspapers, beginning with editorial cartoons, moving to comics, comic strips, and finally comic books.[34] While there is much to be said for this genealogy, the specific aesthetic of comic book art owes more to the aesthetics of contemporaneous science-fiction magazine illustration than to earlier newspaper illustration. When early comic strips began appearing in the late nineteenth century, both they and the newspaper editorial cartoons of the time still inhabited the Victorian sense of

---

*Think block capital letters of diminishing size aligned at the top, producing that upward sweeping curve to the right that draws the reader's eye up, up, and away toward the contents beckoning inside.

space. Think of the stereotypical Victorian living room in which those newspapers might have been read. While to readers of the time the space was appropriately and decoratively filled, to more modern eyes it looks incredibly cluttered, seemingly every inch filled with bric-a-brac, the furniture ostentatiously ornate, with as many additional curves and curlicues as could be fit on. To kids those rooms practically screamed one message: Don't even think about playing in here. Cartoon panels of that time look the same way to modern eyes: The space is too filled with clutter, with all "empty space" taken up with verbiage.

The science-fiction pulps of the '20s and '30s did away with all that. They were part of a much broader shift that reigned everywhere in the culture, reflected in the imperative to replace what were now seen as old-fashioned excessive adornments with a more sparse functional simplicity. Driven by new technologies and styles, this streamlined aesthetic signaled speed, efficiency, technology, the new and the modern. One saw it everywhere, even in such areas as women's clothing, where the frills and bows of the Gibson girl's flowing garb gave way to the sleek tight dress of the flapper, as well as in its corresponding simplified business suit for men. Even personal appearance changed, with slimmer bodies ascendant over the corpulence that used to signify wealth. The old neoclassical building style with all its ornamentation was replaced by modern architecture with its functional forms, creating the skyscrapers over which Superman would soon be leaping in single bounds, modern design and technology innovations replaced those older train engines with newer speeding locomotives, making Superman's demonstrations that he was more powerful and faster than they were all the more impressive, and the horse-carriage-like appearance of the early automobiles gave way to the sleeker sedan that Superman would be hoisting over his head.

Those science-fiction cover illustrations, in which men emerged from slim needle-point rockets in sleek space suits, captured and extended the new modernistic style. (That's why the actual moon landing, with its spindly-legged spacecraft and those bulky space suits, carried with it a slight tinge of disappointment for those of a certain age, notwithstanding all the genuine excitement and enthusiasm it generated. This just wasn't how we'd pictured it for all these years!) The superhero comics captured this modernized aesthetic. To kids, the streamlined sense of space, with all that adult clutter eliminated, offered a huge expansive playground for the imagination. It practically screamed its message: No adults allowed!

Beyond the artwork, the origin stories of most superheroes show their protagonists' powers coming from the world of science—though it must also be said that they bend the rules of science past the breaking point. Superman's outer-space origin sets him firmly in a science-fiction universe, and Batman's scientific expertise, crucial to his success as a great detective, is as important to his crime fighting as are his physical abilities. Yes, there are counterexamples: The Marvel pantheon includes Thor, the Norse God of Thunder, and Dr. Strange, the Sorcerer Supreme who is Master of the Mystic Arts. But the comic book universe is much more populously inhabited by the likes of the Fantastic Four, Spider-Man, Iron Man, the Hulk, Ant-Man, the Black Panther, and so on. The leader of the Fantastic Four, Reed Richards, and all of these just named are not just scientifically based but are actually scientists themselves.*

Siegel and Shuster pinned their utopian but still scientific hopes on their superman. For them, the "super" in Superman didn't just mean an individual variation that created a more powerful man; it meant a new and more advanced type of human who would supersede the present stage of humanity as the next stage on our evolutionary ascension. In contrast to later explanations that attributed Superman's powers to Earth's lesser gravity and its yellow sun, as opposed to Krypton's red sun, as Siegel and Shuster originally imagined it Kryptonians were able to leap those leaps and lift those weights even back on their home world. "He had come from a planet whose inhabitants' physical structure was

---

* Of the DC Big Three of Superman, Batman, and Wonder Woman, only Wonder Woman, the Amazon Princess, comes from a fantasy world. Both she and Captain Marvel were written primarily by non-Jewish creators and imported into comics the whole panoply of classical mythology.

millions of years advanced of our own."[35] So even though Superman was an alien, he literally embodied the promise of our own future.

Science fiction holds out the promise of a different (although not always better) tomorrow. When Superman became the first comic book figure to get his own magazine, he was not yet "The Man of Steel"; rather, he was "The Man of Tomorrow." Bringing the man of tomorrow into the world of today, so that we may thereby catch a glimpse of the world to come, is a very Jewish idea. Especially on the Sabbath, but at other times as well, observant Jews consider themselves to be in a sense simultaneously inhabiting the two worlds: the world as it is now and the world as it will be—that is to say, the world as it ought to be.

To understand the dramatic shifts science fiction wrought upon the popular imagination and particularly the Jewish influence at play here, we will examine the writings of one of the most celebrated science-fiction writers, Isaac Asimov. Asimov was raised by Orthodox parents, but he himself was not religious, and even held a somewhat dark view of religion. Nonetheless, Asimov always insisted he was very Jewish, and in any case we are concerned here with the Jewishness of his writings, not his personal life.

Asimov's most influential contribution to science fiction came in his robot stories. Most of the early stories were eventually collected in the volume *I, Robot*, in which Asimov invented the Three Laws of Robotics.* These laws, completely new when Asimov first wrote them, have become such an intrinsic part of the science-fiction genre that most writers just assume they are in operation in their fiction, knowing that readers will make the same assumption. In fact, they are taken so much for granted that if in any work of science fiction a robot violates these principles we feel something is wrong, and an explanation is required. The precise wording has varied, but basically the Three Laws of Robotics are:

---

* From these stories also come the very word *robotics*, invented by Asimov, though he didn't at first realize that he had coined a new word, as well as another new word for a new technology Asimov made up, to which fans of *Star Trek: The Next Generation* are greatly indebted, "positronic" technology, like the extraordinary brain possessed by the android Data.

1. A robot may not injure a human being or, through inaction, allow a human being to come to harm.
2. A robot must obey orders given by human beings except when such orders would conflict with the First Law.
3. A robot must protect its own existence as long as such protection does not conflict with the First or Second Law.

These principles are first articulated in Asimov's 1942 robot story "Runaround" but are already implicit in his first robot story, "Robbie," in which, to the great surprise of some of the other characters in the story, a robot saves the life of a human child. Many of Asimov's robot stories are ingenious examples of the dilemmas and paradoxes, and often great humor, which arise from conflicts generated by these deceptively simple principles. The "robot Descartes" of the story titled simply "Reason" is a classic example. Here a robot, using the same principles used by Descartes to prove the existence of God, deduces that since it is obvious by the natural light of reason that a creator must be superior to its creations then, as the robot is obviously superior to these human beings, they therefore cannot have created him as they claim to have done. There must instead be a robot creator responsible for the grand scheme of things that has, for its own mysterious purposes, planted these false beliefs in the minds of these poor, deluded humans. Much of the meaning and reading pleasure to be found in the story are generated by the ensuing scenes of mounting frustration on the part of the humans who have to deal with this overweening robotic arrogance.

Before Asimov, the genre model for artificial humans such as robots was still *Frankenstein,* where the monster rebels against and destroys his creator. Mary Shelley's romantic novel remains the classic warning tale of the perils of unbridled science, especially when new technology transgresses far enough to create new forms of life. This was what people expected of robots. The moral of the story was expected to be that humans should not try to attempt to create humanoid creatures, for such unnatural creations defied the natural order and would therefore bring destruction down upon the heads of their creators. The very word *robot* comes from Czech playwright Karel Čapek's 1921 play *R.U.R.,* which stands for "Rossum's Universal Robots." "Robot" is derived from the Czech word for "worker," and in the play the "artificial people," i.e., the "robots" created by the company of Rossum's Universal Robots, rebel against and bring about the destruction of the human race. Čapek is said to have retrospectively come to the conclusion, after he had finished the play, that he had written a version of the Jewish legend of the golem. Asimov's stories played off the fact that many people would think of robots in this way, and his Laws of Robotics are specifically designed to counter this view, bringing humans to have greater faith and trust in science and technology.

Likewise with Superman. Before Siegel and Shuster, the dominant view was that a superman—that is to say, a new type of superior person—would obviously look with disdain and contempt upon us inferior beings, and would use his superiority to attempt to rule over humanity. In science fiction of the day, this plot line seemed intrinsic to the concept of a superman. In some versions his evil nature seemed to arise naturally out of his own psychological makeup, while in others it emerged as a response to the fear and hatred with which humanity viewed him, thereby turning humanity's fears of a superman into a self-fulfilling prophecy.[36] (A story line of this type would emerge years later in the [Jewish] Magneto character of the X-Men.)

Asimov's robots and Siegel and Schuster's Superman were groundbreaking and influential because they shattered the previous mold in which such characters were cast. Their creators reversed their moral polarity from bad to good, turning them from villains into heroes. The definitive transformations of these paradigms manifest the Jewish ethical imperative to strive for a better world, sustained by the belief that it will come.

Also key to the story we are telling here is Asimov's major opus, *The Foundation Trilogy*, which in 1966 received the distinctive honor of being awarded a special onetime Hugo Award (the science-fiction equivalent of the Oscars, named after Hugo Gernsback) for "Best All-Time Series." In this story, set in a far future under a crumbling galactic empire, scientist Hari Seldon invents the science of "psychohistory" (the real branch of historical analysis that goes by this name is something quite different from what Asimov intended by the term). Psychohistory develops from Seldon's realization that if human behavior is examined on a sufficiently large scale, such as the population of the entire galaxy, present circumstances and trends can be mathematically extrapolated with sufficient accuracy to enable one to predict the future. Seldon is disturbed by his finding, based on the application of his method, when he learns that after the coming fall of the empire the galaxy will sink into a thirty-thousand-year period of barbarism. At first seeing this as only a theoretical exercise, Seldon comes to realize that his new science may actually have a practical application. If a plan were to be set in motion mobilizing a large enough critical mass of people over a sufficiently extended period of time, this would inject a new variable into the situation that would change the outcome of the equation. While finding that some period of future decay and loss accompanying the fall of the empire is inevitable, Seldon then sets in motion a daring and complex plan aimed at shortening the coming thousands of years of a dark age into just a single millennium. The individuals involved must initially not know of the plan, for such self-knowledge would introduce unmanageable complications into the enterprise (much as it is often the case that subjects in a scientific experiment must not know the true object of the experiment, for this would change the nature of their participation in it).

Thus Seldon maneuvers to have carefully selected persons dispatched to a remote world to produce an Encyclopedia Galactica, a vast compendium of available knowledge, without knowing that their true purpose is to be the founders of a colony whose task will be to emerge into prominence after the fall of the empire and guide the galaxy back to rational civilization. The story of the foundation thus established is told in the three volumes of the trilogy, originally published between 1942 and 1953, and joined decades later by additional volumes Asimov wrote to satisfy the clamoring demands of his fans and publisher.

So what makes this a Jewish story? There is no religious sensibility in the story of the *Foundation Trilogy*, let alone a specifically Jewish religious sensibility. In fact, here, as in most of his writing, Asimov treats religion largely as superstition fueled by scientific ignorance.

Looking back to some of the criteria I discussed in the introduction, note the two key elements: First, the Jewish elements of the work need not be explicit, nor do the characters need to be explicitly identified as Jewish, but an informed reader should be able to see how Jewish themes or ideas are central to the work. Second, we should be able to see some line of transmission by which the writer could plausibly have come into contact with the Jewish elements present in the book. The latter is easy: Asimov was a Russian Jewish immigrant who came to America when he was three, and whose parents spoke to him in Yiddish. In fact, while he is clear that his characters are not Jewish, one can hear the voice of the Jewish immigrant experience in the seemingly Yiddishist dialogue of some characters. As Asimov explains:

> Sometimes . . . it was necessary for me to have a character whom, for various nefarious purpose of my own, I wanted the reader to underestimate. The easiest trick was to give him a substandard version of English, for then he would be dismissed as a comic character with at most a certain limited folk wisdom. Since the only substandard version of English I can handle faultlessly is the Yiddish dialect, some of the characters in *The Foundation Trilogy* speak it.[37]

As for the Jewish themes of the work, many of the different elements of Jewish thought we've discussed are seamlessly merged in *Foundation*. The story hinges on the intelligibility of history, on the discovery that behind seeming chaos and unpredictability there lies the unfolding of a discernible trajectory where the uninformed would see only disconnected and perhaps meaningless events. The reader's engagement with the story requires only faith in reason, not the suspension of disbelief required by fantasy. The combination of Jewish commitment to rationality, embodied for modern consciousness in science, the Jewish idea of meaning unfolding in history, and Judaism's messianism make futuristic science fiction a natural avenue of exploration for the Jewish imagination.

Thus the Jewishness of Asimov's *Foundation Trilogy* lies not in the Jewishness of its author, nor in any of the work's elements being explicitly Jewish, but rather in the way in which the central preoccupations of the trilogy are central themes of Jewish thought and experience. This is the nature of the claim I've been making about Superman and other comic book superheroes being Jewish characters. In claiming Superman for a Jewish tradition, I am not reducing Superman to being only a Jewish character, not taking away from his more universal appeal. One always arrives at universal appeal from some particular place, and I am demonstrating how the Jewish tradition is Superman's ancestral home.

The men who took their imaginative leaps into the new world of tomorrow through their comic book superhero creations thought they were leaving the Old World behind and moving into a shiny, streamlined, and glorious future. I herewith humbly submit for your consideration the proposition that, whatever future they imagined, they brought their past with them in the tradition of illustrated books, in the legends of the golem, and in the very historical and philosophical impulses for looking to the future instead of the past.

3

THE COMIC IN COMICS

Mad in the Original Yiddish

S ome purists hold that it's somehow degrading to the medium to call them "comics," suggesting that one should at least call them comic *books*, if not graphic novels. I disagree. There's something important about focusing on the comic aspects of the comic book superhero tradition. These aspects are deeply connected to the Jewish elements of the form.

Jewish humor is always held up as one of the trademarks of Jewish culture. The legacy of Jews in the history of American comedy is extraordinary: from groups like the Marx Brothers and Three Stooges, who transitioned from vaudeville to early films; to Jack Benny and George Burns, who brought us from radio to television, where Milton Berle and Sid Caesar were early comic superstars; to filmmakers such as Woody Allen and Mel Brooks; to comics such as Larry David and Sarah Silverman, to more-than-comics such as Bette Midler and Billy Crystal.

All humor shares certain characteristics, so it's challenging to find anything that specifically identifies a Jewish sense of humor. But philosopher Ted Cohen makes a good start in his book *Jokes: Philosophical Thoughts on Joking Matters,* remarking that first of all "it is the humor of *outsiders.*" He goes on to note:

Jews have no monopoly on jokes, nor on good jokes, nor even on jokes of a particular kind, and yet there is a characteristic association of Jews with a certain joking spirit, and that spirit has become an aspect of American joking.[1]

Incongruity is essential to humor. To simultaneously have within one's view the world as it is and the world of the future (whether embodied by the awaited Messiah or by Superman) brings with it a critical perspective on the world in which we live. In this framing, the world as it ought to be becomes the standard by which we measure the world as it is. And we find it wanting. This critical distance is a prerequisite for a sense of humor because the perception that something is humorous always involves a contrast between *is* and *ought*, between how things are and how they're supposed to be. We laugh in the precise instant we perceive the incongruity, when we simultaneously hold both worlds in our minds. That's why a joke isn't funny when it has to be explained, because the explanation can inhabit only one world at a time. Standing with one foot in the world as it is and the other in the world to come is also the classically prescribed attitude for the observant Jew.

I was once invited to a Passover Seder in which the participants were asked to bring something that symbolized liberation to them to be placed on a Freedom Plate, created as a supplement to the traditional Seder Plate that holds the ritual foods and objects, to be used during the ceremony, when each person around the table would be asked to explain why they had brought what they had brought. I brought a Jewish joke book. When my turn came, I explained that to me the moment of laughter was precisely the moment of liberation, for laughter celebrated the joy of moving from this world to the next.

This deeply ingrained double vision, always comparing things as they are against things as they should be and noting the discrepancy, is a principal source of Jewish humor, as well as one of the sources of Jewish progressive political activism. Combined, these two create the stance of the Jewish political satirist, from Lenny Bruce to Jon Stewart. It's also the source of much of the comic in comics, where the portrayals of the ideals to which we aspire reveals the flaws the rest of us mere mortals.

Another aspect of the perspective that shapes Jewish humor comes from the status position of Jews in most cultures: The downtrodden and oppressed always have a better sense of humor than those in power. Those in power see only their own world, while those below are always aware of both environs, what gets called the upstairs and the downstairs in the context of British class relations between masters and servants, or the big house versus the slave quarters in the U.S. context of masters and slaves. This is what the great American intellectual leader and theorist of race W. E. B. Du Bois had in mind when he wrote at the turn of the previous century of the "double-consciousness" of the American Negro.[2] It is the experience of always simultaneously seeing and experiencing oneself not just through one's own eyes, but also through the eyes of the dominant culture.

Every form of oppression, be it anti-Semitism, racism, sexism, or some other form, is a power imbalance between dominant and marginalized groups. Such a power imbalance always brings with it an information imbalance, where those at the bottom always know more about the lives and views of those at the top than vice versa. So employees will know a great deal about the personal likes and dislikes of the boss (which clothes can I get away with wearing? How much salty language is okay at the office? etc.), but the boss usually knows very little about the personal tastes of the employees. He who must be obeyed has no need of such knowledge, while those who must obey need it for survival. Much of the humor of the oppressed takes what they know are the negative views held about them by those in power and turns these stereotypes around. ("Yankee Doodle" was originally a derogatory term used by the British against the colonists, who then seized upon it as a badge of pride. The same dynamic underlies contemporary use of the term *queer*.) Oppression makes such humor necessary as a survival strategy to retain one's dignity and sanity under continually threatening conditions. As *Mad's* Al Jaffee put it, "Oppressed people resort to humor. . . . They can't afford to get angry."[3]

In the U.S., Jewish humor has influenced—perhaps more accurately, infiltrated—the humor of the mainstream culture in a specific way. Jews have been allowed a view into the mainstream through the glass ceilings or walls that still keep them out. The tone of American Jewish humor therefore has less the feel of a complete stranger's hostility and more the gentle mocking of someone who has his foot far enough in the door to play the role of the insider's outsider, more the remotely related black sheep of the family than the outcast scapegoat (though to be sure there's enough of the latter attitude still around).

One quality of Jewish humor is that it deflates authority, bringing it back down to earth. It doesn't allow anyone to get too highfalutin, a quality that is rooted in the Jewish experience of oppression. It derives from the segregation of Jews from the non-Jewish population. The non-Jewish authorities who rule the lives of Jews loom large as a distant other, so they are comedically cut down to humanized size in order to cope with them. (Getting away with a joke on the tsar's officers was always good for a laugh.) Even within the Jewish community, the all-too-human foibles of the rabbi were a constant source of humor.

Jewish humor is embedded in the Yiddish language, which is still the source of much Jewish humor—and the mother tongue of the boyhood homes of many of the early comics creators. Yiddish arose when German Jews were walled off into ghettos within larger German cities. As a result, the medieval German that they all spoke at the time was left to develop on its own within the ghetto walls, cut off from the formal institutions of the surrounding society. What developed was a less formal, more folksy language, which came to be known as the *mamaloschen*, or "mother tongue." This gendering had a specific impetus: Within that isolated medieval Jewish world, the "high" culture, the world of the religious scholarship carried on by "great men," was carried on in Hebrew. Yiddish was the language of the domestic world, the language that women spoke among themselves, simultaneously admiring and gently mocking the public world of men. To be sure, the men spoke Yiddish too when they joined women in the domestic sphere. A bilingual and even trilingual culture—Yiddish, Hebrew, and the language of the surrounding society—breeds the outsider sensibility of the humorist, and cultivates the linguistic playfulness one often finds in Jewish humor. For those who share this heritage, the barbed arrows of Yiddish humor are aimed at bringing down any putting on of airs, deflating any pretentiousness of the "great men." It is through this lens that Jews with this background see any humor of this sort. So for those of us who come to the scene with this Yiddish sensibility, when Clark has fooled everyone about Superman's secret identity and looks out at the audience to give us a wink at the end of the story, we intuitively understand that he's winking to us in Yiddish.

The worldview of a people is embodied in their language. Yiddish is a language of the common people, a folkish language, a "demotic" language, if one wants the technical term used by linguists for the vernacular, common tongue. It's an extraordinarily down-to-earth language, full of wonderfully rich expressions that bring everything back to hearth and home. If a politician or anyone is getting on your nerves, probably with a long boring speech, you may say they have *hakt a chainik*, or "banged on a teapot." A *kochleffel* is a "cooking spoon," but it's also someone who stirs up trouble.

One reason comedians speaking in other languages resort to select words of Yiddish is that so much of its vocabulary sounds like what the word means (the formal word for this quality is onomatopoeia). Does anyone really need to be told they're not being praised if they hear themselves called a shlub, a shnook, or a shmuck? And said correctly, with that Germanic guttural *ch* sound that English speakers have trouble with (as in *Chanukah*), doesn't *chazzerei* sound like what it means, i.e., "junk food"? A *tchotchke*, meaning a "cheap knickknack," couldn't possibly be something expensive, could it? In their graphic glory, Yiddish curses are a subject worthy of admiring study in their own right, e.g., "All your teeth should fall out except one and that one should give you a toothache" or "You should grow like an onion, with your head in the ground and your feet up in the air."

The idioms and expressions of Yiddish continually force one away from the abstract into the concrete, into the nitty-gritty of ordinary experience. For example, there are few better examples of an abstract idea than Einstein's theory of relativity, expressed in the equation $E=mc^2$.

A 1930s explanation of the theory from the greatest Yiddish comedy team, (Shimon) Dzigan and (Israel) Shumacher, illustrates the genius of Yiddish translation from the abstract to the concrete. Astonished that his friend has never heard of the great Professor Einstein, let alone the theory of relativity, one explains it to the other this way: "If you have seven hairs in your soup, it's a lot. If you have seven hairs on your head, it's very little. That's relativity!"[4]

Yiddish is an incredibly graphic language, so it's not surprising that so many comics fall back on it at certain moments, especially when deflating any kind of formality or pretentiousness. It's also not surprising that its basic sensibility, if not its vocabulary, found expression in the graphic language of comic books.

The greatest expression of Jewish humor (or *any* humor) in comics was *Mad*, which started as a comic book in 1952 and later became a magazine. *Mad* was a Jewish production through and through. On the inside front cover of the first issue "the Editors" described how the readers came to be holding it in their hands:

> We decided we wanted to add another mag to our line. . . . We were tired of the war, ragged from the science-fiction, weary of the horror. Then it hit us! Why not do a complete about-face! A change of pace! A comic book . . . Not a serious comic book . . . But a COMIC comic book.[5]

It came to routinely claim that it was produced by "the usual gang of idiots," but the real mad genius behind *Mad* was Harvey Kurtzman, editor, writer, and artist. Born in Brooklyn in 1924, he was physically short in stature, as befitting his name (*kurtz* is Yiddish for "short"). It was Kurtzman's vision that shaped the entire *Mad* enterprise: He drew most of the early covers, wrote and illustrated many of the stories, and his firm guiding editorial hand was everywhere. Just as the comics shop of Will Eisner trained many of the leading cartoonists, some of those who became leading satirists got their start under Kurtzman: Monty Python's Terry Gilliam and John Cleese first worked together under his direction, and he gave Robert Crumb his start.

This founding generation drew with a combination of expressive artistry and parodying tone. Famed caricaturist David Levine may have put it best, as noted by journalist Menachem Wecker: "A reporter once asked Levine what he draws in—presumably an inquiry about his medium. 'I draw in Yiddish,' he replied."[6] Levine's revealing portrayals of the people of our times, which appeared regularly in the *New York Review of Books,* are somehow simultaneously both accurate and exaggerated, as is much of the visual style pioneered by *Mad.* It seems that Yiddish is the quintessential language of irony and satire in image as well as text.

When you take the people of the book, with centuries of an interpretive tradition of reading between the lines and looking for deeper levels of meaning, and then put them under oppression for additional centuries, where they have to monitor and encode what they say in public, this is the verbal and visual language that you get. It's the satirist's visual style, and it's perfect for comics. It straddles the distinction between accuracy and exaggeration. It has to be realistic enough to be instantly recognizable, but sufficiently distant from actual accuracy to be recognized as fantasy. For this visual style to work it has to be simplified to the point where the image is immediately grasped as a joke. In order for comics art to move us forward in the story, for it to fulfill its narrative function, the reader shouldn't have to pause too long to decipher the image.

For American youngsters of the 1950s, *Mad* was a subversive publication that broke through the cultural blandness to which they were expected to conform. Gloria Steinem, who worked as Kurtzman's assistant for a period, said, "There was a spirit of satire and irreverence in *Mad* that was very important, and it was the only place you could find it in the 50s."[7] When asked, "Which cartoonists contributed to your understanding of comics generally, or to a specific visual vocabulary?" Art Spiegelman replied:

My most central influence was Harvey Kurtzman's *Mad.* It's what doomed me to cartooning. His *Mad* (different from the *Mad* that came after) was a thoroughly radical invention. He left after the first twenty-four issues. It was postmodern avant la letter in that it fed off other media, and fed it back to itself through a cracked lens, and was very self-referentially engaged in its own form.[8]

Years later Kurtzman asked Spiegelman to lecture on his own work in the class Kurtzman was teaching at the School of Visual Arts. Instead, Spiegelman arrived with a fully illustrated lecture on Kurtzman's work. He demonstrated the important influence of Kurtzman's "rigorous structure and jazzy rhythms" and declared, "*Mad* was an urban junk collage that said, 'Pay attention! The mass media are *lying* to you . . . including this comic book. I think Harvey's *Mad* was more important than pot and LSD in shaping the generation that protested the Vietnam War." This according to Spiegelman's own comic strip retelling of the event in the two-page story "A Furshlugginer Genius."[9]

Mad spoofed popular culture, and in its early years as a ten-cent comic book, before it became a twenty-five cent magazine, it especially spoofed other, more "serious" adventure comics. The only hero who grabbed their attention so much that he was spoofed twice in the first half dozen issues was Tarzan—"Melvin" in the second issue, then "Melvin of the Apes" in the sixth. What do you expect from a bunch of inner-city Jewish guys who understood the urban jungle but seldom saw a real tree?

Yiddish abounded, appearing more frequently after the first few issues as the gang gained confidence in what they were doing. By the time of "The Lone Stranger," the last story of the third issue, the Stranger asks his sidekick Pronto, "*Vas ist los?*" ("What's up?"), a precursor to Mel Brooks as an Indian chief shouting, "*Loz em gehem!*" ("Let them go!") in *Blazing Saddles,* both actually more linguistically authentic than the speech of Hollywood's usual Indians. After all, there were *some* Jews in the old West, but no Native American *ever* uttered the invented "kemosabe" that Tonto called the Lone Ranger .[10] "*Mad* also gave a wink to Jewish readers with the constant use of Yiddishisms (such as *fershlugginer, schmaltz, oy,* and *feh*), Kurtzman's way of tossing matzah balls at the white-bread WASPy veneer of his competitors' comics," explains Al Jaffee. "*Mad* made fun of pretentiousness, they made fun of the nobleman."[11]

And who was more noble, more high-flying, and thus more in need of being brought back down to earth, than Superman? One of the fan favorite spoofs of those early issues, reprinted innumerable times since, was "Superduperman," written by Harvey Kurtzman and drawn by Wally Wood (who at one time worked on Will Eisner's *Spirit*). If you look closely, the lettering on his chest, where Superman's S symbol is, keeps changing what it says from panel to panel: first it's the seal of "Good Housebreaking," then it shifts to others including "Yale," "For Rent," "100% Wool," "Fragile," "Body by . . ." (mocking the "Body by Fisher" emblem displayed on GM cars), "Preshrunk," and the EC and RCA Victor logos. Superduperman is actually the "incredibly miserable and emaciated looking" Clark Bent, "man assistant to the copy boy," pathetically infatuated with girl reporter Lois Pain, both of the *Daily Dirt* newspaper. The "story," if you can call it that, has Superduperman fighting Captain Marbles, transformed into his fighting red suit with a dollar symbol on his chest when boy reporter Billy Spafon yells, "Shazoom."[12] In typical *Mad* fashion, this parody rips into its own medium, the comics, and pulls no punches.

Mad moved quickly from first spoofing other comics generically—horror stories, detective and adventure tales, westerns, science fiction—to mocking specific characters like those above. It then expanded its targets to include films and TV shows, and after that anything in the culture was fair game, but its preferred targets remained other media creations. It often self-reflectively broke the fourth wall to address its readers. "I know you're going to fall in love with me," says the square-jawed hero to the slinky seductress, "because I'm the hero of this story." One important way it radicalized its young readers was that its satire consistently pulled back the curtain to reveal the hackneyed clichés underneath what was being presented as the latest hot new "creative" product, showing it to be really just another repackaging of the same old shtick. Yes, some of *Mad*'s humor was formulaic and juvenile, but that was kind of the point. When those lowbrow zingers so consistently hit their targets dead center, you've thereby proven just how infantilizing the culture really is. You've established that adult authority in politics, advertising, and popular culture is not to be trusted, whether it comes from Washington, Madison Avenue, or the offices *of Mad* itself.

> *Mad* was a revelation: it was the first to tell us that the toys we were being sold were garbage, our teachers were phonies, our leaders were fools, our religious counselors were hypocrites, and even our parents were lying to us about damn near everything. An entire generation had William Gaines for a godfather: this same generation later went on to give us the sexual revolution, the environmental movement, the peace movement, greater freedom in artistic expression, and a host of other goodies. Coincidence? You be the judge."[13]

Mad was published by Bill Gaines, son of the Max Gaines who helped discover Superman, and who was instrumental in creating the comic book format. Under Bill Gaines, his EC comics company (originally "Educational Comics") had been publishing a number of successful crime, science-fiction, horror, and war comics. But by 1955 their only publication left standing was *Mad,* the others having folded under the onslaught of the anti-comics crusade of Senator Estes Kefauver's Subcommittee to Investigate Juvenile Delinquency of the Committee on the Judiciary. Those hearings decisively changed the fortunes of the comics industry, and will be discussed in greater detail in the next chapter. It was ironic that it was Gaines's publications that ended up being singled out for special condemnation as morally corrupting because, as one commentator wrote, "What set EC apart from its competitors was a commitment to moral themes. Story lines often dealt with the evils of abusive relationships, misguided patriotism, and racism." Furthermore:

> A *Hartford Courant* editorial, for instance, referred to comics as "the filthy stream that flows from the gold-plated sewers of New York"—a code for "Jewish businesses." Comic-book burnings became a familiar sight across the country, and some of the so-called "disgusting" literature was seized by police. The

attorney general of Massachusetts called for the banning of Gaines' humor comic *Panic* after it ran a spoof of "A Visit from St. Nicholas" (commonly known by its opening line, "'Twas the Night Before Christmas"), charging that it was actually stirring up a *bona fide* panic by "desecrating Christmas."[14]

Attention to the language used above reveals the link between the anti-comics crusade and anti-Semitism. Criticism of comics was couched in language resonant with anti-Semitically coded terms calling it a dirty Jewish business, and a mild holiday spoof was called a "desecration" of Christmas.

The offending spoof was by Will Elder, born Wolf William Eisenberg to Jewish Polish immigrants in the Bronx in 1921, who took the name Elder after he returned from World War II army service. In the army, he had put his drawing skills to use illustrating VD posters and making maps, including one of Omaha Beach for the Normandy D-day landing. After D-day, he joined the land forces to fight in the Battle of the Bulge and elsewhere. Elder was the third of the triumvirate at *Mad* (with Harvey Kurtzman and Al Jaffee) who had all first met when they attended New York's High School of Music and Art together. The spoof consisted of the actual text of "'Twas the Night Before Christmas," illustrated by Elder in his distinctive style, which is instantly recognizable to anyone who ever even glanced at *Mad*. It featured stellar examples of the kind of humor that typified the genre, with Marilyn Monroe as one of the "sugar plums" and Elder's self-portrait accompanying Santa inserted to illustrate the line that Santa "turned with a jerk."

Remember those silly little doodles in *Mad* on the sides of the page, the ones that had nothing to do with the story? That was pure Elder, and he put them there because he was driven to fill any available space with additional jokes. He called it "chicken fat," after that staple of Jewish cuisine: "the part of the soup that is bad for you, yet gives the soup its delicious flavor."[15] Elder's compulsive drawing created in readers a compulsion to go back and reread the magazine, correctly convinced that they'd missed things the first time around. Elder had illustrated the story "Ganefs!" (from the Yiddish for "crooks") in *Mad*'s first issue, and among his claims to fame were his many popular media spoofs for *Mad,* including those in which he skewered comics characters with his own creations, such as "Woman Wonder," "Mickey Rodent," "Starchie," "Poopeye," and *Playboy's* (in)famous long-running comic strip that he later did with Kurtzman, "Little Annie Fanny." "Little Annie Fanny" was literally a comic "strip," since in every episode Annie's clothes came off as the story went on.

The spirit of *Mad* in the '50s led directly to the tone of Marvel comics in the '60s. Marvel grew out of the earlier Timely Company, and in the '60s they grew to become the major powerhouse in the industry. We'll see in another chapter how this humor shows up in their characters themselves, but here I'm talking about the way Marvel created an atmosphere of inviting the readers behind the scenes for a folksy chat, a schmooze, with its friendly gang of creators in the "Bullpen," Marvel's version of *Mad's* "usual gang of idiots" who created it all. The direct and gently self-mocking address to the reader, creating a loyal community of fans, came directly from *Mad.* The chief vehicle for this was Stan Lee's monthly "Soapbox" column, in which he let loyal fans of Marvel in on what was happening with the personnel behind the scenes, as well as providing plenty of opportunities to plug forthcoming products. The Yiddish term *fershlugginer* (meaning "messed up," "wacky"), cited earlier as commonplace in *Mad,* actually showed up five times during the 1967–1980 run of Stan's "Soapbox" columns, according to the official count in *Stan's Soapbox: The Collection.*[16]

A central element of the success of Marvel in the '60s and '70s was the humor of some of its most popular characters, a humor marked by the mocking Yiddishist sensibility we've been discussing. Heroes such as Spider-Man and the Thing often didn't take themselves, or anybody else, that seriously. In the '80s, however, mainstream superhero comics took a darker turn, becoming more violent and gritty in both story and art, a trend marked most notably by the mid-'80s publication of Alan Moore's *Watchmen* and Frank Miller's *Dark Knight.* These characters were *very* serious about what they did. This is also the period in which a new generation of writers and artists came to the fore. To be sure, there continued to be Jews prominent among these comic creators, but the earlier Jewish comic sensibility, a sensibility that came out of a New York Yiddish culture where memories of the Old Country were still vibrant, no longer dominated the tone of the industry. When that older, founding generation left the mainstream superhero scene, they took with them much of the comic in comics.

After that, the Jewish elements in comic books became more visible elsewhere, for example in the later graphic novels of such pioneers as Will Eisner and Joe Kubert, then later Art Spiegelman and others. We'll follow this story in the rest of this book.

4

WAR AND PEACE

The Rise and Fall of the Superheroes in and After World War II

The signature event for the entry of comic book superheroes into World War II was also the introduction of the most enduring comic book hero to emerge from the war. The cover of the first issue of *Captain America* famously showed him socking Hitler on the jaw, sending him reeling. Bringing real figures from current affairs into the comics world was unprecedented at the time—the closest they got was usually generic foreign dictators from unspecified countries. That cover image is all the more remarkable when one recalls that it appeared in December 1940, before the U.S. had entered World War II.

Captain America was the creation of comics' first dream team, Joe Simon and Jack Kirby. Later we'll hear much more of Kirby, who rightfully came to be called the "King of Comics" in the '60s, when he partnered with Stan Lee at Marvel Comics. Simon and Kirby intended that cover and all their Captain America stories to be recruitment posters and inspirational stories for U.S. mobilization for the war. The comic was published by Timely Comics, the corporate predecessor of the later Marvel Comics. Timely was a family affair, run by Jewish businessman Martin Goodman. Simon and Kirby were the creative stars of the outfit.

We'll return to that cover in the last chapter of this book, to see how Michael Chabon revisits it in fictionalized form in *The Amazing Adventures of Kavalier & Clay,* using it to explain the real meaning of the comic superhero genre in its entirety. That image has become so iconic that it appears twice in the recent *Captain America* film. On one occasion the film shows multiple copies of the actual comic being distributed, with its cover clearly visible. Then, in the "Captain America" stage show that's part of the story, a "Hitler" tries to sneak up on Cap, but Cap spots him and delivers a roundhouse punch in the style of that classic cover, to the same effect. It's a tribute to the power of Jack Kirby's art—nobody's punches ever packed a wallop like those drawn by Kirby, where the energy rippled out to the four corners of the page and beyond, often from a four-cornered pinwheel pose in which Cap's legs were impossibly stretched and splayed in opposite directions, and one arm would be delivering a solid upward roundhouse swing while the other would be extended out in the other direction and holding his iconic red, white, and blue shield.

The Timely/Marvel company was willing and eager to send Captain America and its other superheroes wholeheartedly into battle against the Nazis, and this was the focus of many of their adventures in this period. Besides Cap, their principal characters were the Sub-Mariner and the Human Torch. The '40s Torch was a different character from the later '60s character of the same name and roughly same appearance who was a member of the Fantastic Four. This earlier Human Torch was really an android Torch, rather than a human being, who had the power to turn into a flaming superhero. The Sub-Mariner was the same one who was reintroduced later, Prince Namor of the undersea city of Atlantis. Namor was more an antihero than a villain, never purely evil, but often fighting against the surface dwellers because of their mistreatment of his people. His double-edged relationship with us air breathers—both sympathetic and hostile—made possible a key war-related shift in Namor's relationship with the Torch. Before the war, they battled against each other in epic fire-versus-water-themed battles, but once the war broke out, they fought together as allies on the U.S. side. Each of Timely/Marvel's big three had all sorts of adventures, but as Captain America was the only fully human character of the group, his adventures leaned toward a more human scale, tending to end with some kind of slugfest between an outnumbered Cap and Axis soldiers or spies. Namor's and the Torch's adventures, in contrast, sometimes veered toward science fiction, involving the thwarting of Nazi plans to develop secret superweapons at hidden bases.

Before the outbreak of the war one could already feel the sense of impending war in the comics. Local crooks were slowly but surely being replaced as villains by grand schemers bent on world domination, often with foreign names and with great resources at their disposal. When war finally came, although U.S. entry was prompted by the Japanese attack on Pearl Harbor, superheroes fought against the Germans much more often than against the Japanese, reflecting the comics' Jewish creators preoccupations with Europe and the Holocaust. The number of swastikas appearing on the covers seemed driven more by how many of them one could fit into the image than by any realistic sense of where they would actually have appeared on weapons and uniforms.

When the superheroes added taking on the Nazis abroad to their agenda of fighting for justice at home, they were following the Jewish community's support for the Roosevelt administration's policies. Before the Pearl Harbor attack that brought the U.S. into World War II, the politics of those in support of the U.S. joining the war versus those who were opposed lined up differently than one might expect coming from the perspective of today's political alignments. To a great extent, the liberals who supported the New Deal's domestic agenda were worried about the prospect of U.S. involvement in a foreign war, and how that might derail progress on domestic social issues. And conservatives who opposed the New Deal domestically tended to be in favor of an aggressive, militaristic U.S. foreign policy that would insert the U.S. into the conflict. The Jews were conspicuous among identifiable demographic groups for their vigorous support for both a domestic social justice agenda and wholehearted U.S. enlistment in the war against the Nazis. The other demographic group that lined up with Jewish opinion was the comic book superheroes.

In this pre–Pearl Harbor period, isolationist sentiment was strong, stronger than many realize when they look back on this period through the filter of the all-out support for the war effort that came after the Pearl Harbor attack. In this early period, both Jews and superheroes were pro-engagement. Nonetheless, both communities were split on the question of just how openly or aggressively to display their support for U.S. entry into World War II. The two leading comic book companies, both controlled by Jews, took opposing stances, and in these differing strategies one can see the same division that existed in the larger American Jewish community. On the one hand was a feeling of urgent need to be very vocal to get the country mobilized against the Nazi threat—this was the approach taken by the upstart outfit Timely/Marvel—versus, on the other hand, a more establishment, assimilationist stance that was leery of rocking the boat of mainstream America too much, thus opting to soft-pedal the pro-entry views—which was the strategy of the much more corporate National/DC company, home of Superman. It's a pattern of conflict within the Jewish community about how to deal with anti-Semitism that repeats itself over and over again, with some taking the position that you should confront it as vigorously as possible with all means available, versus others arguing that if you ignore it and don't alienate your genteel/Gentile friends, it will eventually go away.

There were a very large number of comic book superheroes being published at this time, though many of them required some gimmick of a particular power or costume to tell them apart. They had all sorts of names, but none of the lesser known figures ever achieved the readership of the few industry leaders, and some were quite short-lived, to be replaced by other near clones. Captain seemed to be a particularly popular rank; Captains America and Marvel were joined by Captains Courageous, Fearless, Freedom, Flag, Battle, Victory, Devildog, and others. Then you had Minute-Man, Bullet Man, Hydroman, Pyroman, V-Man and the Hangman, plus the Shield, American Eagle, American Crusader, Black Terror, Blue Beetle, Defender, Conqueror, Flame, Arrow, Angel, along with some women joining the fight too, among them Liberty Belle, Pat Patriot, Miss Victory, and Miss America.[1] In fact, partly because of the sheer volume of comics publishing, the heyday of the comic book superheroes, part of their Golden Age, as it's called by comics aficionados, was in the World War II period. Young American GIs went off to war with the adventures of their favorites folded in their pockets.* It was estimated that one out of every four magazines sent to the troops abroad from the U.S. was a comic book.[2] Sales in the nascent comics industry tripled between 1940 and 1945.

The war provided the superheroes who went to war with not just the stories but also the visuals they needed to firmly define themselves. The evil of the Nazis might have made them the perfect villains, but remember that much of what now comes to mind when we picture Nazi evil is the concentration camps and other aspects of the Holocaust. These weren't all that well known to the general public then, even though information was indeed available to those who sought or wanted it. Then the images were of the Axis war machine, and all those tanks, planes, submarines, hand grenades, and other weapons of modern warfare—with the vivid explosions they caused—really allowed the superheroes to strut their stuff. Bodies smashing against other bodies is just combat, but super bodies smashing against all that metal and machinery, or destroying it by other astounding means like heat rays or power beams, allow you to really experience super deeds. The superheroes were either American or clearly identified with the U.S., so their thrilling adventures furthered identification with the war effort. Kids could join Captain America's "Sentinels of Liberty" club and help be on the lookout for saboteurs and spies.

The National/DC company took a much more subdued approach to the war effort, as a result of which Superman, the first and greatest, was largely kept out of combat, with only a few exceptions. After all, if Superman really got into the war it would be over. That's the upshot of a two-page specially commissioned story his creators Jerry Siegel and Joe Shuster produced for *Look* magazine in 1940 to answer the ques-

---

* The ocean liner *Queen Mary*, used for troop transport in World War II and now permanently docked in Long Beach, CA, houses a glass-enclosed exhibit of items left on board by the troops. Their comic books are prominently displayed there.

tion of what would happen if Superman entered the war. They took an unexpected tack in that *Look* story. Instead of depicting the massive battles scenes one might expect, the comic shows Superman grabbing Hitler and Stalin, one in each hand, to haul them before a meeting of the League of Nations in Geneva.

But this story was outside the universe of the official comics narrative of Superman, as was a later brief strip that appeared in 1945 in *Overseas Comics,* produced and distributed by the U.S. military for its personnel. It's a comic tale in both senses of the word: Hitler invites Superman to join the Nazi race of supermen, and Superman flies to meet him. Superman declines right to the *Führer's* face, and Hitler throws a tantrum. The story's appearance in an official army publication was designed to boost morale by picturing Nazis as buffoons and removing any remaining vestiges there might be of the Nazi aura of invincibility or being super soldiers, fostering American identification with the invulnerable Superman we've got on our side. For the same morale-boosting reasons the Sunday *Superman* comic strip also ran a "Service for Supermen" campaign, in which Superman engaged not in combat with the enemy, but in doing personal service for our troops, as when a seaman asks Superman to go to his hometown to "beat the ears off a skunk that's tryin' t' beat my time with my girl friend while I ain't around to protect my interests," or when in the same one-page story he goes zooming through the sky with a civilian, putting him "through a hair-raising series of aerial acrobatics" so he gains enough self-confidence to enlist.[3]

In the regularly published comics, the writers eventually got quite creative in explaining why Superman wasn't in the war. It turns out that Clark Kent volunteered, but when it came to the eye test he absentmindedly used his super X-ray vision and ended up looking through the wall to read the eye chart in the next room, thus failing the test.

The difference between Captain America's slugging it out with the Nazis overseas versus Superman's taking care of business as usual on the home front reflected not just the business strategies of the two corporations, Timely and National, but also mirrored differences in the personalities of the creators of Superman and Captain America. Siegel and Shuster were in reality more like Clark Kent than Superman, and in their *Look* and U.S. military Superman stories they made comic use of the comics character. Kirby, on the other hand, was a street fighter, and his Captain America jumped into the thick of battle. Kirby once famously volunteered to beat up a hoodlum who tried to muscle in on Will Eisner's comics studio, where Kirby worked as a young man. Kirby said that of all the characters he created, he was most like the battling, bruising Thing of the Fantastic Four (whose name was Benjamin Jacob Grimm, his first and middle names being Kirby's father's first name and his own, respectively).

Superman encountered World War II on a much more regular basis in the series of cartoons that played in movie theaters in the '40s. Produced by Fleischer Studios, the animation was sophisticated for its time and still holds up well today. And while it takes us a bit afield from the war, a couple of pages spent on Fleischer are well worth the detour—after all, World War II was not won by bullets alone. From comics to the USO shows for the troops, both military and civilian morale needed to be kept up through entertainment.

Owned and operated by brothers Max and Dave Fleischer, the Fleischer outfit was one of the only animation studios owned and largely staffed by Jews. The contrast between its style and that of its major competitor, the Disney studio, was clearly East Coast Jewish versus West Coast WASP. It mirrored the Timely-versus-National rivalry in that a more staid, established and establishment house style (Disney) faced off against a rough-and-tumble outsider outfit (Fleischer).[4] While Disney characters were sweet and sentimental, and were depicted in rural and suburban settings, the major Fleischer characters were racy and raucous, and appeared in urban and ethnically inflected environments. Disney had Mickey and Donald; Fleischer had Betty Boop and Popeye. A battle between the anthropomorphized animals of the two studios would have been barnyard friends versus street strays. Even the same animals, when animated by the two studios had a very different look and feel. The Disney dogs were the ones living comfortably in backyard doghouses in those white-picket-fenced yards; the cats were the ones sleeping on a comfy pillow by the fireside while Grandma knitted; and the horses were the sleek ones out in the meadow. In contrast, Fleischer cats were the ones knocking over garbage cans and howling in the alley; the dogs were the ones chasing those cats and snapping at the heels of passersby; and the horses were the swaybacked ones pulling milk wagons over cobblestone streets.

An early Fleischer creation was the regrettably largely forgotten Ko-Ko the Clown. Each episode of the black-and-white *Out of the Inkwell* series began with Ko-Ko climbing out of the inkwell used by the cartoonist shown drawing the cartoon, and each episode ended with him crawling back in (always ink to ink, as in "ashes to ashes"). The Ko-Ko cartoons took place in two worlds simultaneously, the white pages and black line drawings of the animated world, and the real world, where we'd see the cartoonist. Within this framework, Ko-Ko was always trying to escape, thwart, or get even for the endless obstacles and difficulties his creator placed in his way. His relation to his creator was the classic Jewish comic response addressed to their Creator on being the "chosen" people, given the history of persecution that seemed to accompany the honor: "Thank you, really, but maybe you could choose somebody else once in a while?"

A more enduring Fleischer staple, Betty Boop, displayed the attitudes of her New York ethnic working-class roots. Betty Boop was racy not just in the sexual sense but also in terms of race. Her musical jazz numbers with Cab Calloway and Louis Armstrong are still terrifically entertaining. Betty Boop was the first sex goddess for countless adolescents, as is recognized in her recent parody reincarnation in the Comedy Central TV show *Drawn Together*. It wasn't only because she was "just drawn that way," as Jessica Rabbit later claimed in Kathleen Turner's inimitable voice in *Who Framed Roger Rabbit*. It was the stories, too, which also contained elements in which she was empowered through her sexuality. As described by cultural historian Richard Koszarski:

> In *Boop-Oop-a-Doop* (January 16, 1932) she is sexually harassed by her employer, and resists strenuously. By the time Bimbo [a doglike character] and Ko-Ko (back from retirement) get around to saving her, she has the situation well in hand. "He

couldn't take my boop-oop-a-doop away," she boasts in triumph. *Betty Boop's Big Boss* is even more complex, with Betty blatantly using her sexual powers to edge out a mob of other women for a rare depression-era job. When her new boss begins stroking her breasts and chasing her around the office, army, navy and air forces rush to her rescue. But Betty, as usual, makes it clear that she knows how to rescue herself. At the end of the film Betty and the boss are again in each other's arms, this time on her terms.[5]

The actress who voiced her, Mae Questel, was also the voice of Olive Oyl. She became known to a later generation as the gigantic Jewish mother looming in the sky over Woody Allen in his "Oedipus Wrecks" segment of the film *New York Stories*. (When I've told people who remember the film who she was, I've sometimes gotten a response of "I *knew* I knew that voice from somewhere").

The Superman cartoons fed back into the comic book story lines in amusing ways. A 1942 comics story has Lois agreeing to go to an afternoon movie with Clark, but she wants to go to the Empire Theatre, where they're showing a Superman cartoon, because she's missed the first few in the series, so Clark obligingly recaps the first one for her: "Superman sent a mad scientist to prison—but he first had to battle a heat ray and smash the savant's laboratory." As they sit in the theater and the opening credits roll, declaring that the film is based on *Action Comics* and *Superman* magazines, Lois says, "I don't believe I've ever seen those magazines," and Clark thinks to himself, "How they know so much about me is a puzzle. Perhaps they're clairvoyant." (The scene is an early example of product placement and media integration, not to mention intertextuality). His real problem is how he's going to prevent Lois from seeing the scenes where the on-screen Clark changes into Superman. He contrives to have her go out into the lobby with him for water when something is supposedly stuck in his throat (Lois: "Hurry— I don't want to miss that film"; Clark: "I didn't realize I was this thirsty"), and then when they're back in their seats he knocks her purse over so she's crawling around looking for it and he "clumsily" kicks it out of reach just when she's about to get it so that her eyes are off the screen for just long enough.

It was the heroic rather than the comic Superman who actually caught the attention of the Nazi propaganda machine. They were aware of Superman's (i.e., Siegel and Shuster's) Jewish origins, and thought them significant enough to comment on. An article in *Das Schwarze Korps* (*The Black Corps*), an SS newspaper, attacked Superman and his creator in its issue of April 25, 1940. How could anyone imagine that a Jew and an American could create a superman? The real supermen, of course, were the Aryans.

Here's how the piece began:

> Jerry Siegel, an intellectually and physically circumcised chap who has his headquarters in New York, is the inventor of a color-ful figure with an impressive appearance, a powerful body, and a red swim suit who enjoys the ability to fly through the ether.
>
> The inventive Israelite named this pleasant guy with an over-developed body and underdeveloped mind "Superman." He advertised widely Superman's sense of justice, well-suited for imitation by the American youth.
>
> As you can see, there is nothing the Sadducees won't do for money!

The classic anti-Semitic themes are here: Jewish men as feminized, physically and intellectually weak, conniving and greedy. The acknowl-edgment of what would otherwise be a virtue, "inventiveness," is here turned into a vice, as it's used for money-grubbing exploitive purposes, with the Americans dumb enough to be taken in by the schemers. Some of American comics art turned the tables on this kind of deni-grating anti-Semitism by depicting negative and physically exaggerated stereotypes of the enemy in their portrayals of especially Japanese but also German soldiers.

With the end of the war, the superheroes lost their best foes. It's a truism that heroes are defined by their enemies; for example, instead of featuring thrilling action scenes, the postwar *Superman* covers took a dramatically—or rather, comedically—sharp turn, showing a Superman with too much time on his hands, reduced to showing off with cute stunts. You can see it in a representative half year's run of covers of 1946 issues of *Action Comics* in which Superman is drawn successively chopping down a tree with one swipe of his hand, getting hit in the face with a custard pie, sitting underwater without any breathing apparatus playing chess against a fully outfitted deep sea diver, levitating prone onstage in a magic show, kidding a window washer working high on a skyscraper while sitting on thin air next to him, and lying down while "Trick-Shot Shultz" uses his forehead as a golf tee.[6] There's never been a more striking contradiction between what the title on the cover promised and what the image depicted. It may have addressed the adults' need for comic relief after the war, but this wasn't what superheroes were supposed to be for.

The Jewish sons of immigrants who created the first wave of superheroes had succeeded all too well in their attempts to embody the immigrant's American dream in their pages. They'd become assimilated. They'd left the working-class urban streets behind for new homes in the middle-class suburbs. And their characters seemed to have made the same transition. They lost that urban ethnic edge that gave them their vitality and became bland WASPs, trading in their outsider status for badges of respectability.

It wasn't just a matter of the plots. The art itself had lost much of its earlier dynamic quality, even as it became more polished. National, now DC, still dominated the superhero field, and the house style for Superman had been established by Wayne Boring. There's no better way to say this: Boring's art was just too boring. As skilled as he was at drawing the human figure and giving Superman his classic appearance, Boring created layouts that were often static. Characters just stood and spoke to each other, neatly positioned at midlevel in the middle of repetitively rectangular panels. John Romita, a classic artist on *Spider-Man*, said that if you drew Spider-Man just standing on the ground, you were wasting the character. Even if he wasn't in action and was merely having a conversation, he should still be hanging upside down, or clinging to walls, or in some other distinctively Spider-Manly agile posture.[7] In that sense, Superman and the other superheroes of the DC universe were being visually wasted.

The Silver Age of the comics is mostly associated with the Marvel characters we shall meet in the next chapter, but it started when DC editor Julius "Julie" Schwartz revived some Golden Age characters who had faded away, first and most notably the Flash and Green Lantern, who were then followed by others such as Hawkman. In their earlier incarnations, these characters had mystical or supernatural origins—the Flash was the reincarnation of Mercury, and Green Lantern got his powers from a mystical green flame. Schwartz took much of the DC line in a strong science-fiction direction, so the new Flash gained his powers from an accident during a scientific experiment, and Green Lantern now got his powers from an alien who had crash-landed on Earth. In the new DC look the old boyishly enthusiastic modernism that had kept the rough edges of guys still looking back over their shoulders to where they'd come from gave way to a super-sleek modernist look of those who'd made it out and were papering over where they'd been. Though the characters were still placed in the cities, the crisp lines and clean backgrounds of artists such as Gil Kane and Carmine Infantino proclaimed a suburban aesthetic of wider streets outdoors and Scandinavian furniture indoors.

The end of World War II took the driving energy out of superhero comics in the late '40s and into the '50s, but what really almost killed comics was the attack on the industry taking place out in the real world. In 1954, the U.S. Senate's Subcommittee to Investigate Juvenile Delinquency of the Committee on the Judiciary held fateful hearings on the comic book industry, led by its chair, Senator Estes Kefauver. The hearings were spurred by the publication, earlier that year, of Dr. Fredric Wertham's *Seduction of the Innocent,* which blamed juvenile delinquency on comic books for their encouragement of violence and degenerate sexuality, and argued, among other things, that Batman and Robin were living out a homosexual's dream. (Dick and Bruce living together in that well-appointed all-male mansion and dressing up in their costumes, especially that one with Robin's bare legs!)

The most famous testimony at the hearings was given by Bill Gaines, publisher of EC comics, which published a series of crime, war, horror, science-fiction, and humor comics (including *Mad*, discussed in the previous chapter). Gaines's responses to Fredric Wertham's criticisms when he was called to testify as a witness right after Wertham at these hearings were also one more chapter of long-standing internecine Jewish warfare. Wertham (originally Wertheimer) was a middle-class Jew from Germany, while Gaines and most of the other comic book creators had Eastern European working-class roots. Their disagreements echo those of generations of middle- and upper-class assimilated Western European Jews looking down on the primitive products of the culture of the Eastern European small towns and villages, the shtetls, with the Eastern European Jews thumbing their noses right back at them.

The committee had arranged to have hearings on the relation between comics and juvenile delinquency in New York as part of a countrywide tour designed to gain publicity for its cause, and for Senator Kefauver, who was maneuvering for a possible presidential candidacy. Gaines actually volunteered to testify at the hearings. In contrast, the other, older comics publishers tried to stay out of the spotlight, understanding all too well that nothing good could come when public moral crusaders began to rally forces, based on their own earlier experiences, or on stories they'd heard from the comics industry's birth out of disreputable junk-magazine publishing.

Gaines began his testimony with a prepared statement that laid out a decent defense of comics as harmless entertainment, in the process of which he took time to accuse Wertham of basically being a prudish philistine for his arguments identifying comics as a source of juvenile delinquency and general moral degradation in U.S. culture. "It would be just as difficult to explain the harmless thrill of a horror story to Dr. Wertham as it would be to explain the sublimity of love to a frigid old maid," he declared.[8] Then, as he was being questioned by the committee, Gaines faltered and began vacillating between defending his comics as delivering positive messages, and assuming a contradictory position of defending comics as pure entertainment that delivered no message at all. Here's the most well known part of his testimony, recorded in the Congressional Record and broadcast on television, part of his direct exchange with Senator Kefauver:

> *Senator Kefauver: (holding up a recent copy of EC's* Crime SuspenStories*)* Here is your May 22 issue. This seems to be a man with a bloody ax holding a woman's head up which has been severed from her body. Do you think that is in good taste?
>
> *Gaines:* Yes, sir; I do, for the cover of a horror comic. A cover in bad taste, for example, might be defined as holding the head a little higher so that the neck could be seen dripping blood from it and moving the body over a little further so that the neck of the body could be seen to be bloody.[9]

Wertham was worried about the problems of crime and violence in society. He thought that if the baser impulses of the lower classes were indulged, as they were by all the lurid sex and violence in comic books, their propensity for violence would go unchecked. He very much had in mind the experience of the rise of fascism in Europe. For their part, those in the comics industry saw in Wertham an advocate of censorship, of the state attempting to curb the freedoms and control the minds of the people. In other words, when the Jews on both sides of the argument looked at the other side, they saw Nazis. No wonder feelings ran so high.

Comics fans still have incredibly angry feelings about Wertham to this day. Comics writer and historian Mark Evanier satirically titled a collection of his essays on comics *Wertham Was Right!* and puts it this way, after discussing such classic comics villains as Lex Luthor, the Joker, Dr. Doom, etc.:

> But ask any comic fan who's the greatest villain of them all, and it's No Contest: Dr. Frederic Wertham, M.D. He's the man who almost single-handedly killed the comic book field; who

brought on the dreaded Comics Code, who gave comic book writers and artists a public image only slightly more prestigious than heroin distributors, but without the attendant perks.[10]

Gaines versus Wertham had its notoriety, reaching the front page of the *New York Times,* though it never reached the heights (or depths) of the similarly Jewish class-consciousness-infused Duel of the Hoffmans in the following decade, when in the Chicago 7 (originally 8) conspiracy trial defendant and Yippie radical Abbie Hoffman shouted at upper-class presiding judge Julius Hoffman in Yiddish that the way he was conducting the trial was *"A shande far de goyim"* ("A disgrace before the Gentiles"). Asked in routine fashion to state his name at the beginning of his testimony, Abbie pointedly declared before Judge Hoffman, "My slave name is Hoffman. My real name is Shaboysnakoff. I can't spell it." That wasn't so much a confession of ignorance as a *"J'accuse"* hurled against assimilationists.[11]

Seeing the writing on the wall from these hearings, the industry adopted its own "Comics Magazine Association of America Comics Code" in a successful attempt to head off government censorship by self-censoring instead. Every comic book would now display on its cover the Comics Code Seal of Approval. One really should read the whole document, but here are some excerpts to give the flavor of it:

> Crimes shall never be presented in such a way as to create sympathy for the criminal, to promote distrust of the forces of law and justice, or to inspire others with a desire to imitate criminals.

> In every instance good shall triumph over evil and the criminal punished for his misdeeds.

> No comic magazine shall use the word horror or terror in its title.

> All scenes of horror, excessive bloodshed, gory or gruesome crimes, depravity, sadism, masochism shall not be permitted.

Scenes dealing with, or instruments associated with walking dead, torture, vampires and vampirism, ghouls, cannibalism, and werewolfism are prohibited.

Suggestive and salacious illustration or suggestive posture is unacceptable.

Females shall be drawn realistically without exaggeration of any physical qualities.

Respect for parents, the moral code, and for honorable behavior shall be fostered. A sympathetic understanding of the problems of love is not a license for morbid distortion.

Passion or romantic interest shall never be treated in such a way as to stimulate the baser emotions.[12]

It took the wind out of the sails of comics, and eviscerated the industry.

Comics continued to be published, but with a much diminished readership. The superhero genre especially suffered. The Cold War just didn't generate the heated excitement of World War II; attempts to replace heroic fights against the Nazis with supposedly more true-to-life tales of FBI and secret service agents trying to root out Communist spies just didn't pack the same wallop. By the time of the early '60s comics were sorely in need of revitalization. The needed shot in the arm came courtesy of Stan Lee and Jack Kirby at Marvel comics.

Jack Kirby, the Thing (of the Fantastic Four) drawn as Jewish.

5

IT'S A JEWISH THING

Not-So-Secret Identities
in the Marvel Bullpen

By the 1960s, the founding generation of writers and artists of those early comics had gotten much of what they had prayed for personally, and the industry they had created was much the worse for it. They had succeeded all too well in their assimilationist journey, and the comics paralleled that: They had become clean, safe, and suburban, their characters now part of the mainstream establishment more than outsiders. Likewise the art was cleaner and more sophisticated, but lacked the energy that came from the struggles of the generation who'd come out of the city tenements.

The infusion of new energy the comics desperately needed came, above all, from Stan Lee and Jack Kirby at Marvel Comics. Lee and Kirby took the comics back to the city streets, Lee with his characterizations and Kirby with his art. This return to urban grittiness came with an undeniable raw power, palpable in Kirby's art, a visual translation of the energy of the ethnic streets of New York.

There never was or will be another artist whose work is as synonymous with superheroes as Jack Kirby. He was a powerhouse and defined the look of Marvel in its glory days. Other artists who worked there were told to draw like Kirby, sometimes directly from his layouts. Kirby's superheroes had a dynamic force that no one else could approach. In Will Eisner's seminal text *Expressive Anatomy for Comics and Narrative*, the only art included other than his own is Kirby's, five full pages of it in a chapter on "Posture and Power."[1]

Kirby's figures exploded off the page. It wasn't just how muscular they were, it was that you could *see* those muscles propelling them forward, *feel* the speed at which they moved, and practically *hear* when a punch landed. When his characters weren't forcefully propelling you along with them from one panel to the next in furious action, they were coming right at you from pages where Kirby positioned them straining against the front plane of the panel, massive hands reaching toward you at the front of radically foreshortened arms.

And it wasn't just the superheroes. It was those machines as well. Nobody made technology come to life like Kirby. His super vehicles and weapons went on forever, and the more you looked—which you kept doing because they were such showstoppers—the more they seemed to grow and expand before your eyes: An engine at the back or a weapon at the front would be attached to a turret that swiveled on a wheel mounted on a massive block with uncountable dials and segmented protrusions on it that tapered off and then re-expanded into another segment of the machine with its own new array of contraptions and connections. And yet with all that going on, the machines never looked fragmented, but somehow came together as overpowering, organic wholes.

Those who watched Kirby work were amazed at the speed with which he drew. That velocity made itself felt on the page. He was so extraordinarily capable of communicating energy in his drawings that he developed a new way to literally depict energy, in a technique that came to be known as the "Kirby krackle" or "Kirby dots." To show a field of energy, say surrounding a person or emanating from a machine or just swirling in space, he'd draw a pattern of black dots of different sizes, usually against a much lighter color, typically a flaming orange. According to artistic orthodoxy it shouldn't have worked; black is supposed to be a receding color and round black dots should pull the eye into the background, suggesting black holes. Using black dots to give viewers a feeling of strong energy crackling toward them was counterintuitive. But in Kirby's hands it worked spectacularly and became one of his many trademarks.

Kirby's own energy came to him as almost his birthright from New York's Lower East Side, where he was born Jacob Kurtzberg on August 28, 1917, to Rosemary and Benjamin Kurtzberg. His father was a tailor who went to the synagogue every day, but young Jakie was soon selling newspapers and fighting other neighborhood tough guys as part of a gang.[2] He got his professional start at the Fleischer animation studio, working on cels of Popeye. Before he became the King of Comics at Marvel, Kirby had been half of the first dream team in comics, working with Joe Simon, also a Jewish tailor's son. (Simon claimed he had an advantage over Kirby right from the start: Kirby's father only made pants, while Simon's made whole suits.)[3]

The Simon and Kirby team created characters in almost every genre of comics, not just superheroes but western gunslingers, fantastic monsters, kid gangs, swashbucklers, starring in crime adventures or mysteries, horror tales, war stories, and even good old funny pages. When superhero comics were in their postwar slump, Simon and Kirby created the romance genre comic book with the *Young Romance* title in 1947. When comics briefly tried to follow the movie 3-D fad in the 1950s they created a comic that was distributed along with 3-D glasses, *Captain 3-D*.[4]

At Marvel, Kirby and Lee brought comics into a new era. And while neither of them made much of their Jewishness, their jump forward in comic art and sophistication was accompanied by an important shift in the way Jewishness worked its way into their creations. If we look back at Superman, the Jewishness I describe is below the surface, implicit in the work, and one needs to perform a degree of decoding and analysis to see it and to understand how the story traces its way back to the Old Country. In the Marvel age the characters themselves start to take on a more visibly Jewish tone and attitude.

The Jewish content is not yet fully explicit, as it will be in the more recent graphic novels we take up in the later chapters of this book, but it is nonetheless clearly there.

Lee and Kirby's most groundbreaking work was the Fantastic Four. As surely as Siegel and Shuster's introduction of Superman in 1938 inaugurated the comic book superhero genre, the introduction of the Fantastic Four in 1961 initiated a decisive shift. If one can sufficiently suspend disbelief to talk about "realism" in the superhero genre, then the Fantastic Four was immediately recognized as more "realistic" than anything seen before. Here were characters who reacted as ordinary people might if they suddenly found themselves inadvertently possessed of superpowers. They were reluctant heroes who bickered among themselves, worried about paying the rent, and generally dealt with the travails of daily life. Despite having superpowers, they were really everymen rather than supermen. It was the introduction into the superhero genre of the attitude of cutting through pretentiousness that we saw earlier is characteristic of Jewish humor. In a reversal of the process, as noted earlier, by which Superman's metamorphosis over the years from mischievous outsider into near-saintly do-gooder was a de-Jewification of the character, by introducing superheroes with all-too-human character flaws, Marvel accomplished a re-Jewification of the superhero.

Fantastic Four #1 tells the story of how Dr. Reed Richards leads a flight into outer space in a rocket ship he designed, piloted by his friend Ben Grimm. He is accompanied by his fiancée, Susan Storm, and her younger brother Johnny. Though initially carrying out a government project, they launch prematurely without official clearance in order to beat "the Commies" into space. But the ship is bombarded by cosmic rays, which its shielding isn't strong enough to withstand. It crash-lands on its return, and the astronauts find themselves transformed. Susan Storm turns invisible, and names herself the Invisible Girl. Johnny ignites into flame, which gives him the ability to fly, becoming the Human Torch. Reed Richards's body becomes elastic and stretchable, and he dubs himself Mr. Fantastic. Ben Grimm's body takes on a monstrous shape—imagine an NFL linebacker with a thick coating of orange rocks over his entire body—that makes him super strong, and he takes the name the Thing.[5]

Right from the beginning, the Thing became the most popular member of the Fantastic Four, being both the most tragic and the most comic figure. Unlike the others, the Thing could not return to an ordinary-looking human body, so he was deprived of the normal life the others could still lead when not out superheroing. He had a skeptical attitude, sarcastic wit, and an irascible personality that gave the quartet much of its appeal, bringing cantankerous humanity and humor into the general derring-do, and constantly charging the foe with his signature "It's clobberin' time" battle cry. The Thing could be counted on to mock plans for world domination or whatever other evil was being perpetrated by a given supervillain, as well as what he perceived as Reed Richards's sometimes overbearing pomposity in explaining whatever counterplan he'd strategized to save the day. The Thing's mode of address was always intended to deflate authority—he'd regularly call Mr. Fantastic "Stretch" or refer to the Torch as a "hothead" just to provoke him.

As it turns out, the Thing is actually Jewish. This revelation occurred in 2002, forty-one years after the character was introduced. During the story, he heads back to his old "Yancy Street" neighborhood because he believes it might be the Day of Atonement, and he wants to return something that he had stolen as a kid from the neighborhood pawnbroker, Mr. Sheckerberg. The theft had earned Ben admission into the Yancy Street gang: "Sheck's very own personal Star of David thing! The only thing in his store that's, like, not for sale," as another kid in the gang described it. It turns out Mr. Sheckerberg is now being squeezed for protection money by a bad guy named Powderkeg. During the ensuing battle, there is an explosion and Sheckerberg is thrown to the ground. Ben can't tell if Sheck is alive or dead. Frustrated that he "can't do nothing," Ben stands over Sheck's body and says, "No, there is one thing. . . . Lessee . . . Been a while . . . Sh'ma Y'Israel Adonai Eloheinu Adonai Echad . . . uhm . . . Baruch Shem K'vod Malchuto L'olam Va'ed."

But Sheck turns out to be okay and tells Ben, "It's good, too, to see you haven't forgotten what you learned at temple, Benjamin. All those years in the news, they never mention you're Jewish. I thought maybe you were ashamed of it a little?" Ben replies, "Nah, that ain't it. Anyone on the Internet can find out, if they want. It's just . . . I don't talk it up, is all. Figure there's enough trouble in this world without people thinkin' Jews are all monsters like me." After some other conversation, Sheck says, "Remember the tale of the golem, Benjamin? He was a being made of clay . . . but he wasn't a monster. He was a protector," after which he tells Ben to keep the Star of David, to protect it until he needs it back. The story ends with Powderkeg all wrapped up, ready for the police to pick him up. "You're really Jewish?" he asks Ben. "There a problem with that?" the Thing replies. "No! No," Powderkeg stammers, "it's just . . . you don't look Jewish."[6]

In a later story, we learn that Ben returns to the old neighborhood every year to celebrate Chanukah, and he tells young Franklin Richards (son of Reed and Susan), "Me and Kitty Pryde [of the X-Men], we're the world's two—count 'em, two—openly Jewish super heroes," making one wonder if perhaps there are others still closeted.[7] (Meanwhile, over at DC Batwoman is now a Jewish lesbian.) His Jewishness now crops up from time to time in the stories, as for example when he's in a hospital talking to an unconscious Human Torch, he says, "Haven't been to temple in a long time. I wonder if there's a prayer for somebody in your condition."[8]

The Thing's coming out as Jewish followed a long trend of explicitly Jewish comics and graphic novels entering the mainstream, a trend we'll discuss in later chapters. It produced a good deal of commentary. Leonard Pitts, widely syndicated Pulitzer Prize–winning columnist for the *Miami Herald* and admitted lifetime "comic book freak" wrote, "I just found out Ben is Jewish. Though truth is, I always suspected as much."[9] Pitts tellingly cites two factors he relates to the Thing's Jewishness: "It's probably significant that he was an outcast, an object of misunderstanding and fear. And that his humor helped him cope."

The Thing's humor is the kind of anarchic antiestablishment humor that came out of New York's Lower East Side, exemplified in Superman's day by the Marx Brothers. It had the decidedly Yiddishist flavor that came with that territory. As early as issue number three, when Reed warns that they are facing "one man whose powers seem to be greater than ours," Ben replies, "Power—shmower!! Just let me get my hands on him again."[10] So when Pitts refers to Ben's humor as an indication of his Jewishness, he is specifically tuning in to a certain kind of Jewish humor.

When discussing their creative histories or personal biographies, neither Stan Lee nor Jack Kirby made much of their Jewishness, although Kirby came to explicitly acknowledge its importance to him in later years. In a spoof story he wrote that Marvel published called "What if the Marvel Bullpen Had Become the Fantastic Four?" Kirby cast himself as the Thing, and Lee as Mr. Fantastic. He once drew a card for his nephew showing a smiling Thing with "Blessings for Hanukah" written in Hebrew on his chest. As Mark Evanier, comics writer and Kirby's sometime assistant, tells it:

> "If you'll notice the way the Thing talks and acts, you'll find that the Thing is really Jack Kirby," Jack once explained. "He has my manners, he has my manner of speech, and he thinks the way I do. He's excitable, and you'll find he's very, very active among people, and he can muscle his way through a crowd. I find I'm that sort of person."[11]

Lee's and Kirby's assimilationist name changes might raise suspicions today about their attitudes toward the Jewish aspect of their lives, but such things were common enough in those days. Here's how Lee tells the story in his autobiography:

> Being only seventeen at the time and not yet having become the incredibly sophisticated and knowledgeable superperson that I am today, I somehow felt it would not be seemly to take my name, which was certain to one day win a Pulitzer, and sign it to mere, humble comic strips. Thus, I was caught up in the fantasy

of using a pen name, something suitable for strips, while saving my real name for the saga that would make me immortal.[12]

Lee was born as Stanley Martin Lieber on December 28, 1922, to Celia and Jack Lieber in Upper Manhattan, and later legally changed his name. I might accept the completeness of his explanation were it not for the fact that he begins his autobiography by identifying his parents only as "Romanian immigrants" but not as Jews, and the book hardly mentions his Jewishness. He gets around to mentioning that his parents were Jewish fairly late in the game, in the context of saying that the mixed marriage with his Episcopalian wife, Joanie, made it difficult for them to adopt a child so they finally gave up on it. It's perfectly legitimate for someone not to think their Jewishness had much of an impact on their work, but such a gap in his life story seems too much like avoidance for me to fully accept it. And I'm not the only one—when the *Forward,* the major Jewish newspaper in the U.S., interviewed Danny Fingeroth about his new book on Stan Lee, they asked him about how Lee "seemed to disavow any kind of Jewish element in his comics."[13] It's not like Lee's family origins are irrelevant to the story of his professional career. His first break in the business was being hired at Timely, Marvel's predecessor, which happened only because he was a young relative of the publisher, Martin Goodman. At eighteen, Lee was basically a gofer for Simon and Kirby. Gradually they let him write a bit: in order to qualify for magazine mailing rates, comics had to have at least two pages of text. Lee's first writing assignment was such a text story in *Captain America.*[14]

In a radio interview with New York's Radio WNYC, when Lee was asked how much he thought Jewishness informed the medium of comic books, he replied, "You know, I have no idea. I never really thought of it. It is strange when you mention it that the best-known characters were done by Jewish writers. I guess that is an odd thought."[15]

Setting the question of Jewishness aside for a moment, Lee's reference to characters being done by writers is telling, for he has been widely criticized for not giving enough credit to his artistic co-creators.

This is especially significant because what came to be known as the Marvel style of working, which he pioneered, actually shifted more of the storytelling responsibility to the artist. Rather than being asked to illustrate detailed scripts, artists would be given outlines and left to tell the story visually, with the writers filling in the captions and word balloons later. Many industry insiders think this change in the production process, rather than any of the specific characters he created, is ultimately Lee's most important contribution to the industry, as it allowed for the fuller flowering of what is, after all, a visual medium.[16]

Kirby's own strong inclination toward having the art rather than the words drive the story had been strengthened by his early apprenticeships in the Fleischer and Eisner shops, where he had more free rein than he might have had elsewhere. And when Lee took over running Marvel he was probably inclined to be a bit deferential toward his former boss Kirby, who was already a star. The Marvel style came out of the distinctive synergy between the two.

A good illustration of the Lee-Kirby working relationship emerges from one of their mid-'60s story conferences. They decided they needed to make the Fantastic Four's adventures more compelling by upping the ante on the super villains. They pulled out all the stops and came up with a godlike galactic wanderer named Galactus, who fed off the energy released when he destroyed planets. Kirby went off to work, and returned soon enough with drawings of pages for *Fantastic Four* #48. Its last panel features the dramatic first appearance of the new, colossal Galactus. But there was something else introduced in this issue as well: Zooming through space was a monochrome flying figure riding a surfboard. "Who the hell's this?" asked Lee. Kirby explained that a powerful figure like Galactus would surely have a herald preceding his arrival. That celestial rider of the skyways was the Silver Surfer, who soon became one of Marvel's most popular superheroes.[17]

The run of the few issues that begins with #48 constitutes one of the best examples of the unparalleled creativity of the Lee–Kirby team, and especially Kirby's contribution to it. The Galactus saga spans three issues, #48–#50, in which the Silver Surfer comes to increasing prominence. One of the hallmarks of Lee-Kirby stories was the interplay between vastly cosmic plots and very personal scenes, with that sensibility of having a down-to-earth foundation for even the most high-flying of characters. Issue #51, "This Man . . . This Monster," was a classic, deeply moving story that demonstrated the human tragedy afflicting Ben Grimm because of his transformation into the Thing. The splash page, with the Thing directly facing the reader in a torrent of rain, is one of Kirby's images in the groundbreaking and definitive exhibit "Masters of American Comics" (originally mounted by the Hammer Museum and the Museum of Contemporary Art in Los Angeles in 2005, later split between the Jewish Museum in New York and the Newark Museum in New Jersey, appropriate as a good number of the featured artists are Jews).* Stretching even further on the cover of the next issue, *Fantastic Four* #52 boldly proclaims that it is "Introducing the sensational Black Panther," generally acknowledged as the first African-American superhero.

So, over the course of just a few issues they went from an epic battle for the fate of the entire galaxy, to the Thing's personal emotional story of being a permanent outsider, to breaking racial barriers in the medium, a move very much in line with the typical Jewish tone of the politics at Marvel, a liberal bent that included strong support for the civil rights movement. (Steve Ditko, whom we'll meet shortly, was the notable exception to the liberal orientation of the Marvel shop. He was an odd man out in many ways, being politically on the right, notoriously publicity-shy, and not Jewish.)

After the Fantastic Four, Lee and Kirby's next creation was another man-monster, the Incredible Hulk. The story line was that after being accidentally bombarded with gamma radiation, when Dr. Bruce Banner got angry he was transformed into the large and incredibly powerful Hulk. In like manner radioactivity gave birth to a number of superheroes in this period. In 1945 the United States had dropped two atomic bombs on Japan, and their subsequent impact on the national popu-

---

*Art Spiegelman withdrew his support for the exhibit because of this segregation.

lar culture very much depended on which side you were on, meaning whether you had dropped those bombs or had them dropped on you. In 1950s Japanese popular culture, atomic energy created monsters like Godzilla, but in 1960s U.S. popular culture, it created superheroes. To the victor go the spoils.

Since the Thing's transformation was permanent (with some very temporary exceptions), people forget that after their rocket ship's crash landing Ben's original transformation into the Thing was triggered by his getting angry, and when Johnny first "flames on" as the Human Torch, he says, "When I get excited I can feel my body begin to blaze." It seems, then, that in Lee's imagination men turn into monsters when they get angry or aroused. Is it too much to speculate that in the Lieber household it was perhaps impressed upon young Stanley that nice Jewish boys don't get angry, that they're supposed to be, dare we say it, "mild mannered," like our old friend Clark Kent? Although recent writers added the idea that the Hulk's overwhelming rage stems from having been abused as a child, this wasn't Lee's original conception. For him, ordinary anger was enough to make someone feel compelled to warn people, in a line from the opening sequence of the *Incredible Hulk* TV series that's become part of our common popular culture lore, "You wouldn't like me when I'm angry."

Marvel writers and artists continued to explore the theme of the persecuted outsider in their work, most notably in tales of the X-Men, the team of superpowered mutants introduced by Lee and Kirby in 1963.[18] In the 1980s, the artist-writer team of John Byrne and Chris Claremont introduced a new X-Men character Kitty Pryde, who is identified as Jewish. She hails from Deerfield, Illinois, a city with a sizable Jewish population and, as Shadowcat, can "phase" through solid matter. The nemesis of the X-Men is another mutant named Magneto. Over time a backstory was developed that identified him as a child survivor of Auschwitz named Max Eisenhardt (a quasi pun for someone with the power of magnetism, since "Eisenhardt" evokes the German and Yiddish *hart* and *eisen,* or "hard iron"). The leader of the X-Men, Charles Xavier (Professor X), first meets Magneto in Israel under Magneto's adult alias, Erik Lehnsherr.[19] The analogy between the persecution of the Jews and persecution of mutants became a theme of the ongoing story. In one issue, after Magneto has switched to the side of the good guys, he and Kitty visit the Holocaust Center in Washington, D.C., on Holocaust Remembrance Day ("Yom HaShoah" in Hebrew), and Magneto says: "Then . . . it was the Jews. My nightmare has ever been that tomorrow, it will be the mutants."[20] When in issue #150 Magneto discovers that he came close to killing Kitty and he expresses his shock that he almost killed one of "his people," the statement is left ambiguous as to whether he means Jews or mutants.[21] A 2008–2009 miniseries, *X-Men Magneto: Testament,* greatly embellished the story of Magneto's boyhood during the early years of the Holocaust. The theme of persecution was strongly picked up in the popular *X-Men* films.

Marvel's most popular character, Spider-Man, cocreated by Lee and artist Steve Ditko, was introduced in a story told in *Amazing Fantasy* #15, August 1962. Teenage Peter Parker is bitten by a radioactive spider and gains the proportionate strength and agility of a spider, the ability to cling to walls and other surfaces, and a spider-sense that warns him of danger. Being a science whiz, he invents web-shooters, which he wears around his wrists with the control buttons in his palms (unlike in the 2002–2007 film trilogy, which have the webs shooting out from his body as part of the biological transformation caused by a bite from a genetically modified spider), from which he can shoot out superstrong webs for many different purposes, using them as lines from which he swings through the city, as cords to tie up criminals, to make a web in which to catch people, etc. Originally just seeking fame and fortune as Spider-Man, he turns to crime fighting only after a tragic incident in which his Uncle Ben, who along with his Aunt May has been raising him, is killed by a burglar. Peter realizes that this is the same burglar he had earlier let run past him to escape the police, just because he hadn't wanted to get involved.[22] Unlike Superman, motivated by his ideals, and Batman, driven by vengeance, Spider-Man becomes a superhero out of guilt.

Now, it's a little too neat and simplistic to claim Spider-Man as a Jewish character just because of the guilt factor. This is a much over-used and abused stereotype. As a religion, Judaism has no monopoly on being guilt-inducing. But if we locate Peter's story and his guilt in their specific place and time, then there is an important Jewish dimension here.

Spider-Man is a post-Holocaust American Jew, and the guilt that plagues and motivates him is a specific post-Holocaust American Jewish guilt. It is guilt about not having done enough to save one's people, about having passively stood by in the face of the crime and having let it happen. This is Peter Parker's personal tragic past, and it is the tragic past of Jews in the latter half of the twentieth century. Because of our gendered ideals of heroism, according to which we expect men to come dashing in to the rescue, that burden landed particularly heavily on the shoulders and consciences of Jewish men, including those who created comic book superheroes. Kal-El's and Bruce Wayne's personal tragedies were deaths they could not possibly have prevented, and it's worth noting that these two characters were created before the Holocaust had permeated the Jewish psyche. Peter, in contrast, is forever haunted by his personal failure to act. He has learned the hard way that, as the last panel of the story famously says, "With great power there must come—great responsibility."[23]

In naming him "Spider-Man" and not "Spider-Boy," Lee and Ditko signaled that they would give this young character the same respect they would an adult. Much of the enormous success of Spider-Man was due to their ability to present and examine the emotions of a maturing adolescent from the critical vantage point of older men, but without ever condescending to him or his problems. By taking Peter Parker seriously, Lee and Ditko demonstrated that they were taking their readers seriously as well.[24]

Here's Lee's explanation of part of the character's tremendous appeal:

[A]t that time all the comic book heroes were adults. . . . So Spidey was probably the first comic book hero that teenagers themselves could identify with. . . . You may have noticed that Peter Parker never lived in Gotham City, or Metropolis, or any other place that was obviously a fictional city. Nope, his very first story planted him firmly in Forest Hills, a part of New York City. So readers could really visualize him web-slinging around the streets of New York and its environs.[25]

It wasn't just the naming of Spider-Man's physical location as New York that made him a New Yorker; it was his whole style—indeed, the style of the whole book, wherein Peter's friend (and later enemy) Harry Osborn called him "Boychik"—that embodied that whole New York Jewish sense of humor.[26] Lenny Bruce famously said that if you're from New York, you're Jewish even if you're not, and if you're from the Midwest, you're not Jewish even if you are. In this sense, Spidey was clearly Jewish. Peter Parker was a teenage version of Clark Kent, with scientific instead of journalistic leanings, though he was less of a shlemiel and more of a shlimazel than Clark. (The classic definition: The shlemiel is the guy who spills soup on the shlimazel).[27] With Peter, though, it wasn't an act. He reminded you of the line from the song "Born Under a Bad Sign," popularized by the rock group Cream: "If it wasn't for bad luck, I wouldn't have no luck at all."[28]

Placing him not just in New York but specifically in the neighborhood of Forest Hills in the borough of Queens was New York insider's code. I should know, for that's where I grew up, as my son used to proudly inform his friends when he was younger, "My Dad comes from Spider-Man's neighborhood."[29] The population of Forest Hills is heavily Jewish, mostly of Eastern European descent, a good number of them Holocaust survivor families, as is mine. It was certainly known as a Jewish neighborhood, and it was clear to me from the beginning that Spider-Man was Jewish. Peter Parker's Aunt May was the stereotypical Jewish mother, always overprotective of Peter: "Don't forget your scarf and galoshes today, dear." His odd power of a spider-sense that warns him of impending danger is the internalization of that paranoia. It's Woody Allen's old persona turned into a superhero—who else but a Jew would have as a superpower a tingling feeling that makes him start to worry even *before* he can identify where the danger might be coming from?

Comparing Spider-Man with Superman is extremely informative. The first chapter of this book showed that Superman is a "non-Jewish Jew," a concept developed by Isaac Deutscher to designate a Jew who denies his Jewish heritage and adopts a universalist outlook, but who does so to pursue ethical values he or she has inherited precisely from the Jewish tradition. Superman, who on the surface is as non-Jewish as they come, is nonetheless a deeply Jewish character. Spider-Man, on the other hand, has personality traits that make it much easier to imagine him as Jewish, such as his humor and anxieties, but at a deeper level he is really more of an everyman figure.

To understand the full significance of this contrast we need to take a longer historical view, putting both these figures in the context of changing conceptions of masculinity in the United States. The change is reflected in the language used to discuss masculinity, specifically in the concepts of "character" and "personality." One *displays* a certain *personality*, but one's *character* is the *basic* stuff you are *made* of. In the words of historian Thomas Winter:

> Historians . . . have seen *character* and *personality* in juxtaposition, linking them to a shift in U.S. culture from a producer society to a consumer society. . . . This interpretation associates *character* with the values of a nineteenth-century producer culture, offering a self-sustained notion of the self, grounded in ideals of independence, sobriety, self-control, and civilized morality, whereas *personality*, as a new notion of the self, came into being alongside an emerging consumer culture, requiring the ability to play act, to win friends, and to influence and convince others.[30] [Emphasis added.]

The *man of character* answers only to his own internal moral code, no matter what others may think, whereas he who possesses a *masculine personality* is concerned to appear masculine to those around him. Superman was created when the development of our more commercial mass and consumer culture was already under way and the ideal of *personality* was already on the scene, beginning to undermine the older ideal of *character*. Superman harkens back to an older concept of manly character: He is the strong, silent type, in contrast to Spider-Man's wisecracking wise guy. (Think Gary Cooper versus Bruce Willis.) Spider-Man is perhaps more reflective of the reality of masculinity in the late decades of the twentieth century: often unsure of himself, not entirely clear on how he is going to solve problems, generally improvising his way through life, as are men in the brave new world where gender and professional roles are less clearly defined than in the past.

These concepts illuminate the shift from the original Golden Age DC superheroes to the later Silver Age Marvel superheroes. In that evolution of comic book superheroes, the Jewishness of the characters shifted from their *character* to their *personality*, from the interior, deeper psychodynamics that motivate Superman to the more surface personality traits that manifest themselves in the Marvel superheroes. In stark contrast to Superman, Spider-Man's Jewishness lies in his demeanor, his personality. Spider-Man's *personality* is Jewish, but his *character* is not. In contrast, Superman's *character* is Jewish, but his *personality* is not.

The difference between Superman's and Spider-Man's Jewishness is analogous to the way Jews, as they became more assimilated into American culture, struggled less with identity issues of being strangers in a strange land. They felt themselves to be more native to America, and so became freer to act and create in ways that are identifiably Jewish, not coded or indirect. Jews became significantly more comfortable within mainstream American culture in the space of one generation, from the 1938 birth of Superman to the 1962 introduction of Spider-Man. The change reflects how during this same time period Jewishness itself transformed for many American Jews; from an inner conviction to an outer display, from a way of life to a lifestyle, from ritual observance to ritualistically eating the Sunday bagel that accompanied reading the Sunday comics. Either way, covertly or overtly, Jewish men inscribed their Jewish identities into their comic book superhero creations.

Will Eisner, "The Escapist & The Spirit" splash page.

6

THE PENCIL IS MIGHTIER
THAN THE WORDS

The Spirit of Will Eisner

C omics combine words and pictures into an integrated whole. Nonetheless it is primarily a visual medium, in which visual storytelling dominates the verbal. So a comic book without words is still a wordless comic book, but a comic book without pictures isn't a comic book at all, it's a book. That's apparently why so many of those books are so long; according to the conversion formula in that old saying, it takes them a thousand words to make up for every picture they're doing without.

The Jewish artist who more than anyone else developed comics into an artistic medium was Will Eisner. If Jack Kirby was the King of Comics, then Will Eisner was the "Rabbi of Comics." *Rabbi* is simply the Hebrew word for "teacher," so I trust that doesn't sound too sacrilegious.

If you read any of the numerous pieces written to introduce Will Eisner and his influence on comics, you'll find they often begin with the author bemoaning how hard it is to avoid superlatives in talking about Eisner. I can now testify that they're right. Saying he was a legendary giant doesn't begin to do justice to the man. Everybody, and I mean *everybody*, who has been a creative force in comics jumps at the chance to acknowledge their debt to Eisner. The comics equivalent of the Oscars are named after him: Every year since 1988 the Will Eisner Comic Industry Awards (usually called simply the Eisners) are presented at the industry's oldest and largest convention, the San Diego Comic-Con. His exceptionally long career dates back to the very beginning of the genre, and he took a striking turn toward producing more explicitly Jewish material in his later years.

When it is said that Will Eisner elevated comics to an art form, the focus is usually on the specific techniques he introduced, but it goes deeper than that. His technical skill made it possible for comics to realize artistic aspirations, but it was his unparalleled attention to the form itself that made it possible to have those aspirations in the first place. Eisner always insisted that comics creators must think about the medium itself, about the relationship between the content of the stories they were telling and the form in which they were telling them. He insisted upon this in his many roles—as creator, teacher, or interviewer/interviewee—and he was the first to do so.

It's Eisner's insistent focus on the relation between form and content in the comics or graphic novel medium that made it possible for others to then come along and take it all seriously as an art form. This relation between form and content is always a critical component of art's critical reception. For example, in any work of literature, whatever it's about on the surface, as an artistic work at a deep level it's *also* about the language in which it's written. Or whatever the subject of a painting, as a work of art it's also about the medium or act of painting itself. In that same sense any worthwhile play is also always a work about the theater, photography is always about light, and so on. If there's a distinction to be made between comics as cheap fiction versus comics as literature, or as just a commercial product versus an art form, then the distinction has to do with those working in the medium being critically aware of its formal characteristics. And it's Eisner who introduced that awareness.

Will Eisner was comics' first cinematographer. It's impossible to discuss his work without using the language of film; one is unavoidably drawn to speaking in terms of camera angles and how the shot is composed, and how the story is paced and framed. Movies are "motion pictures," and the pictorial elements drive how they tell their stories. Eisner clearly thought in this language, and his visual sense was so strong that he draws us into that language with him.

He translated this language onto the graphic art page by moving in two directions. First, he moved the camera into different positions. While most artists drew comics figures at eye level, Eisner often went to the overhead shot.* Interior shots often had the camera placed in an upper corner of the room, producing a distinctive dramatic effect, especially when coupled with his noirish sense of shadow. And where did those shadows and angles come from? Said Eisner: "The city is what I know. My drawings are affected by my life in the city. My lighting is a result of living in a city where lights always come from single sources, from above or below. My perspective was learned looking out the window of a five-story tenement building."[1] Second, his images were not separate individual scenes. Rather, each panel stood in strong visual relationship to the preceding and succeeding images. That's why Eisner came up with the term *sequential art* to describe the medium. He showed that what matters in visual storytelling is that the visuals move the story along.

If you're not clear what I mean by visual storytelling, you can try the following little thought experiment. First, imagine your favorite scenes from a few movies, and then imagine yourself describing those scenes to a friend who hasn't seen these movies. Chances are, you'll find yourself saying things like "and then he says, and then she says," etc., etc. Now recall your favorite scenes from movies directed by Alfred Hitchcock, and again imagine yourself telling a friend about these scenes. Chances are that you're no longer saying "he said, she said," but rather "first you see this, and then you see this other thing, and then . . ." *That's* what I mean by visual storytelling. The story is told by the succession of images, not through dialogue. Hitchcock was a master of the craft. That's why he's still so diligently and admiringly studied in film schools.

---

* It's a rare panel of Joe Shuster's, for instance, that doesn't position us at eye level with Superman, no matter where on or above Earth he is.

But in contrast to films, in comics it's we the viewers who are ultimately in the director's chair. One panel can show the hero socking it to the bad guy, while the next shows the villain reeling, but the force of the blow was all in that narrow white space between the panels, the "gutter," where it's the reader's imagination that propelled the action from one static image to the other. No director's vision, no cinematographer's camera, and no actor's skill can match the excitement of the action that occurs as we move from one panel to the next on the comics page, because in that transitional space we, the readers, simultaneously play all these roles, tailoring the film to our own personal fantasies. That's the main reason why comics fans who see the latest Hollywood blockbuster based on comic book superheroes will tell you that despite all the awesome special effects and overwhelming computer-generated wizardry on the screen, deep down they were still disappointed. It's just not how we always saw it in our own mind's eye. This ability to personally tailor the action is also a key and underappreciated reason why the culture of comics fandom morphed so easily into the culture of video gamers.

The distinctive skill of the comics artist, unlike that of the illustrator or cartoonist, lies not in the static image but in the way each image moves the reader on to the next. In emphasizing this, Eisner brought to comic books the Jewish sense of the priority of time over space, which we discussed earlier. Unlike a fully kinetic art form, such as dance or film, comics art is kinetic art rendered on a static page, to create the effect of a moving book.*

Eisner enhanced comics art by expanding the scope of the comics artists' own field of vision. He did so by enlarging the fundamental unit in which comics artists thought, shifting their focus from the panel to the page. Since comic books arose from comic strips, early comic book artists derived their techniques from the format of those strips, where panels were arranged in a linear fashion to be read from left to right.

---

*The kinetic sculptures and paintings of prominent Israeli artist Yaakov Agam provide the foremost contemporary example of the idea that authentically Jewish art should embody this element of time.

Having a page in front of you basically meant you were arranging lines of panels on the page. Eisner taught artists to change the way they perceived a page, starting with a page of space that needed to be allocated. Sometimes the best use of that space would indeed be to divide it up into panels, but that was only one possible solution among many. And if you did use panels, there were myriad variations available. For example, a series of narrow panels would give you a sort of staccato effect, creating a sense of tension or urgency, while a longer panel slowed things down. A different kind of continuity was created if you did away with panel borders altogether and let the eye simply flow from one image to the other, allowing the empty space between them to separate one scene from another. Smaller-panel close-ups brought readers closer to the character's internal emotional state; larger panels showing scenes at a distance led readers to simultaneously register the reactions of other characters. Everything had to be used in the service of the story. The sizes and shapes of the lettering allowed readers to *hear* the story—were the characters shouting or mumbling? Posture embodied mood—were the characters angry, sad, mad, glad? If we continue to invoke the analogy between comics and film, then Eisner brought comics from the old-time era of the silent films into the modern world of the talkies. He insisted that words and pictures had to communicate together, in mutually enhancing partnership, rather than forcing the reader to shift back and forth between word and image, breaking the flow, and possibly losing the reader's attention.

Eisner wrote two instructional books whose titles alone communicate his vision of the form: *Comics and Sequential Art* and *Graphic Storytelling and Visual Narrative*.[2] The title of a third instructional volume, left unfinished at his death and completed by Peter Poplaski, who had worked with him, also communicates Eisner's priorities: *Expressive Anatomy for Comics and Narrative*.[3] It was indeed essential to get the anatomy right in drawing, but that was merely a technical prerequisite and had to always be in the service of telling the story. These books grew out of his courses at the School of Visual Arts, and they remain indispensable guides to the field.

William Erwin Eisner was born in Brooklyn in 1917. His mother, Fanny (Ingber), was born on the boat bringing her family to the U.S. from Romania. His father, Samuel, came from Vienna, where he'd painted murals. In New York he painted stage sets for the Yiddish theater, then worked as a grainer (someone furniture companies hired to paint brass beds to make them look like the then more popular wooden beds), then became a house painter before eventually getting into the fur manufacturing business, where he went broke. Eisner described his family as "lapsed Orthodox" and spoke of his mother as the practical one and his father as the artistic dreamer.[4] It was a common division of labor in European Jewish families—remember the description of "the mama" from the opening song "Tradition" in *Fiddler on the Roof*: "Who must raise the family and run the home so Papa's free to read the Holy Book?"[5]

During and after high school, where he drew for the DeWitt-Clinton school newspaper, Eisner found various ways to use his drawing skills to help support the family during the Depression, doing posters for local merchants and small ads for newspapers.[6] Eisner's first significant entry into the world of comics came when his high school friend Bob Kane suggested he might find work with Jerry Iger, who was editing a boys' magazine called *Wow, What a Magazine!* Eisner went to the offices in a Fourth Avenue loft but couldn't get Iger's attention. Determined, he followed Iger to the magazine's printer, where they were having a problem getting clean reproductions. To their great surprise the young Eisner solved the problem the experienced hands couldn't by the simple means of using a burnishing tool to brush down the burrs on the edges of the plate that accumulate over time and blur the image, It was a trick he'd learned working on his high school magazine and after hours in a print shop. Bob Andelman tells the rest of the story in his authorized biography of Eisner:

The engravers turned to Iger and said, "Who is this guy?"
Not missing a beat, Iger said, "My new production man."

Eisner smiled. . . .

They went back to the *Wow!* office and Iger grabbed Eisner's portfolio for a second, more sincere look. In earnest, he said, "What do you have to sell?" He bought Eisner's first adventure story.[7]

The two soon formed a partnership, the Eisner & Iger Studio, where they both created material for the new comic books that were being published, and also packaged the work of other creative teams. The growing popularity of the comics increased the publishers' need for new material, and the studio would save them from having to separately hire and coordinate writers, pencilers, and inkers by offering them a finished product instead. Figuring out this assembly-line technique for profitable in-house production was the beginning of Eisner's long-standing reputation as one of the best businessmen in the field. That reputation was strengthened as later creators were amazed that he retained the rights to his characters in an era when that was unheard of. Many of those who later became leading talents worked there, most notably Jack Kirby and Batman co-creator Bob Kane. Jules Feiffer even worked there as a teenager for no pay, just to be allowed to hang out!

Eisner tells an only slightly fictionalized version of those years in his roman à clef *The Dreamer,* with the names changed to protect the artists innocently dreaming of better days, and the higher-ups not-so-innocently taking advantage of them. Billy (Eisner) describes how the shop they're going to set up will work to his partner Jimmy (Iger): "I'll sit in the center and lay out stories . . . pass the lettered pages to the pencil and ink people along the left wall. . . . [T]hey'll pass the inked pages up the other side of the shop for background and cleanup," to which Jimmy responds, "Hmmm . . . looks more like an Egyptian slave galley . . . than a comic book studio!"[8] Introducing the assembled talent, Billy points out Jack King (Kirby): "The world of adventure comics was made for him. King is a ghetto kid! He comes out of a gang-ridden neighborhood. There he acquired his respect for power and anger. That gives thrust to the way he executes adventure stories. Where else but in comics can one put to work this kind of drive with a natural talent for drawing? . . . Comics is a world of bad guys and good guys. . . . That is why Jack King is here."⁹

Eisner left the studio partnership with Iger to create the character most associated with him, the Spirit. The eponymous comic appeared as a seven-page color comics insert section in Sunday newspapers across the country. It ran weekly from 1940 to 1952, and had distribution of up to five million readers. *The Spirit* also appeared as a daily strip in newspapers, occasionally in comics, and even as a short-lived radio show. Spirit merchandise appeared from time to time, even including a pop-up book adaptation of an old Eisner story in 2008, the year of Frank Miller's very different take on the character in his film *The Spirit*.¹⁰

Eisner started each story of *The Spirit* with a dramatic splash page, a single composition taking up the entire page to get the reader's attention. These are the most often reprinted examples of Eisner's work, and deservedly so. In these we can see clearly how Eisner thought in terms of entire pages, instead of panels. Normally the title of a comic feature would appear at the top of the page, always written in the same place and in the same way. But here the words *The Spirit* would be part of the image itself, and dramatically different every time. The word *the* was usually small, but *Spirit* would be something to behold: it could appear in the shape of buildings, fences, clouds, flames, tracks in the snow, paper blowing in the wind, in a sign or newspaper headline, written on an income tax form or postcard, or backwards as if seen in a mirror. Or it might just be made of huge sprawling letters with the characters sitting, standing, leaning, lying on or running through them.

The Spirit was really Denny Colt, "criminologist and private detective," who had been taken for dead and buried in Wildwood Cemetery, but really had only been in a unique state of suspended animation after being bathed in experimental chemicals. Upon awakening in the cemetery, Colt decided to let the world continue to believe he was dead and fight crime in his new identity as the Spirit from his secret hideout under the cemetery, which he entered through his grave. Leading the supporting cast was the pipe-smoking Police Commissioner Dolan. Dolan's daughter Ellen was the "good girl" in the story, the one who wanted to wed rather than bed the Spirit. The Spirit's sidekick was Ebony White, a black boy in all the connotations of that term; a character who was seen as a comic relief figure at the time, in the vein of the role Eddie "Rochester" Anderson played vis-à-vis Jack Benny or the sort of characters you'd find in *Amos 'n' Andy*, but understood as condescendingly racist when looking back from a contemporary perspective.

The Spirit was a crime fighter, of course. More than that, though, he was the vehicle for Eisner's take on—and takedown of—the whole mainstream comics crime-fighter and superhero genre. Though he was technically a masked figure, the little domino mask spread across his eyes didn't really hide his face or facial expressions. The Spirit had a few monikered villains as his foes—the Octopus, Mr. Carrion—but that wasn't at the heart of his derring-do. Usually he was up against what the extraordinary comics historian and artist Jim Steranko calls "worn-out felons, bowery pickpockets, nickel and dime shoplifters, street corner punks, city hall grafters, shabby con men, furtive sneak thieves, stripe-suited pimps, weak-willed winos, sweat-stained stoolies, baggy pants torpedos and a rogues' gallery of other three-time losers."[11] Steranko also obligingly provides a wonderful description of the femmes fatales in the Spirit's life:

> The sexiest females ever to slink across a comic page were Eisner's women. Other artists have drawn them more voluptuously but never with more character. They were felines with cigarette holders lounging on sensuous lips. All were varied blends of Veronica Lake, Marlene Dietrich, Joan Crawford, and Lauren Bacall. . . . They would frequently introduce themselves from full page splash panels with such Mae West repartee as . . . "The name is Powder, like in gun powder—I blow up just as quick and I'm twice as deadly!"[12]

There was cartoon violence and sexiness in *The Spirit*, but it was all so tongue-in-cheek one couldn't take it seriously. The kisses may have been passionate from the women's side but they were within the bounds of the old "one foot on the floor" rule for college dormitories. The Spirit got pummeled more often than he beat up the bad guys and fell into more traps than he set. His general approach to things was as disheveled as his "costume": a blue hat, sometimes knocked off or crumpled even when on, blue gloves that never came off, a red tie that was often loose and flapping in the wind, and a blue suit that usually looked like a Clark Kent hand-me-down that he'd slept in the night before. The self-mocking tone of it all was presumably what Jules Feiffer, who worked on *The Spirit* for years under Eisner's direction, meant when he said he grew up presuming the Spirit was Jewish (notwithstanding the annual "Christmas Spirit" story).[13] Eisner hadn't wanted a mask on the Spirit and he added it only at the publisher's insistence. Looking back, Eisner said, "I could never understand why any crime-fighter would go out and fight crime. Why the hell a guy should run around with a mask and fight crime was beyond me."[14]

A strong sense of irony thoroughly colored all of *The Spirit*. The tale might be populated by everyday tenement dwellers, or noirish gangsters, or some memorable oddballs, but one came to expect to see the moral universe basically restored if nonetheless perhaps somewhat disturbed or disheveled by the ending, which often delivered a comic comeuppance to those who deserved it. But it wasn't just that many of the stories had ironic or twist endings; the irony operated at a more fundamental level. The way Eisner integrated text and image is key to his acclaim and influence, and in *The Spirit* he often accomplished this integration by having the tone of the story and the tone of the art work against each other in creative tension rather than smoothly blending. While in their characterizations the tone of the stories tended toward greater realism than was found in standard superhero fare, even when the plot was outlandish, the art was less so, moving more in the direction of cartoon and caricature. This opposition enabled Eisner to accomplish the seemingly impossible task of reconciling the contradictions otherwise inherent in having a seven-page comic book story placed as a weekly insert feature in newspapers: The cartoonish look made it appear to belong with the funny papers, while the adult content made it suitable for more extended newspaper space. Anyone who has learned how to really work within institutions—or maybe more precisely to work with but really around them, as outsiders like Jews have had to learn how to do—has learned that they can generally be satisfied by presenting the mere appearance of conformity instead of actually strictly conforming. Eisner gave both newspaper and comics readers what they were looking for, while simultaneously moving each audience with his own brand of storytelling.

Spirit stories often had surprise endings and in later years turned more toward human interest or humorous material, with the Spirit himself sometimes appearing as little more than a tangential figure or bystander. One favorite is "The Story of Gerhard Shnobble." The Spirit doesn't even make an appearance until midway through this tale, and his only function is to be so wrapped up in doing his own thing that, like everybody else, he never notices the real action, or his impact on it. The title character, the apparently innocuous Gerhard Shnobble, has recently lost his job, and decides he will become famous by leaping from a tall building and flying, an ability he had discovered he had as a child but had suppressed, even forgotten, in order to fit in with the world around him. Shnobble leaps into the air—only to be shot and killed by a stray bullet intended for the Spirit. The tone here is not what one expects from the comics:

> And so . . . lifeless . . . Gerhard Shnobble fluttered earthward . . . but do not weep for Shnobble. . . . Rather shed a tear for all mankind . . . for not one person in the entire crowd that watched his body being carted away . . . not one of them knew or even suspected that on this day Gerhard Shnobble had flown.

The Spirit's influence was enormous, and those who remember reading him in their youth retain a special affection for him. Novelist John Updike recalled:

After the relatively innocent good-against-evil adventures of Superman, Batman and Plastic Man, Will Eisner's Spirit made an alarming and indelible impression. . . . The vertiginous perspectives, the long shadows, the artist's blithe violation of the tidy limits of the panel, and curious moral neutrality of the noir hero—all this formed, for me, an unsettling transition into what I now realize was the adult world.[15]

In 1978, Eisner published what is generally considered the first graphic novel, A Contract with God and Other Tenement Stories.[16] (To be fair, it wasn't actually the first graphic novel to be published, but the first to successfully popularize the concept and the term.) We know it's a graphic novel because it says so right there on the cover: "A Graphic Novel by Will Eisner." But that's the only place the phrase appears. On the back cover the book is said to be "a powerful collection of graphic stories . . . in a unique format." A Contract with God is four stories with only a shared location among them. The phrase doesn't appear in Eisner's preface either, in which he tries to describe what he's doing with a surprising degree of what he calls "a certain sense of uneasiness." He writes:

> The text and the balloon are interlocked with the art. I see all these as threads of a single fabric and exploit them as a language. If I have been successful at this, there will be no interruptions in the flow of narrative because the picture and the text are so totally dependent on each other as to be inseparable for even a moment.[17]

The term graphic novel took a while to catch on. When Jules Feiffer came out with Tantrum the following year, the book jacket called it "a novel-in-cartoons."[18] The acclaimed 2002 film Road to Perdition was based on Max Allan Collins's 1998 graphic novel of the same name. In his introduction to the sequel Collins reports that at the film's premiere, "Reporters shouted (as my wife Barb and my son Nate and I were going down the red carpet), 'What's a graphic novel?' A number of reporters thought that meant the novel had been 'graphic' in the violent sense."[19]*

Some of the most acclaimed practitioners of the form have come to not care for the now-standard term *graphic novel* popularized by Eisner and others. Art Spiegelman is the creator of *Maus,* arguably the most acclaimed graphic novel of all time (discussed at length later) and the one that finally convinced skeptics that the form could be treated seriously. When an interviewer mentioned to him that he's considered the father of the form, Spiegelman declared, "I want a paternity test."[20] Literary critic Elif Batuman reports the discomfort with the term of some other notable creators:

> As Marjane Satrapi [*Persepolis*] puts it, graphic novels simply enable "the bourgeoisie to read comics without feeling bad"; according to Alan Moore [*Watchmen*], they allow publishers to "stick six issues of whatever worthless crap they happened to be publishing lately under a glossy cover and call it *The She-Hulk Graphic Novel.*" Moore and Satrapi, in common with many others, want their work to be known as "comics."[21]

The first four pages of *A Contract with God* show Eisner at his most distinctive, both in his artistic style and in the kind of stories he liked to tell. The first page opens on the setting of the piece. A large font of all capitals declares "A Tenement in the Bronx" and we read that "at 55 Dropsie Avenue, the Bronx, New York—not far from the elevated station—stood the tenement." Below this is a drawing of three-, four-, and

---

*When Eisner talks about wanting to create adult graphic novels, he means neither "adult" nor "graphic" in the ways these reporters might have imagined. "Adult" films are radically misnamed. They're where people indulge their juvenile fantasies, the opposite of mature adult behavior. It was the slam-bang, strong on action but weak on character development style of both mainstream comics and pornography that was precisely what Eisner wanted the medium to leave behind. Sex and violence are certainly part of the adult world Eisner portrays, but they're not the focus.

five-story apartment buildings, seen receding toward the left as if we're standing in the street in front of them, with taller buildings behind them. As on most of the pages in the book, the borders of the page are supplied by the reader. That is to say, because the elevated train station at the left and the building at the right are more or less straight vertical lines, our eye creates the equivalent of the panel frame there. Whereas lines that are actually drawn in order to form a frame close around the interior space and thereby keep the viewer at a distance, the openness of these pages draws the reader in.

The next three pages work together as a long zooming tracking shot, with the camera continually dollying in closer, moving left to right and top to bottom. The left-hand page offers a bird's-eye view of the neighborhood, with accompanying text giving the history of its tenants. From up above all seems peaceful. As we move in, the action intensifies. The text below the drawing says the neighborhood "teemed with a noisy neighborliness," which is a lead-in to the right-hand page, where we swoop closer into an alley and down to one of the lower levels. There two women are leaning out of their windows talking to each other from opposite sides of the alley, craning their necks forward to catch up on the latest gossip while hanging laundry out to dry on the clotheslines that extend between their buildings. When we turn the page we find ourselves right in the thick of things, even lower to the ground and closer to the action. We see another woman extended farther out of her window, looking up with a raised fist and yelling at a woman in the window above her, who is obliviously shaking out her carpet, the dirt from which rains down from above.

We've now arrived at our destination, ready for the show to begin. The accompanying text confirms our relationship to the neighborhood: "Within its walls great dramas were played out. There was no real privacy—no anonymity. One was either a participant or a member of the front-row audience." In these opening four pages, Eisner has transported us visually into and through the neighborhood and deposited us in our front-row seat.

The book takes its title from the first story, "A Contract with God," written on the story's title page on a large round piece of stone. The first three words are capitalized and in Roman lettering but the last word looks very Hebraic; the O and D are not closed but have openings on the left, and all three letters have a flourish of serifs at their tops, typical of Hebrew lettering. At the bottom of the page, quite small in comparison to the stone, a stooped figure is walking in a heavy rain, through a puddle and past a fire hydrant. The rain is drawn in Eisner's trademark fashion—long lines streaming down the page threatening to inundate the figures, so much so that it is surprising that the page doesn't feel damp in your fingers. Because Eisner used this so frequently his friend Harvey Kurtzman jokingly dubbed it "Eisnershpritz"; *shpritz* being Yiddish literally for "spray" and idiomatically for rain.

"A Contract with God" is the story of Frimme Hersch, who brought with him from the Old Country a stone on which he had written a contract with God as a boy. "Frimme" functions simply as his first name but it would immediately register with any Yiddish speaker as derived from *frum*, meaning "religiously observant" or "pious." And that's the point of the story. After the death of his daughter, whom he has loved ever since she was left on his doorstep as a baby, the pious man throws his contract out the window, both literally and figuratively. In doing so he invokes an old and honored Jewish tradition. Judaism is at its foundational core a covenantal religion, founded on the covenant sealed at Sinai between God and the Jewish people. The terms of that contract as presented by God are essentially: You will obey my laws and I will be your god. For any contract to be valid both parties must be bound by it, and it follows that if one party fails to fulfill their contractual duties then the other party is thereby released from their obligations. A commonly held Jewish view avows that this basic principle remains valid even for this divine contract. This conception animates such stories as that of Elie Wiesel's play *The Trial of God*, based on events he witnessed in a Nazi concentration camp: If God has abandoned the Jewish people, then God has violated the terms of the contract in which God promised to be their god, and may be held accountable for this. Frimme Hersch angrily shouts out such a challenge to God: "You violated our contract! If God requires that men honor their agreements, then is not God, also, so obligated??"

There's an ancient rabbinic story that elaborates the centrality of this covenantal basis of Judaism, claiming that God offered the same contractual deal to other peoples as well, but the Jews were the ones who chose to accept God's terms.[22] Thus the phrase translated as the "chosen people" could just as accurately be translated as the "choosing people," the ones who chose to honor and keep the divine laws. The Jews as a "chosen people" in this regard does not have the connotations of being elite, or elect, or better than other people, as is often implied in certain Christian traditions. One of the reasons this matters is that were this generally understood, one of the pillars of anti-Semitism might be weakened.

Having abandoned his faith, Frimme Hersch becomes a wealthy real estate tycoon through unethical business practices, including overcharging the synagogue for the rent for its space in the old tenement at 55 Dropsie Avenue, which he now owns. In the end, he repents his shady business practices and turns over the deed to the building to the rabbis, but only after they have agreed to write him a new contract with God. He vows to go back to living the rest of his life piously again. Immediately after he defiantly declares to God that "this time, you will not violate our contract!" he suffers a fatal heart attack.

The story has a postscript. A young Hasidic boy is trapped in the alley next to 55 Dropsie Avenue by "three toughs." He fights back by throwing stones and they run off. One of the stones is Frimme Hersch's old contract that he had thrown out the window. The text reads, "And that evening on the stoop of the tenement, Shloime Khreks signed his name below that of Frimme Hersch . . . thereby entering into a contract with God."

The book tells three other slice-of-life stories of people whose lives have come to reflect the sordid nature of their surroundings. An anti-Semitic building superintendent is driven to suicide, a street singer has a shot at a better life but drowns it in too many shots out of the bottle, and a group finding temporary escape from their troubles one summer in the Catskills in upstate New York finds that while they can take themselves out of the city, they can't take out of themselves the character flaws the city has put into them.

Eisner told tales of the inner city in later graphic novels, some of them picking up the story in this very same building. *Dropsie Avenue: The Neighborhood* gives us the longer historical overview, taking us from the neighborhood's beginnings as Dutch farms into the postwar years, and *A Life Force* takes us through the effect of the Nazi period in the U.S.[23] In all these works, the stories of Jews are front and center, and names of characters are often Yiddish-English puns that highlight the meaning of the story. In *Invisible People,* which tells stories of the anonymous people we often pass by in the big city, the lead character in one story is Hilda Gornish, *gornisht* being Yiddish for "nothing."[24] The city itself is as vibrant a character as any of the people in it, and the effects of this urban environment on its inhabitants are palpable. Here Eisner's backgrounds are never merely decorative; they are part of the story. That's another lesson he tried to impress upon his students: Nothing on the page should be there incidentally; everything one draws should serve a storytelling function.

In his last two graphic novels, Eisner shifted even further to producing explicitly Jewish material. In his 2003 graphic novel *Fagin the Jew,* he offers a very different take on Charles Dickens's renowned 1838 novel *Oliver Twist* and its major villain, Fagin. The only character in Dickens's novel referred to by his religion, Fagin takes in orphaned boys and teaches them to be thieves and pickpockets. His scheming, cruelty, and rapacious greed have become legendary. The character is one of those rarities in literature who has transcended the work out of which he was born to become an archetype of evil in general, and an evil Jew in particular. Fagin's only peer as a partner in this crime in English literature is the character of Shylock in Shakespeare's *The Merchant of Venice.* In his foreword, Eisner connects the stereotype of Fagin to his own use of stereotype with Ebony, the Spirit's black sidekick, He explains that while he didn't see it at the time, he came to recognize the offensive nature of the character, and found through his teaching experiences that he had to come to terms with the issue of using physical and characterological stereotyping in narrative art. He writes:

> So it is with this background and an awareness of the influence of imagery on the popular culture that I began to produce

graphic novels with themes of Jewish ethnicity and the prejudice Jews still face. . . . Upon examining the illustrations of the original editions of *Oliver Twist*, I found an unquestionable example of visual defamation in classic literature. The memory of their awful use by the Nazis in World War II, one hundred years later, added evidence to the persistency of evil stereotyping. Combating it became an obsessive pursuit, and I realized that I had no choice but to undertake a truer portrait of Fagin by telling his life story in the only way I could.[25]

The story of how Moses Fagin came to be Dickens's Fagin is in the classic Eisner mode of urban tales. It's a story of how the downtrodden came to the city looking for a better life, only to be further trodden down by the city, in this case London. We learn how Fagin, once a moral and upright young lad of promise, was betrayed and cheated, his mistreatment fueled by anti-Semitism. Though innocent, Fagin is accused and punished for every theft that occurs in his vicinity simply because he is a Jew. Spending years unjustly imprisoned in a penal colony, then in indentured servitude, Fagin works his way up from utter destitution to the miserable station in life in which we first encounter him in *Oliver Twist*. In the backstory Eisner invents for Fagin, we see that in embracing this life the fictional nineteenth-century Fagin made the same existential choice made by twentieth-century playwright Jean Genet. "I decided to become what crime made of me,"[26] as Jean-Paul Sartre quotes in his book on Genet, *Saint Genet: Actor and Martyr*.

Eisner has done his historical research and shows that Fagin was a victim of intergroup class tensions between Sephardic and Ashkenazic Jews, in addition to anti-Semitism against Jews on the whole. Eisner's afterword addresses how he chose to portray Fagin physically, with a rounded face that stands in stark contrast to the sharply pointed noses and chins of anti-Semitic caricature:

The Jewish community of London around 1800 consisted of two main groups, the Sephardim and the Ashkenazim. The Sephardim came from Portugal and Spain to settle in England after fleeing the Spanish Inquisition. Because they were mostly educated, they were able to achieve an accepted position in the English community . . . and for the most part became professionals, tradesmen and financiers.

. . . [T]he "lower class" who arrived during the eighteenth century were mostly Ashkenazim. They came from Germany and Middle Europe, where they had lived in small villages until driven out by intolerance, repression, and pogroms. Rural life and peasant culture had rendered them less educated and cruder in their ways. As a result, when they arrived in London they had difficulty assimilating. Like all new, poor immigrant arrivals throughout history, they clung to old ghetto habits and social behavior. Impoverished and illiterate, they took up marginal occupations in the grimier quarters of London. It is reasonable to assume that Fagin came from such origins.

In my opinion, the limning of Jews by illustrators of Dickens' time was most likely inaccurate with regard to Fagin's appearance. Because of their Eastern European origins, Ashkenazic Jews likely had features that had come to resemble the German physiognomy. . . . However, the popular illustrations of Jews, including Cruikshank's [Dickens's illustrator], were based on the appearance of the Sephardim, whose features when they arrived were sharper, with dark hair and complexions, the result of their four-hundred-year sojourn among the Latin and Mediterranean peoples. . . .

My version of Fagin is based on the more Germanic face, which I believe is more truthful.[27]

In addition to his round face, Eisner gave Fagin a white beard and a bulbous nose. In sum, while most depictions of Fagin visually reinforced anti-Semitic stereotypes by making him look like the devil dressed up, Eisner's Fagin looks like a ragged Santa Claus. In *Fagin the Jew*, Eisner challenges anti-Semitism in both text and image.

Eisner's last graphic novel, published posthumously in 2005, was *The Plot: The Secret Story of the Protocols of the Elders of Zion.* The Pro-

tocols of the Elders of Zion is a fraudulent anti-Semitic document first published in Russia in 1903, purporting to report the secret plans of the Jews for world domination. Supposedly the manuscript contained the records of a secret meeting of the Council of Jewish Elders, who oversee this conspiratorial plot. Despite the fact that it was definitively proven to be a hoax long ago, it keeps being reprinted, circulated, and taken to be true, making it perhaps the most successful forgery in modern history. Even today a Google search about the *Protocols* will as usual direct you first to Wikipedia, but then to a site that warns of "World Conquest Through World Jewish Government" and presents it as an authentic document.[28]

In Eisner's brief introduction he twice refers to the *Protocols* and the anti-Semitism it spreads as "vampire-like."[29] He means that anti-Semitism generally and the *Protocols* specifically keep resurrecting themselves even when they should be dead and buried. But one wonders if Eisner might also have had in mind a host of other old and disturbing associations between vampires and Jews, joined in the popular imagination in a brotherhood of bloodsuckers. As he once said, "I grew up on movies, that's what I lived with. The movies always influenced me." Many have noted how his art seemed particularly influenced by the German Expressionist films of the 1920s.[30] He must have known F. W. Murnau's classic 1922 silent film *Nosferatu*. The unforgettable physical appearance of the film's vampire was precisely the physiognomy that Eisner had spent so much time in *Fagin the Jew* demonstrating was a classic anti-Semitic depiction of the Jew: a figure with long, angular features, skulking in dark streets and doing the devil's work. Vampires and Jews were believed to drain the blood of innocents, both literally (the old blood libel again) and, in the case of the Jews, also metaphorically, as they were thought of as financially sucking people dry in their dirty business dealings. And of course they're both repelled by the Christian cross. In the classic 1931 film *Dracula*, Bela Lugosi even wears a star of David as Dracula.

Eisner shows us the origins of the *Protocols* in the antimodernist scheming of Tsarist Russia. Conservatives in the court of Tsar Nicholas II (the last tsar of Russia, overthrown and executed by the Russian Revolution of 1917) were opposed to the moves he was making in the direction of modernization and Westernization. One conservative militantly anti-Semitic schemer named Rachkovsky hit upon the idea of attempting to convince Tsar Nicholas that the pre-revolutionary turmoil promoting Western-style modernization was a Jewish plot to undermine Russia by bringing it under foreign domination. Such theories were in the air anyway, and Rachkovsky theorized that a document demonstrating the existence of such a plot would turn theory into fact and would turn the tsar definitively away from the pro-modernization camp. Of course no such plot or document existed, but that wasn't going to stop Rachkovsky. He was an assistant director of the tsar's police department, notorious for its use of forged documents to make its cases. He found the perfect man for the job in Mathieu Golovinski. Golovinski made a living forging whatever documents the police needed, and supplemented his income by writing anti-Semitic polemics for the right-wing press. Golovinski modified the text of an obscure book written for an entirely different purpose by Maurice Joly in 1864, *The Dialogue in Hell Between Machiavelli and Montesquieu.* Joly's intention had been to oppose what he saw as the tyrannical rule of Louis-Napoléon in France, so he put into the mouth of Machiavelli, identified in the public mind as the theorist of despotic rule, what would be recognized as the policies of Louis-Napoléon. Golovinski essentially rewrote and embellished Joly's *Machiavelli* as the *Protocols of the Elders of Zion.* It was published in Russia and placed in the hands of Tsar Nicholas by Sergius Nilus, a mystic at court who was a competitor of Rasputin for the attentions of Tsarina Alexandra. The plot was a success in that it played a significant role in turning both the tsar and Russia strongly against both modernization and the Jews.

Eisner's narrative follows the *Protocols* as they resurface in different times and places throughout the twentieth century. In each case, he tells how various people establish that the *Protocols* are a forgery. There is a famous exposé in the *Times* of London by respected international correspondent Philip Graves in 1921, a 1935 trial in Switzerland, a 1937 court decision in South Africa, a 1964 U.S. Senate Judiciary

Committee report, a continuing stream of articles and books globally—with people convinced each time that *this* time the lie will surely be put to rest once and for all. Yet various editions and translations continue to appear in Poland, Italy, Brazil, Lebanon, Egypt, Spain, Argentina, India, Syria, Japan, Mexico, with renewed publications appearing in Russia and the U.S.—perhaps most notably, the *Protocols* were vigorously promoted in the 1920s not only in Nazi Germany but also in the United States, by Henry Ford in his *Dearborn Independent* newspaper.

Eisner inserts himself into the story as doing research for a "graphic book" on the subject beginning in 1993. In 2001, he encounters a small group on a university campus in San Diego who are part of an ethnic student demonstration and have the book with them at a picket line. Telling them that it has been proven to be a fake, one responds, "Well . . . Well . . . Ah, maybe the Jews *used* this book to make their plans," with others echoing, "Yeah," and, "Even if it *is* a fake, people should read the book because it *reveals* the *Jews*." When Eisner protests, "That doesn't make sense," others of the group respond with, "Listen, mister, are you a *promoter* of Jews, eh, eh?" and, "Aha! You *are* a *Jew*, *right*?" Then, revealed for the first time in a panel, one can read one of the signs they're carrying, which says, "Down with Jews." In saddened silence, Eisner watches the group walk away, still holding up their signs.

On the book's last page, superimposed on flames rising from a burning synagogue in the center of the page, surrounded by pages fluttering to the ground with news of the desecrations of Jewish synagogues and cemeteries and anti-Semitic slogans painted in classrooms in the U.S. and Europe, the text reads, "2004 the *Protocols of Zion* is still sold in bookstores around the world."

The last work Eisner completed is a humorous short story in which he returned to the Spirit, to team him with Michael Chabon's fictional comics hero the Escapist. If it seems redundant to call a comics hero "fictional," this is one case where it isn't. The Escapist is the name of the comic character created by the protagonists in Michael Chabon's novel *The Amazing Adventures of Kavalier & Clay* (which we'll discuss in this book's final chapter). So the Escapist wasn't really a fictional hero, but a fictional fictional hero. Following the novel's great success, Dark

Horse Comics published a series of comic books in which they kept up the pretense that the Escapist really had been an old-time comics hero whom they were bringing back. They went to great lengths to keep the gag going, providing a running faux history of the Escapist's adventures, supplemented by letters in which readers reminisced about having read *The Escapist* in their youth. The first issue starts with a one page essay by Michael Chabon that begins, "I still remember the first *Escapist* comic I ever came across," and goes on to talk about how he decided to make that character the subject of his fictional history, and to thank "the generosity of the Kavalier and Clay estates."[31]

Eisner's story has the Escapist and the Spirit meeting for the first time, each helping the other escape from their separate cells in which they're being held by P'Gell, a classic female nemesis of the Spirit. P'Gell had captured the Spirit while he was trying to save a courier who was carrying the manuscript of a book by Kavalier and Clay. And she's holding the Escapist to try to get ransom from Chabon. The multiple levels of ironic humor and satire, of cross-referencing with layer upon layer of blurring the lines between fact and fiction, create an actual "amazing adventure." I'll let part of their concluding dialogue end this chapter, beginning when the Spirit has just freed the Escapist from an electric straitjacket:

> Escapist: Thanks, Spirit! But please don't tell anyone about this. . . . Escaping is my specialty, y'see!
> Spirit: You can count on it. . . . And I was saved by a superhero!!! Wow, Eisner will have an ulcer if he ever hears about it!
> (*Both running together on a city rooftop*)
> Spirit: Tell me, Escapist, have you ever wondered what heroes do for society?
> Escapist: . . . Don't have much time to dwell on "Why"! . . . But I guess what we give are . . . instant solutions and happy endings!
> Escapist: (*following the Spirit on to the next rooftop*) Society just wants us to do it again and again! Eh, Spirit?![32]

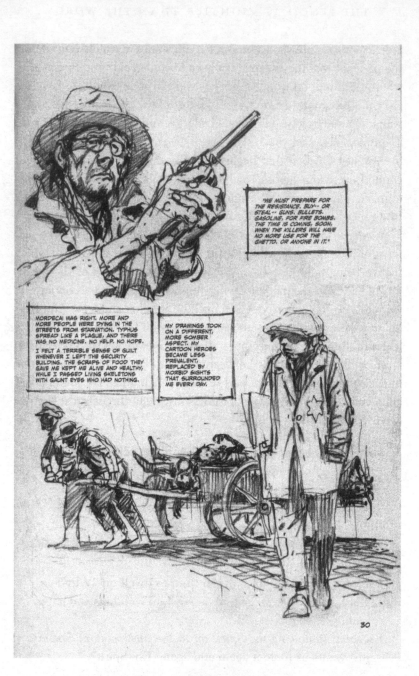

Joe Kubert, Yossel in the Warsaw Ghetto.

7

A JEW AT WAR

The Art of Joe Kubert

Joe Kubert's career parallels Will Eisner's in significant ways. Both had (and Kubert is still having) long and influential careers going back to the beginning of comics. Both are teachers: In 1976, Kubert and his wife, Muriel, cofounded the Joe Kubert School of Cartoon and Graphic Art in Dover, New Jersey, the first accredited school dedicated entirely to "the art of cartoon graphics," from which many of today's leading comics artists have graduated. Among the graduates are Kubert's sons Adam and Andy, now both well-respected comics artists in their own right. And both Kubert and Eisner turned to producing explicitly Jewish work in their later years.

The turn to Jewish themes in Eisner and Kubert's later work could simply be attributed to personal factors. After all, it's not uncommon for creative artists to turn inward in their later years and look back toward their roots. But there are larger tendencies at work here too. In different ways and to greater and lesser degrees, much of their Jewish work is autobiographical. The explosion of autobiographical Jewish graphic novels of which their work is a part came first not from these veterans, but from the emergence of a new creative force, the work of Jewish women graphic novelists. There are alternating and reciprocating waves of influences and debts here; the pioneering work of the men of the founding generation of Jewish comics artists paved the way for the newer wave of women graphic novelists, and then the work of these Jewish women prepared the ground for the later work of these earlier pioneers.

The predominance of women creators in autobiographical comics is striking, as is the Jewish presence within this genre, so much so that Jewish women's autobiographical comics practically constitute a subgenre of their own, only just now being recognized as such. As I write this, the museum exhibit "Graphic Details: Confessional Comics by Jewish Women," the first representative collection, is touring museums throughout the country. It showcases cartoonists as well as graphic novelists, and includes longtime pioneers and advocates Aline Kominsky Crumb, Trina Robbins, and Diane Noomin of the early underground *Twisted Sisters* and *Wimmen's Comix* anthologies launched in the 1970s. Robbins provides a valuable perspective on this subgenre:

> *Wimmen's Comix* no. 1 also contained the first autobiographical comic ever published, drawn by Aline Kominsky. Autobiography has since become a staple of comics drawn by women, and big chunks of women's comix tend to be about the artist's dysfunctional family, miserable childhood, fat thighs, and boyfriend problems.[1]

Among many other notable projects, Kominsky Crumb and her husband, Robert, lovingly mocked themselves as a mixed Jewish-Gentile marriage for a 2006 cover of *Heeb*, the magazine that more than anything else (with the possible exception of Sarah Silverman) marked the current generational shift in Jewish comedic sensibilities, with wild parodies going where *Mad* would never have dared to tread.

Some of the current generation of female Jewish graphic novelists tell their stories over the course of several volumes. Ariel Schrag chronicles her four Berkeley High School years in her books *Awkward, Definition, Potential,* and *Likewise,* each written in the summer following that year. Two volumes of a projected semiautobiographical trilogy by Miss Lasko-Gross have appeared: *Escape from "Special"* and *A Mess of Everything.*[2] A series of short segments tell episodic tales that cumulatively cohere into a sensitive and humorous coming-of-age portrait of a precocious Jewish girl. "Miss" isn't the author's title—it's her name, from Melissa, and the "special" she's escaping from is special education classes. Her artistic style alone communicates the basic story: We see a bright, perky child emerging from dark or labyrinthine backgrounds that are always threatening to overwhelm her.

Two notable graphic novels by Jewish women use their setting in Israel to focus more explicitly on the development of their Jewish-American identity. Sarah Glidden's *How to Understand Israel in 60 Days or Less* is the story of her Birthright Israel tour (*Taglit*, in Hebrew).[3] These are free and structured tours for Jews ages eighteen to twenty-six who have never been to Israel, designed to give them a positive experience of the country. She's sympathetic to the Palestinians and suspicious of the trip, and therefore taken by surprise by the emotional roller coaster it turns out to be for her. We are privy to the ongoing trial Glidden conducts in her head in which she plays all the roles while trying to decide if she's being "brainwashed" by the experience. Miriam Libicki's *jobnik!* is also a story of an American in Israel, but she's there longer, and in the Israeli army, during the second intifada. Libicki's "drawn essay," "Jewish Memoir Goes Pow! Zap! Oy!," is a personalized history of autobiographical comics that argues that the genre, including work by both Jews and non-Jews, is inherently Jewish in that the confessional mode of its flawed characters is free of Christian notions of sin and perfection.[4]

This turn to more personal stories in graphic novels is itself part of a much broader trend, one of many cultural manifestations of what came to be broadly known as "identity politics," and here again women have been at the forefront of this development. The women's movement of the 1960s brought into public consciousness the idea that "the personal is political." Women's consciousness-raising groups led the way in discussing the political dimensions of what had previously seemed like purely personal matters, from sexual (dis)satisfactions to workplace sexual harassment and other forms of discrimination to the annoying way men wouldn't ask for directions when they were lost. When elements of the civil rights movement morphed into the Black Power movement, this brought questions of racial and ethnic identity into the political arena as never before, and the gay and lesbian liberation movement built on and expanded these perspectives. This idea that "the personal is political" meant that elements of personal life were no longer seen as individual idiosyncrasies, but as being part and parcel of broader political forces. It brought with it the corollary idea that "the political is personal," meaning that one didn't have to leave one's personal identity behind when one entered public and political life, carrying instead only a general and universal identity as a citizen. Rather, one could and should carry into political activity the concrete particular perspectives on political issues one had gained in one's personal life.

This coalescing of the personal and the political in identity politics spawned by the social movements of the '60s was itself a response to broader societal trends having to do with the development of the modern state and economy. As the philosophical "Father of the New Left," Herbert Marcuse, wrote in 1955:

> The traditional borderlines between psychology on the one hand and political and social philosophy on the other hand have been made obsolete by the condition of man in the present era: formerly autonomous and identifiable psychical processes are being absorbed by the function of the individual in the state— by his public existence. Psychological problems therefore turn into political problems.[5]

One can see the impact of this new way of thinking in, for example, how one now positions oneself against something like drunk driving no longer as just a public-spirited citizen looking out for the general welfare, but particularly as a *Mother* Against Drunk Driving, with one's private identity made public and politically relevant. Or one marches in protest not just as a person for social justice but specifically as a member of *Jews* for Social Justice. And so on. This questioning of traditional political assumptions and boundaries also naturally manifested in the arts, creating the conditions for graphic novels to turn from traditional action-adventure stories, in which the creators were invisible behind the characters, to more personally introspective and revealing works.

In addition to the work of the women named above, another excellent example is the autobiographical Jewish graphic novels of the Cleveland curmudgeon Harvey Pekar. (If New York City was the classroom for most of the Jewish comics writers and artists, then Cleveland appears to be a satellite campus—first Siegel and Shuster, and then Pekar). He first became a national mini-celebrity via appearances on *The David Letterman Show,* where his verbal sparring with Letterman amused many. His fame spread beyond the comics and late-night crowd with the release of the major studio film based on his writings, *American Splendor.* In *The Quitter* and *Not the Israel My Parents Promised Me,* Pekar tells the story of his upbringing as the son of Polish Jewish immigrants.[6] We learn how his parents' outsider relationship to American culture formed his own outlook, how much of his youth was spent dealing with his shame about his father's accent, including when he called Harvey by his Yiddish name of Herschel, and about the Old Country interests his father pursued, spending what little leisure time he had studying Talmud and listening to recordings of cantors singing Jewish liturgical music. The heritage of which he was once ashamed is on proud display in his last major work, *Yiddishkeit: Jewish Vernacular and the New Land,* edited by Pekar and Paul Buhle with Hershl Hartman, which is a monumental attempt to tell the history of Yiddish in episodic graphic novel form, with contributions by many artists.[7]

Joe Kubert worked his way into the autobiographical mode in his later years. To understand the significance of Kubert in the comics field, and hence part of the significance of this later work, we need to go back to the beginning of his career and move forward with him along his path.

Joe Kubert has plied his trade continuously since he was twelve years old, at almost all of the major comics publishers, and in most capacities, as artist, writer, and editor. From an early age, for him it was about picking up a pencil and "making a mark" in the world, literally and figuratively.[8] While still in his teens, he was making more money drawing comics than his father brought home from his job as a kosher butcher.

The majority of his work has been at DC, where he eventually came to draw most of their characters at one time or another. His greatest acclaim, however, comes not from the superhero genre but from war comics, especially the character of Sgt. Rock of Sgt. Rock and Easy Company, who appeared in *Our Army at War,* a comic of World War II stories, from 1959 to 1988, and sporadically thereafter. The character was so popular that *Our Army at War* at times outsold DC's superhero titles, and its title was eventually changed to *Sgt. Rock.* The overwhelming majority of the stories were written by fellow Jew Robert Kanigher and illustrated by Kubert.

These were stories of men in combat, but the great power of the stories of Sgt. Rock and Easy Company was that they were about the men much more than the combat. They were character-driven, and the strengths of the soldiers of Easy Company, especially Frank Rock himself, were those of ordinary men trying to survive under extraordinary difficulties. The cover of *Our Army at War* #112 (November 1961) is a portrait gallery of Rock and the other "Combat-Happy Joes of Easy Co.": brawny Bulldozer, steadfast Ice Cream Soldier, sad Zack, winking Sunny, stolid Nick, cigar-smoking Wee Willie, Archie, looking older than the rest, and Junior, looking younger. The stories didn't feature super abilities or great feats. Sure, there were some tales of astounding marksmanship or strength or speed, but the core of the stories was clear in the name itself, Rock. They praised the endurance, steadfastness, stubbornness, and persistent courage required to stand one's ground displayed by what we have now come to call the greatest generation.

Kubert's art etched the weariness of the war-weary into Rock's visage: a triangular face looking haggard and suggesting gauntness without quite getting there that narrowed down from his helmet, its strap undone and flapping, to a jutting jaw with a permanent stubble of beard and, most striking of all, the dark shadows of his recessed eyes. In the bend of the shoulders and the slight buckle of the legs one felt the weight of what Rock carried: the grenades and ammunition belt that always hung on him, the rifle in his hands, and the responsibility for the lives of the men under his command. It was the powerful humanity of Sgt. Rock, the way that you could see the resonance with his men's pain and peril registering on his own face, that accounted for his popularity even at the height of the opposition to the Vietnam War. When Kubert became editor of DC's war and other comics during this period, he started an unusual practice for a war comic. At the end of each story appeared the slogan "Make War No More." "I wanted to make it clear that, despite the fact that I was editing war books, we were not glorifying war," Kubert has explained.[9]

That attitude came across clearly and had a strong impact. I know it affected me personally. During the second Iraq war I was one of the speakers at a "teach-in" held at my university while we were still under the Bush administration. The university has an ROTC program, and during the discussion two young men from the program passionately delivered their opinion that the professors on the panel were fools and stormed out, clearly feeling demeaned if not outright insulted by the criticisms of the war being made. Before the moderator moved on to other questions I interjected to say that I regretted that they had left, that I honored their service, and that those of us who were sharply critical of U.S. policy, as I was, had an obligation to bend over backwards to make clear that in our criticisms we separated the war from the warrior. I was very surprised when that received more applause than anything else anyone had said. Looking back, I think that I was helped to really get that distinction at an emotional level by reading Kubert and Kanigher's war comics during the Vietnam War era, even though they were set in World War II. (Similarly, the TV show *M*A*S*H*, while set in the Korean War, was experienced by its audience as really being about the Vietnam War, which was still going on when the series started.)

Aside from a few scattered and oblique references, until very recently comics about World War II managed to ignore that central part of the war that was the Holocaust, the systematic genocide against the Jews. Kubert brought Rock and Easy Co. directly into confrontation with the Holocaust in the six-issue 2006 miniseries *The Prophecy*. When asked why it took a full sixty years after the end of World War II for Sgt. Rock and Easy Company to first encounter the Holocaust, Kubert said that when he was drawing the strip in earlier decades there was "a tacit understanding" that images of concentration camps would have been too bloody and brutal for their primary audience, whom they took to be ten- to twelve-year-old boys.[10] The cover of the first issue of that miniseries showed Sgt. Rock directly addressing the reader, as he usually did verbally if not also visually to narrate the story, saying, "You ready? You wanna see war? Me an' Easy'll show you the *real war!*"

They parachute in near "Vilnus" in Lithuania, on a special mission to extract "a very valuable object that's gotta be ferried outta here."[11] There they meet up with Jewish resistance fighters who bring them to their object, which turns out to be a young Orthodox rabbi named David, whom some believe will fulfill a prophecy of deliverance. The Allied plan is that when the rabbi reaches an Allied safe haven, they will have him send messages back to Europe in radio broadcasts that will inspire Jews to fight back more vigorously. As they travel to their rendezvous point for the rabbi's extraction, the shock and horror of the men of Easy Co. intensifies as they encounter first a burned synagogue with the charred bodies still inside, then a concentration camp with its mound of corpses, then hidden Jews who tell of other horrors. The Jews they encounter have differing perspectives on what they should be doing: The Orthodox play a crucial role in getting the rabbi to safety; nonetheless, the Jewish resistance fighters sharply criticize them for praying for their deliverance instead of fighting for it. As in the other stories of Sgt. Rock and Easy Co., while the action and adventure elements of war comics were certainly there, the emphasis was on the human element. Kubert consistently held fast to his basic principle: One could honorably depict the struggles of those who fought, and readers could revel in their adventures, without glorifying war.

While Sgt. Rock remains by far the major military character identified with the Kubert-Kanigher team, he's not the only one. In 1965, they took war comics another step away from a chauvinistic celebration of war with their introduction of a surprising new feature. *Enemy Ace* told the story of a *German* World War I pilot, Hans von Hammer, an aristocrat who followed the old warrior's code of mutual respect between enemy combatants. He had a fatalism that saw destiny ruling those who lived and died in the skies. This helped more sharply define the character, allowing him to wax poetic in some high-flying language to accompany the high-flying aeronautical acrobatics. It also shifted readers' attention away from the fact that it really was the "hero" of the feature, and not fate, who was shooting down planes that were on "our" side. Kanigher and Kubert had to toe many a fine line in this feature, which was originally the backup second feature to Sgt. Rock in *Our Army at War*, but eventually became very popular in its own right.

Kubert's reputation as the preeminent artist of war comics led him to be tapped to do the art for a *Tales of the Green Beret* newspaper strip in 1966, inspired by Robin Moore's best-selling book *The Green Berets* and written by Jerry Capp, brother of Al Capp (both originally "Caplin"), who created *Li'l Abner*. Kubert had envisioned it as an adventure strip in the vein of the old *Terry and the Pirates*, famously done by Milt Caniff. He soon quit when, as he saw it, "[l]ittle by little Jerry [Capp] tried to turn it into a political treatise" in favor of the war.[12] It's not that Kubert was a war protester strongly opposed to the Vietnam War (although his wife, Muriel, increasingly turned that way).[13] Like many immigrants and veterans (Kubert was drafted and served from 1950 to 1952, mostly at Fort Dix, with a six-month stint in Germany), he was inclined to believe and support what the U.S. government said about the necessity of the war. But he didn't participate in any flag-waving hurrahs that demonized the enemy and minimized the tragedy of war in order to mount an ostentatious display of heroics.

After Sgt. Rock, the characters Kubert is most associated with are Hawkman, whom he drew during his original incarnation in the '40s, and then brought back in his revival in the '60s; Tarzan, whom he drew in a period when DC held the comics rights to Edgar Rice Burroughs's characters; and Tor, a prehistoric hunter of Kubert's own creation. There's a common theme here. All of these characters allow Kubert to employ his remarkable ability to imbue the human body in motion with extraordinary grace and power. Tarzan and Tor wear only loincloths, Hawkman is one of the most sparsely clothed superheroes (among the men anyway), and you'd be amazed how often the uniforms of the men of Easy Company end up torn and shredded, so their musculature is on full display.

The extraordinary fluidity and economy of Kubert's line allow him to condense the energy of action into subtle fluctuations of the body in motion. Musculature works by counterbalancing tension and release, and the two master comics artists Kubert and Kirby choose to highlight the different moments of that dynamic. While Kirby's superheroes project the powerful release of energy when they have sprung into action, Kubert captures the tension held in the body at the moment action is initiated. The classic Kubert moments occur when Tarzan is right at the point of emerging from his stealthy crouching pose to leap out of the jungle at whatever man or beast he's attacking, when Hawkman comes swooping down about to engage with his foe, and when Sgt. Rock is just releasing the grenade he's hurling at the enemy. It's what makes Kubert one of the most sought-after cover artists in the business. He creates in the viewer a sense of anticipation of what's going to happen *next*, exactly what you want on the cover of a magazine to make the reader want to look inside.

Kubert's strength is in the human scale of the human body rather than in the costumed, super-muscled superhero range. For a time, DC's Sgt. Rock was in competition with Marvel's World War II combat feature, *Sgt. Fury and his Howling Commandos,* drawn at first by Kirby. If you were looking at a figure leaping into action in the midst of the enemy, practically exploding off the page, you were more likely looking at a Kirby page, but if in contrast the characters were visibly more impacted by what was exploding at and around them, you were more likely looking at Kubert's work. Kubert's humanism continually comes through in both art and story, always emphasizing the realistically human, non-overblown scale of the action, whether involving soldiers at war or even the adventures of superheroes.

When the Thing came out as Jewish, it was the most notable such revelation in comics, but the oddest conversion from non-Jew to Jew involves a character created by Kanigher and Kubert in 1976, the Ragman, who fights crime in his impoverished neighborhood with powers of more than human strength and agility, which he gets from donning a suit seemingly made of rags. Kubert still today says that he and Kanigher had no intention of creating a Jewish character, but to me the later development of the character is a striking example of how the creator's background can manifest itself in the creation without the creator

having explicitly intended it, as we've seen in other parts of this book.[14]
Here's a revealing excerpt from the letters page in 1977:

> I would, however, like to comment on . . . the matter of Rory
> Regan's [Ragman] apparent Jewishness. Despite his very
> non-Jewish name, Rory seems, to me at least, to be the com-
> ics' first Jewish superhero. His father looks either Jewish or
> Italian, and junk dealing was a fairly common occupation for
> both these groups at one time. Bette Berg has a Jewish name,
> so let's assume she's Jewish too. The point is that I like the idea
> of a comic book about a Jewish pawn shop owner who is also a
> super-hero. . . .
>   Leo Keil, Brookline, Mass

To which editor E. Nelson Bridwell responded:

> I asked Bob [Kanigher], who stated that if Rory was meant to be
> Jewish he'd have a Jewish name—as Bette does! She's Jewish—
> Rory is of Irish descent.[15]

The character didn't last long in that original incarnation, but was
revived not by his original creators but by others in 1991. The distance
Jewish identity traveled in mainstream comics in the intervening years
can be marked by the words on the cover: "From the ashes of the Warsaw Ghetto to the back alleys of Gotham City . . . the Tatterdemalion
of the oppressed rises again." While the origins of his suit were never
explained in the original series, now it's explained as having kabbalistic
origins, and the Ragman's original powers of strength and agility cor-
respondingly expand to include flight and a kind of extrasensory perception that borders on telepathy. It turns out that after the original
soulless golem was created:

> It was decided by a council of rabbis that the golem should be
> replaced by a human agent. Using the same ancient spell, but
> substituting rags for clay, the rabbis created a living costume.

135

Unlike the golem, this uniform required the presence of a human being to animate it.[16]

Jewish themes dominate the eight-issue miniseries. This time around, the character's name is no obstacle to his being Jewish. The latest Ragman, Rory Regan, is a Vietnam veteran who inherited the suit from his father, who fought in the Warsaw Ghetto. The Ragman eventually has to fight and defeat a reanimated golem, who has become more humanlike with the passage of time. The Ragman now reappears from time to time in the DC universe, his costume now reconceptualized as a Suit of Souls made up of souls of the dead captured in rags.

Having illustrated stories from the Bible for a DC series in the '70s, in the '80s Kubert developed a relationship with the Orthodox Jews of the Lubavitcher sect in Brooklyn when they approached him to do a series of two-page stories for their magazine *Moshiach Times* (*Messiah Times*). These stories were collected in one volume in a 2004 book, *The Adventures of Yaakov and Isaac*.[17] They are instructional morality tales aimed at Jewish boys, complete with study questions, and some are also little history lessons recounted as parables relevant to some incident in the boys' lives. They range from Yaakov showing Isaac how praying every morning taught him the discipline he needed to win a school race, to a tale of Alexander the Great, honored in Jewish history for not suppressing Jewish worship, to a story that may be apocryphal but is claimed to be true, about a World War I incident in which a German soldier about to bayonet to death a French soldier in the trenches hears the Frenchman say the "Shema" ("Hear O Israel . . ."), the traditional prayer observant Jews wish to have on their lips at the moment of death. The German soldier then stops and utters the appropriate Hebrew response, and they both walk away from the battlefield.

Kubert took on real war reporting instead of fictional war stories in his 1996 graphic novel *Fax from Sarajevo*. One of his friends, artist Ervin Rustemagic, was stranded in Sarajevo, Bosnia, with his wife and their two young children in 1992 when the city was attacked by Serbian forces under brutal dictator and war criminal Slobodan Milošević. While trapped, they preserved their sanity by communicating with the outside world through faxes to their friends. The faxes to Kubert and his wife, Muriel, appear in the book from time to time, mostly to back up the story Kubert tells in graphic novel form. Kubert declares his motivation on the book's front overleaf: "In 1945, we told the world, 'Never again.' In 1992, we forgot our promise." The Kuberts had visited the Rustemagics in their home in Sarajevo, the city in which Ervin was born and raised, earlier in the same year of the war, but Kubert explains in the book that he hadn't even known his friend Ervin was of Muslim descent until after the murderous "ethnic cleansing" began. In one of the faxes, Rustemagic asks Kubert to communicate to the Jewish communities of the U.S. how proud and moved everyone he knows in Sarajevo is that the Jews there are committed to standing and fighting with them.[18]

The horrifying story told in the book includes Serbian snipers specifically targeting children because they get paid more for them, and "rape camps" where women and girls are imprisoned. Having left their own home just in time, as it was being flattened by tanks, Rustemagic and his family move from one neighborhood to another in search of shelter. In this hell, he uses his car to pursue the faint hope of escape. Here comic books were valued because, when piled into the car as additional armor, "two or three copies can stop a bullet or a bomb splinter."[19]

Fax from Sarajevo won numerous awards when it came out, including the Eisner Award for Best New Graphic Novel, presented to Kubert personally by Eisner, his employer when he was first starting out more than fifty years earlier. It was a pioneering work in a genre that's come to be called "comics journalism." The most oft-cited examples, along with *Fax from Sarajevo*, are Joe Sacco's *Palestine* and Marjane Satrapi's *Persepolis*, about Palestinian and Iranian experiences, respectively. Several recent additions to this rapidly expanding genre include *The Photographer: Into War-torn Afghanistan with Doctors Without Borders* by Emmanuel Guibert and Josh Neufeld's *A.D.: New Orleans After the Deluge*, about the experiences of Hurricane Katrina survivors in the city.

Kubert's later works became more personal as well as more Jewish. He explores the violence in his own childhood neighborhood in his 2005 graphic novel *Jew Gangster*. It is in part Kubert's consideration of what his life might have been like if things had gone down a different path early in his life. Like so many of the comics creators of his generation, Kubert came from a tough New York City neighborhood. Here he tells a fictional story of a Jewish boy who succumbs to the lure of the streets and enters the criminal underworld of Brooklyn during the Depression. Kubert pays great attention to those streets, which are recognizably the same sort of neighborhood portrayed by Eisner in so many of his books.[20]

There seems to have been something in the air around this time about the theme of Jewish gangsters. In roughly the same period several works addressed issues of violence perpetrated by Jewish criminals. Neil Kleid and Jake Allen's 2006 graphic novel *Brownsville* tells the story of the Jewish gangsters and hit men who came together to form Murder, Inc.[21] More in the comics mainstream, the twelve-issue DC miniseries *Caper*, which ran from 2003 to 2004, tells lurid crime stories of three different generations. The stories appear in four-issue installments, all written by Judd Winick but illustrated by different artists—Farel Dalrymple, John Severin, and Tom Fowler—with the first telling a fictional story inspired by Murder, Inc., but set in turn-of-the-century San Francisco, and the others in different California locations.[22] One saw a marked interest in the topic, even in scholarly writing, starting a little earlier: Rich Cohen's *Tough Jews: Fathers, Sons and Gangster Dreams* (1998); Rachel Rubin's *Jewish Gangsters of Modern Literature* (2000); Warren Rosenberg's *Legacy of Rage: Jewish Masculinity, Violence, and Culture* (2001); and Elliott Horowitz's *Reckless Rites: Purim and the Legacy of Jewish Violence* (2006).[23] These books acknowledge that in the general public imagination "Jewish gangster" seems almost like an oxymoron, a contradiction in terms. Yes, people know about Jewish crooks, but the phrase tends to call to mind images of crooked moneymen rather than killers with bloodied hands.

Which brings us to the crowning achievement of Kubert's explicitly Jewish work, *Yossel: April 19, 1943. Yossel* is an alternative autobiography.[24] That is, it's a personalized version of the popular fiction genre of alternative history, in which variations of historical possibilities are explored: What if the South had won the Civil War, or the Nazis had won World War II, etc. Kubert is a Polish-born Jew who was brought to the U.S. by his family in 1926, when he was two months old. The family had tried to leave months earlier but were denied visas and passage on the ship because his mother was pregnant with him at the time. *Yossel* is Yiddish for "Joe," and in *Yossel: April 19, 1943* Kubert tries to answer the question of what would have happened if he hadn't made the trip, if he had remained in Poland and been caught up in the maelstrom of the Holocaust.

The book was published in 2003, during the period that saw the emergence of the broader trend of autobiographical graphic novels we discussed at the beginning of this chapter. As we have seen, in the early works of the founding fathers of comics, Jewish influences and backgrounds were submerged and have to be decoded to become visible. In today's United States, it feels safer for Jews to be open about their Jewish identities, resulting in more works with explicitly Jewish themes.

Kubert begins the story in a situation as close to his actual background as he can get: the small town of Yzeran in eastern Poland, a father who's continually supportive of his son's love of drawing from the age at which he could hold a pencil in his hand (even though the norm would have been to discourage such childishness as the child grew older), and eventually the beginning of hushed stories among the adults of terrible things happening to Jews. We then see these stories hitting home: the knock on the door, and the order to leave their home immediately, as it is now the property of the Reich. They pack up and go to Warsaw, where they live in a crowded apartment in the ghetto. By the time he is fifteen, Yossel's drawings have changed. No longer imitating the heroes and scenes of the American comics that appear in Polish newspapers, the boy has begun drawing the people around him. In the damp basements of the ghetto where the children play, he meets Mordecai, a character inspired by Mordecai Anielewicz, commander of the Resistance forces in the 1943 Warsaw Ghetto Uprising.

During one inspection of their apartment, a Nazi officer notices

Yossel's drawings of "big, strong muscled men." "Come with me. Now!" he says.[25] In Yossel's telling:

> I will never forget the look of awful dread on Mama's and Papa's faces, as I followed the Nazi officer. . . . I was led to the far end of the ghetto quarters where the somber building that housed the security forces stood. I had never been this close to it before. We went in. My legs trembled as I mounted the stone steps.[26]

Then:

> They gave me paper, pencils, even an eraser. I did sketches of the soldiers and they congratulated me. Pushed cookies and bread in my pocket. Slapped me on my back in friendly gestures. Hours later, I left in a daze. Being able to draw was truly a blessing.[27]

Kubert has said that in his youth his ability to draw was "a life saver" for him, as it kept him out of the kind of trouble he illustrated in *Jew Gangster*.[28] Here, drawing is a lifesaver for Yossel, too, as the Nazis keep him in the ghetto for their entertainment when the rest of his family is put on a transport to Auschwitz. They don't realize that he's using his proximity to spy on them and report back to Mordecai. He eventually learns of the deaths of his family from someone who escaped from the camp and made his way back to the ghetto. Yossel meets his end in the Uprising, going down fighting with Mordecai and his other comrades, burned in the sewers by a Nazi flamethrower:

> I did not feel the pain when the bullets hit me. Only a pressure, like when the rabbi was jabbing me with his finger against my chest to make a point in learning Torah.
> I fired my gun into the light again and again until the hammer clicked empty.[29]
> . . . Was I holding my pencil? Was I drawing? I must be, else, how could I see the heroes, the jungles, the dinosaurs, the aliens from other worlds?
> It felt good to draw again, to shut out the rest of the world, to feed my mind and my heart with that which makes me complete.

No noise. No wetness. No heat. No cold. No pain. Nothing.
"M-Mama."[30]

Kubert draws Yossel in a way that evokes one of the most famous photographs of the Holocaust, taken in the Warsaw ghetto. The photograph shows a young boy, hands held up in the air in terror, at the head of a frightened group of mostly women and children being taken out of a building and forced along the ghetto street by Nazi soldiers, rifles at the ready. As *Yossel* progresses, he comes more and more to resemble that boy, down to even wearing a cap and jacket of the same style once he's in the ghetto.

That photograph was taken by the Nazis themselves during the final liquidation of the ghetto to document their handiwork. It appears in an official report entered into evidence at the Nuremberg war crimes trials, a report declaring their mission accomplished sent back to headquarters in Berlin by commanding General Stroop titled, "The Jewish Residential District in Warsaw No Longer Exists." I've always felt a personal connection to the document since an incident that occurred many years ago. At some point around the end of my college years, my father and I were sitting around the kitchen table of neighbors and friends of my parents from the Old Country. Somehow in the conversation I mentioned this report.

"How do you know the name Stroop?" asked our host, Robert Born.

I explained that it had come up in a book I was reading.

"I remember Stroop," he said. You could see in his eyes that in his mind he had left us and was back there. Having grown up in a community of Holocaust survivors and taking it all for granted, I had simply forgotten that I was in the home of a survivor of the Warsaw Ghetto.

"I remember those black boots," he said slowly, clearly picturing the scene in his mind. "We had to line up when he came for inspection, and when he got out of his jeep he'd stretch out his legs first. Those long black leather boots were so polished that the sun shined off them." I looked at him intently as his gaze returned to the present and us. "I remember Stroop," he repeated.

I had unintentionally triggered a type of conversation that would take place in many homes with greater intentionality, where the children of Holocaust survivors drew out of the survivors stories they hadn't planned on telling. We'll see in our discussion of Art Spiegelman's *Maus* how that impacted the Jewish storytelling voice in graphic novels. Stories reluctantly elicited often emerge with a natural plainspokenness whose unembellished form gives them greater power precisely because of their terseness. The visceral force of his memories that transported him back to that time and place was so strong that some of it seems to have even rubbed off on me, transporting me back to that kitchen even now as I recall our conversation.

In the Stroop Report, the Jews are only occasionally identified as offering resistance or fighting, and are referred to as "subhumans, bandits, and terrorists."[31] German military reports preferred not to acknowledge Jewish resistance. What commander in the field was going to send back a report admitting that the mighty German military machine was having trouble dealing with an inferior race? It's a principal reason that the story of Jewish resistance was untold at first, leading to the mistaken impression that Jews simply passively accepted their fate. Following standard historical practice, the first histories of the war made extensive use of captured German war documents. For professional historians, their creed is often that where there is no documentation, there are no historical facts. The record had to wait to be corrected in later accounts until the documentation of Jewish resistance was recovered, in diaries and letters hidden under floorboards and behind loose bricks or buried in the forests, and until interviews could be conducted in languages unknown to the first wave of historians: Slavic languages and Yiddish. There was Jewish participation in the national resistance movements in the occupied countries; armed resistance within the death camps themselves, including Auschwitz and Treblinka; mass escapes from Sobibor and Koldyczewo; resistance cells such as the Herbert Baum group in Berlin; uprisings in the ghettoes; and fighting partisan groups in the forests of Eastern Europe.

When the full picture is assembled—including the hostility of the local population, the history of anti-Semitism that led Jews in the early years to believe that "this too shall pass," the collective reprisals against resistance, the lack of arms and military experience—the question is not why the Jews didn't resist, but rather how they managed to mount the resistance they did in the face of overwhelming odds and near-insurmountable obstacles. But the picture of Jewish nonresistance has been set in the public mind, and most people still "know" that the Jews just went "like lambs to the slaughter," despite some recent efforts to correct the record. Kubert uses *Yossel* to strike another blow against this canard of Jewish passivity.

The way the book was drawn and printed is deeply integrated into the story itself. It is illustrated in stark pencil drawings, looking perhaps unfinished when compared to the standard form. As Kubert explains in the book's introduction:

> The usual procedure in cartooning is first, to do the initial draw-ings with a pencil, then to apply ink over the pencils with brush and pen. The pencil drawings are then erased, leaving only the ink rendering.
>
> The drawings in this book are pencil renderings. . . . I wanted to convey a sense that these drawings were in Yossel's mind, even though he may never have had the opportunity to put them all to paper.[32]

Further, the paper on which these drawings are printed in the book is gray instead of the traditional white, which makes the work feel more like a historical document and less like a standard comic book.

Kubert continues to be productive, but *Yossel* is clearly a career high-light, both because of the acclaim it has received and because it explains so much of his career. His personal identification with Yossel, infinitely greater than with any other character he's ever portrayed, demonstrates how he always saw war from the point of view of its most vulnerable victims. It explains how the person acknowledged to be comics' greatest war artist always emphasizes the human toll of war and ended up put-ting "Make War No More" into the comics when he became an editor.

The idea that the ability to draw could save one's life in the Holo-caust isn't as far-fetched as it might seem. David Olère survived two years in Auschwitz because he illustrated letters German guards were sending home. A character based on him appears in Pascal Croci's graphic novel *Auschwitz,* using his actual prisoner number, 106144.[33] It also happened to Dina Gottliebova (later Dina Babbitt) as a prisoner in Auschwitz. The infamous "Angel of Death" Dr. Josef Mengele spared her life and that of her mother, Johanna, so that she could draw portraits of gypsy inmates. He thought her paintings captured their skin color better than the photography of the time, important to him because he thought this helped demonstrate their racial inferiority. The drawings were acquired and put on exhibit in the '70s by the museum at the site, whose curators did not know that the artist was still alive. When they refused to return them following her repeated requests after she identified them, an international campaign, which included U.S. House and Senate resolutions, was mounted to get the paintings back to her. The petition remained unsuccessful at the time of her death in 2009 at the age of 86.[34]

As part of that campaign a six-page comic was created to illustrate the situation. Inked by Kubert, with an introduction by Stan Lee, it was written and drawn by Neal Adams, one of the most respected figures in the comics industry, both for his extraordinarily talented contributions on comics pages and also for his behind-the-scenes work as a leading champion of creators' rights. The story was reprinted for wider circulation in the last issue of the six-issue miniseries *X-Men Magneto: Testament* that for the first time told the story of Magneto's youth as a Jew prior to and during the Holocaust.

If one needs any additional reason why I should have singled out Will Eisner and Joe Kubert for the extended treatment they've received in this book, here's what Adams has to say:

> When people ask, "Who do you like in comics?" the two people I mention are Will Eisner and Joe Kubert. Everyone else is a skilled artisan. When it comes to human beings, it's Will Eisner and Joe Kubert, and then it's hard to keep counting.[35]

8

OF MICE AND SUPERMEN

Art Spiegelman's *Maus*

C oming to terms with the enormity of the Holocaust in either words or images has proven to be an enormously challenging task, so much so that some have declared it to be impossible. In this vein, Elie Wiesel, the most prominent keeper of the flame of the memory and legacy of the Holocaust among the survivors, has maintained that one must in many ways maintain a respectful silence in the face of that evil, or at least, as he graphically puts it, if one dares to speak one should not say anything one would not be willing to say in the presence of the bodies of the murdered children. In the face of such a grave cautionary admonition, attempting to adequately deal with the Holocaust and its legacy in a medium that requires both words and images working in tandem might seem to be doubly impossible. The genius of Art Spiegelman's groundbreaking graphic novel *Maus* is that it uses the unique graphic novel medium to cut through this Gordian knot and accomplish precisely that.

The creation of *Maus* and the reception it received were made possible by the conjunction of the maturing of a medium and the maturing of a new generation of creators and audience, what in Jewish circles is called the "Second Generation," that is, the children of the survivors (e.g., Spiegelman and me and the rest of our cohort). With good reason, many of the survivors who arrived in the U.S. after the war said relatively little about their experiences. Most obviously, it was too painful for them. And they didn't want to pass the pain on to their children. Further, even when they were willing or even desired to speak, they had difficulty finding a receptive audience, not really because of anti-Semitism, though there was that too, but more because people were simply unwilling or unable to take it all in. While a significant number, like Wiesel, felt called upon to act as witnesses and make sure that what happened was not forgotten, for others their own reluctance to tell their stories dovetailed perfectly with the reluctance of others toward hearing them, and those stories threatened to disappear into the past. It seemed better to let history lie buried with the dead.

But the children of the survivors weren't satisfied. They (we) sensed something was missing, something in our parents' past that made them less present to us in the present. Some part of them had been left "back there." What was it? We started to ask questions, to insist that yes, we really did want to know what had happened to our parents and to our missing relatives, whose presence we also missed even though we had never known them. And yes, we could bear the burden of this knowledge without succumbing to it. Into this generational tug-of-war between the children's growing wish to have the past of the Holocaust revealed, not as mass historical phenomenon but as intimate family history, versus the survivors' resigned weariness that "it's enough already with such stories," to invoke *Maus*'s survivor's words, stepped *Maus*, which brilliantly uses the graphic novel medium's fusion of words and pictures to capture the difficult but also creative tensions between the urge to conceal and the need to reveal. What cannot be said can perhaps be shown, and even if we cannot really show the reality of the camps and other horrors, we can nonetheless illustrate the revealing/ concealing intergenerational conversations about them, and thereby illuminate the past even if we still remain in the dark about much of it.

Spiegelman's *Maus: A Survivor's Tale* dramatically changed the landscape for graphic novels. It demonstrated what the medium was capable of and that there was an audience for it. It's the single work fans hold up to show skeptics that the medium can deal with serious subject matter and can move adults to deep emotions and reflective thought. It remains the only graphic novel to have received a Pulitzer Prize, a Special Award in 1992.

The prize had "Special" status because people simply didn't know what to make of this genre-shattering work. The *New York Times* originally had it on their bestseller list under "fiction," but changed its categorization to "nonfiction" after they received a letter of protest from Spiegelman. In it he expressed sympathy for the problem of classification he'd created for them by telling a factual story in such unprecedented fashion, through a graphic novel in which all the people were drawn with the heads of animals (primarily mice, cats, dogs, and pigs). He playfully suggested that perhaps what was needed was a special new category: "nonfiction/mice."[1]

As I noted in the introduction, a key question in coming to terms with any work of art is the relationship between form and content, between its medium and its message. That's going to be the principal focus of the discussion of *Maus* here.

Maus tells two interwoven stories: the experiences of Vladek, Spiegelman's father, during the Holocaust, beginning in the prewar period in his native Poland, and the story of Spiegelman's relationship to his father, as he gets Vladek to relate the stories that are eventually put into *Maus*. With the postmodern self-reflexive consciousness of his generation, Spiegelman tells us the story of the telling of Vladek's story, even as he's telling us that story. Interspersed throughout the work are moments when Spiegelman shows himself pondering how he's going to draw the book, including moments where he breaks through the "fourth wall" and directly addresses the reader. By making his drawing hand so conspicuous he joins in contemporary postmodernist ideology's rejection of any idea of an "invisible hand" at work bringing the world to order.[2] In his words, looking back on the work years later:

> The story of *Maus* isn't just the story of a son having problems with his father, and it's not just the story of what a father lived through. It's about a cartoonist trying to envision what his father went through. It's about choices being made, of finding

what one can tell, and what one can reveal, and what one can reveal beyond what one knows one is revealing. Those are the things that give real tensile strength to the work—putting the dead into little boxes.[3]

Maus's dominant and defining imagery is that the Jews are drawn as mice and the Nazis as cats. *Maus* is German for "mouse," and the iconography captures the obvious predator and prey relationship between cats and mice, as well as the Nazi ideology of Jews as vermin. When I teach this work, I begin with a class discussion in which the students compile a bestiary of the animals depicted. I used to be surprised if they mentioned cats (Nazis) before mice (Jews), but now I've come to expect it. I've realized that while for me this is obviously a story about Holocaust victims, thus starting with the mice/Jews, for most of my students their primary frame of reference is that this is a story of World War II, which for them is about Nazis, hence they are first drawn to focus on the cats/Nazis.

Once you have the Nazis as cats, then the symbolism of dogs as their natural enemies comes into play, and it's a clear choice to draw the Americans as dogs. The other major players in the story are the Poles, drawn as pigs. When I ask my students for anything that would account for an association between Poles and pigs, some of them hesitantly bring up Polish sausage, as well as less savory associations with calling someone a pig in which one might mean they are unclean, or greedy, or boorish, and so on. But after I've written on the board "mice = Jews" and "cats = Nazis" (or sometimes "cats = Germans" if that's how they've put it, which gets us into an interesting discussion about the book not differentiating between the two, and what that might tell us about its point of view), when I come to "pigs =" or "dogs =" I pause. I ask, "What about Jewish Poles or Jewish Americans? Mice, or pigs/dogs?" They pause for a moment, and then they're clear that the answer is "mice." So for the rest of the bestiary I write on the board notations like "non-Jewish Americans" or "Polish non-Jews" for what these animals represent.

There are other creatures featured in the book, though not as prominently, and sometimes for only a handful of panels. Toward the end of the story, after the war, British officers make a one-panel appearance in a jeep at a displaced-persons camp, drawn as fish (fish and chips, anyone?). A gypsy fortune-teller is depicted as a moth, specifically a gypsy moth, of course, reflecting Spiegelman's fondness for visual puns. The occasional French person is a frog, and in a postwar sojourn to Sweden the Swedes are elk.* Postwar we also encounter small mice with catlike stripes, the children of a mixed marriage.

So now comes the payoff question. What does our bestiary tell us about from whose point of view this story is being told? Who in the book sees the world this way? For which character is the basic categorization of persons Jew or non-Jew, as evidenced by our having seen how being Jewish visually trumps any other identity? (Only if the person is not Jewish do we then get to see what nationality they are.) We realize that this is the worldview of Art's father, Vladek, and that the way the work is drawn thus literally draws us into seeing the world through his eyes. (Students will also bring up that the Nazis saw the world this way, which then leads us into a discussion of the extent to which Vladek's worldview is one imposed on him by his experiences of persecution.) This is essential information for understanding Vladek, and it's communicated through Spiegelman's artistic choices in the graphic novel form. You couldn't very well write a novel that so relentlessly hammers this point home. One cannot imagine a novel in which each time Vladek spoke to someone the author would insert a line reminding us that Vladek fundamentally saw this person as either a Jew or a non-Jew.

Reflecting the general intergenerational tension of which they are a part, Vladek and Art are, at many points in the book, at odds over the telling of Vladek's story. Art is constantly trying to pull more information from his father, and his father resists. Spiegelman is wrestling with the paradox also expressed by renowned Jewish poet Adrienne Rich when she writes about writing about her father: "[I]n order to write this I have to be willing to do two things: I have to claim my father . . . and I have to break his silence, his taboos; in order to claim him I have in a sense to expose him."[4]

---

* Spiegelman was born in Stockholm, although this doesn't enter into *Maus*.

They differ not just about whether to tell Vladek's story, but how to do so. Words are often not adequate for Vladek and other survivors when they want to communicate something of real importance. At such moments the survivors want to *show*, not *tell*. We see this at moments when, at key points in the story, Vladek wants Art to learn some skill upon which he thinks his son's survival might someday depend if the worst happens. At these times Vladek interrupts Art's note taking and gets Art's pencil and pad out of his hands and shows his son what he wants him to know: how to repair shoes, or how to build a secret bunker in a home in which you can hide yourself and your family when they come looking for you: "Show to me your pencil and I can *explain* you . . . Such things it's good to know exactly how was it—just in case."[5] Art's therapist, also a survivor, responds in the same vein when Art asks him what it felt like in Auschwitz. He doesn't answer by attempting to tell him but instead attempts to demonstrate some taste of it by scaring him: "BOO!" he shouts, causing Art to jump in his chair. "It felt a little like that. But Always."[6] The choice of a primarily visual over verbal medium for this work—a graphic novel instead of a novel—honors the nonverbal communication mode of survivors despite the fact that the medium is alien to them.

Spiegelman addresses the classic conundrum of dealing with the Holocaust artistically, the problem of articulating the unspeakable, by using the graphic novel form. Vladek's reticence to speak becomes Art's imperative to draw. Like many children of Holocaust survivors, Art has learned to listen to his father in and through his silences.[7] *Maus* bridges the Holocaust and post-Holocaust generations not just by its content, intermingling Art's and Vladek's stories, but in a form that strives to indissolubly blend verbal and nonverbal communication.

The form of the book is both comforting and disconcerting, and it uses this confounding conjunction with astounding skill and success. As a comic book it initially appears to most of its readers to be child-ish, and not just generically in a children's genre, but specifically the most childish of the childish, a book of talking animals. The deep associations we all have with cartoons of talking animals, especially mice, relax the reader's defenses in reading a book about the Holocaust. The book can then get in under the reader's defenses, and end up indelibly conveying the horrors of these events to the reader's imagination more graphically than would another medium.

The absences of key figures in Art's life haunt the story of *Maus*. We learn about his mother Anja's impact on him in four pages in volume 1, which are drawn in a different idiom from the rest, with fully human figures in a stark style that invokes block woodcuts. These pages are a reprint of an autobiographical story Spiegelman drew years earlier in 1972, *Prisoner on the Hell Planet: A Case History,* which opens with Artie addressing himself to the reader with a forlorn expression: "In 1968, when I was 20, my mother killed herself. She left no note."[8]

The second missing member of the immediate family is Art's brother, Richieu, who perished in the Holocaust. Fearing for his safety in the ghetto where they were confined, Vladek and Anja had given him into the care of an aunt living in a ghetto in another village that appeared to be safer. When the Germans came to evacuate that ghetto to Auschwitz, at a time when the Jews had come to realize what that meant, the aunt used the poison she always carried around her neck to kill herself and the children in her home, both her own and Richieu: "I won't go to their gas chambers! . . . And my *children* won't go to their gas chambers."[9] Vladek's memory of that lost brother, to whom Art felt he could never measure up, permeated Art's childhood.

Each volume of *Maus* ends with a sad commentary on how Art still feels the presence of these missing family members. At the end of volume 1, Art discovers that when Vladek was depressed after Anja's suicide he had destroyed all the extensive diaries Art's mother had kept. In the last panel Art repeats to himself what he had called his father in his initial moment of rage at this discovery: "Murderer."[10] It's the accusatory lament of Art when he's so completely immersed in his role of autobiographical storyteller that he has, in that moment at least, completely conflated the teller and the tale. At this moment destroying how a person has told their life is for him tantamount to actually taking the life of that person. With stunning irony, in a book full of true murderers, the only one explicitly called that is Vladek, the survivor.

Vladek's invocation of Art's brother at the end of the work is also stunning. In the last panel of the tale Vladek is falling asleep, with Art standing dejectedly at the foot of the bed. "I'm *tired* from talking, Richieu, and it's *enough* stories for now . . . ," Vladek says.[11]

Vladek's Holocaust stories are ordinarily extraordinary, by which I mean that when one hears survivors' stories they routinely seem absolutely extraordinary, incredibly harrowing, and fraught with the unimaginable. Vladek's story includes a particularly wide range of experiences, including military combat, flight, hiding, capture, managing to survive in Auschwitz, great losses, loyalties and betrayals, and the problems of picking up the pieces after the war. This variety of Vladek's experiences on which *Maus* draws is one of the elements that make it so successful in communicating the realities of the Holocaust. The subtitle of *Maus's* second volume, *And Here My Troubles Began,* is Vladek's way of beginning to relate what happens after he arrives at a camp. Its effect on the reader when uttered is chilling, because by that point Vladek has already endured so much that seems unendurable.

The single most reproduced page in the work, deservedly so, appears at the beginning of chapter 2 of volume 2, titled "Auschwitz (Time Flies)." It warrants our extended attention. The heading "Time Flies" appears at the top of the first page, and within each panel Art's narration sends us flying back and forth in time at dizzying speeds, from Vladek's personal experiences as well as their larger historical context to various stages of Spiegelman's work on *Maus* and its reception, and even a brief flash-forward to the baby Françoise and husband Art are expecting.

But there's visually even more going on than this narration. Throughout the page there are flies buzzing around Art. So it appears that "time flies" is a kind of verbal/visual pun. The obvious meaning of the phrase is that of the common expression, meaning that time passes very quickly. In that meaning, "time" is a noun and "flies" a verb, i.e., what time does is fly. But it can be read differently too, making "flies" a plural noun and "time" its adjectival modifier, meaning that we're talking about a group of an odd type of fly, one that flies through time. That is to say, if we were to ask what kind of flies we were seeing, we would then be told that these are "time flies." We discover in the last panel that these flies have indeed been accompanying us through the time travels of Art's narration, for when we pan back in that last panel to see Art at his drawing board, we also see that piled up at his feet is a mound of skeletal corpses of mice, looking like the mounds of corpses in the concentration camps. We now realize that what the flies have been doing all this time, though previously unbeknownst to us, was flying around those corpses. Those flies thus occupy a space that is both verbal and visual, situated in both the past and the present all at once. They are the ever-present buzzing of the spirit of history in our ears, the post-Holocaust embodiment of the Jewish "Holy Ghost" that makes one of the father and the son.

The layout of this page uses the rhythms of the graphic novel medium to maximum dramatic effect. The top half of the page, with its four rectangular panels, has moved us quickly from one narrative point to the next. But the single large panel that takes up the bottom of the page applies the brakes, allowing for its greater impact. That last panel brings the dizzying time travel to a crashing halt in a visually dramatic collision of past and present. It's not just the time flies and the mouse corpses. Visible right through and just outside the window of Art's studio in the present is a guard tower and the barbed-wire fence of Auschwitz. From off page at the right come the last words: "Alright Mr. Spiegelman . . . We're ready to shoot! . . ." In this visual context, that alert of being ready to shoot takes on ominous multiple meanings.

But those time flies and all the rest we've already discussed aren't the only visual oddities here. If one allows one's eye to pan back to see the forest rather than the trees one might notice that the oddly angular black shadows that occupy much of the background in the individual panels form the partial contours of a swastika when connected and seen as a whole. The nearly subliminal swastika looming in the background is a device Spiegelman uses elsewhere as well; at one point when Vladek and Anja walk through a crossroad in their travels the crisscrossing of the converging paths forms a swastika. Spiegelman believes, as do many others, that the eye takes in such things to create an emotional impact even if they don't consciously register. Here the graphic novel form is used to uniquely communicate how ubiquitously life in the Holocaust universe is lived in the shadow of the swastika.

This page begins a unique sequence of seven pages in which Spiegelman draws himself and others not as the animals they would normally be but as humans wearing the masks of these animals. (I leave out of consideration a sequence in which during the Holocaust Vladek is out in public passing as a non-Jew, and is therefore drawn as a mouse wearing the mask of a pig. There the mask indicates a disguise; that is not the case here.) These masks pose questions about how one presents oneself, not just in an artistic representation but also as a matter of personal authenticity. Both these issues are implicated on this page and the next in Art's resistance to the commercialization of *Maus*. That resistance takes its toll—by the bottom of the second page of this chapter Art has shrunken down to the size of a child, and as a dog-masked American hounds him to approve a *Maus* clothing line, asking him what percentage he wants, Art is reduced to bawling in response, "I want . . . I want . . . my *Mommy!*"[12] He finally returns to adult size only following a session with his therapist, in which they discuss Art's feelings of being inadequate to the task of accurately representing Auschwitz. It's both a serious and humorous debate—when the therapist greets Art at his door with his dog, Art wonders if he can include a drawing of the dog in the book or whether that will "louse up" his entire project of having animals represent people.[13]

Art's therapist asks him to consider that he himself may be a survivor. At the root of Art's insecurities is that Vladek remains trapped in the Holocaust and has managed to draw Art back there with him, so that none of Art's accomplishments stack up against the feat of surviving under those conditions. Vladek survived, and now Art's task is to survive living with the survivor, for the book abundantly demonstrates that Vladek is a difficult person to live with. There are many instances where Spiegelman doesn't shy away from presenting both Vladek and himself in unflattering lights. As one gets to know Vladek, it becomes crystal clear that oppression doesn't make people virtuous, it just makes them oppressed. It's part of Spiegelman's ethical and artistic commitment to be as accurate as possible, a deliberate rejection of what in the first chapter of this book I referred to as Christian hagiography, the tendency to treat subjects deemed worthy of biographies as saintly. This illustrates why Miriam Libicki refers to autobiographical graphic novels as a Jewish genre—because they reveal warts and all, unburdened by Christian notions of sin and perfection.

The "Time Flies" page is one example among many others in the book that powerfully illustrate how Art, as a child of Holocaust survivors, has inherited his father's way of simultaneously inhabiting two different times, the present and the past. *Maus* opens with a prelude illustrating how Vladek lives in the past, to the detriment of his relationship with his son, in two pages set in "Rego Park, N.Y. c. 1958," the only part of the book placed in Art's childhood.[14] (Rego Park, by the way, is right next to Forest Hills, Spider-Man's and my old neighborhood.) Artie is hurt and comes crying to his father, who is sawing a wooden board in front of their garage, to tell him, "I—I fell, and my friends skated away w- without me." Vladek stops sawing and says, "*Friends? Your friends?* . . . If you lock them together in a room with no food for a week . . . *then* you could see what it is, friends! . . ."

That sudden irruption of the past into the present, capable of being triggered at any random and unforeseeable moment, transforms everyday commonplace difficulties into existential challenges that test survival skills. Earlier, when I wrote of the affinity of Jews for science fiction, I noted how observant Jews live simultaneously in two worlds, that of the present and that of the future messianic utopia. Vladek has survived a world turned upside down, so his consciousness is the reverse of this. He simultaneously lives in the present and in the past dystopian world that was the hell of the Holocaust. It's a mentality that marks the collective consciousness of post-Holocaust Jews. It's especially strong in the survivors themselves and is often passed on to their children. Recall the discussion of Willy Loman as Jewish in this book's introduction. The same time-warped consciousness that separates a man from his surroundings and sends his mind into the past, opening up a generational rift that separates father from son, afflicts Willy Loman too. For Willy, a son's business setback is enough to trigger his cry expressing the vision in his mind that "the woods are burning, boys, you understand? There's a big blaze going on all round us."[15] Much of what makes both *Maus* and *Salesman* so powerful is the way in which their form matches their content. Their main characters don't really move between past and present in flashbacks; rather, they simultaneously inhabit both time frames. That's how we come to really feel the impact of the tragedies that have befallen them, as we watch with horror a man falling out of time, utterly displaced and detached from the moorings of his surroundings. Spiegelman explains why the comics form is especially well suited to express these ideas:

> What is most interesting about comics for me has to do with the abstraction and structuring that comes with the comics page, the fact that moments in time are juxtaposed. In a story that is trying to make chronological and coherent the incomprehensible, the juxtaposing of past and present insists that the past and present are always present—one doesn't displace the other the way it happens in film.[16]

Maus is a complex work, and in retrospect one can see that Spiegelman had been working his way toward it for some time. Included in a collection of Spiegelman's early work, *Breakdowns: Portrait of the Artist as a Young %@&*!*, is his earlier attempt at telling the story of *Maus* using the mice-versus-cats metaphor. Here one can clearly see that in the initial renderings of this 1972 three-page story, Spiegelman was working closer to standard cartoon depictions, with the mice even having more Mickey-like ears than the final version.[17] In other works before *Maus* he was experimenting with various nontraditional and experimental comic techniques in which the smooth flow of the narrative was interrupted in order to draw attention to the medium itself, such as intermingling different illustrative styles on the same page or even in the same panel, or altering the sequential order of the flow from one panel to the other.

Maus remains his signature work, but since then Spiegelman has also written some children's books for the very young in comics form, and for adults he has branched out in several directions. In the very oversize book *In the Shadow of No Towers* he dramatizes the events and impact of the 9/11 World Trade Center attack, which occurred very close to where he lives with his family.[18] He occasionally returns to drawing himself as a mouse in this book, as in a sequence of four panels when he tells the reader, "I remember my father trying to describe what the smoke in Auschwitz smelled like. . . . The closest he got was telling me it was . . . 'indescribable.' [A silent panel] . . . That's exactly what the air in Lower Manhattan smelled like after Sept. 11!" Honoring the important Jewish principle of acknowledging one's teachers, Spiegelman devotes part of the book to reprinting some early turn-of-the-century newspaper comics that influenced him.

Spiegelman returned to *Maus* in a major way in 2011 with the publication of *MetaMaus,* an in-depth commentary on *Maus.*[19] *MetaMaus* is for Spiegelman simultaneously both a celebration and exorcism of the role of *Maus* in his life. Like others who have produced a work declared to be a milestone work of genius, he feels greatly gratified by the recognition even as he chafes at how this single work has come to define and confine him, to the neglect of his larger body of work. He relates how, when his daughter was younger and was asked what her father did for a living, she said, "Daddy draws mice." He intends *MetaMaus* to stand as his definitive reckoning with the questions and comments *Maus* has generated.

The bulk of the text consists of interviews with Spiegelman conducted by English professor Hillary Chute, chosen by Spiegelman because of what he considered her "lucid takes on my work and that of others."[20] The book also includes numerous samples of Spiegelman's work, not only pages from the final version of *Maus* but preliminary notes and sketches for it, documents on which he drew for his research, examples of the work of other artists who influenced him, publishers' rejection letters for *Maus,* interviews with Spiegelman's family about what they think of it all, and family trees for both his parents, including a four-page genealogical chart of "A Branch of the Spiegelman Family Tree," two pages of which consist almost entirely of blank boxes that speak volumes about the erasure of knowledge in Holocaust survivors' family trees. It also includes Spiegelman's account of struggling to find imagery needed to faithfully render the unimaginable, especially regarding life in the death camps.

The *MetaMaus* book comes packaged together with a hyperlinked DVD that contains the complete *Maus* accompanied by Spiegelman's audio commentary, audio and transcribed versions of his interviews with Vladek, family photos, articles by Spiegelman and others, and more. Between the book and DVD, there is an enormous amount of information about the prior history and behind-the-scenes creative work that went into *Maus*. Reading it is like taking a course in how to think of the structure of a comics page, such as how to take into account how readers' eyes assimilate visual information so that you can guide them to take note of what you want them to see and emphasize. One learns how Spiegelman struggled with how to translate a nonlinear narrative onto the printed page. It's nonlinear not just because of the back-and-forth movement between the time frame of the Holocaust story and the time frame of Vladek's telling that story to Art. There's also the problem of the sporadic and even contradictory nature of the story Vladek tells. It's a problem historians regularly confront—sometimes first-person eyewitness recollections just don't match up with what we know of historical events, a general problem compounded by the radical spatial, temporal, and moral dislocations that were inevitable when one entered what survivor and writer Primo Levi and others called "the Holocaust universe." In one notable sequence in *Maus* to which Spiegelman calls attention in *MetaMaus*, Art is seeking Vladek's confirmation of the well-documented existence of a prisoners' orchestra in Auschwitz. No, Vladek is quite sure there could have been no such thing, and as we see Vladek and Art walking along in the present having this conversation, the background shows Vladek in the camp passing right by the orchestra, but with his view obscured by other prisoners being marched between them. The combination of words and pictures in a single panel uniquely enables Spiegelman to simultaneously honor both the historical record and his father's memories, even when they contradict each other.

There's also much here about how Spiegelman sees the relationship between the wider culture and *Maus*, as well as comics more broadly. He recounts how he grew up with a sense that, as Holocaust survivors, his parents were different from many others. Starting to draw comics for him represented "my assimilation into the American culture in ways that were closed to my parents, and it gave me a zone of safety from them."[21] It was a way for a Jew to enter the mainstream and, as at the beginning of the comics industry, it was a creative form that required only paper and pencil.

Discussing his early comics reading, Spiegelman sees Holocaust themes where others might not. He departs from a widely accepted analysis among scholars of the period claiming that the popularity of the horror genre in both films and comics in the U.S. during the 1950s reflected deep and to some extent unconscious fears of the threat of communism. (A classic example would be to see a film like *Invasion of the Body Snatchers* as a metaphoric and cathartic engagement with fears of communist "brainwashing.") But Spiegelman had a different take on the comics of the period: "I came to think that all the EC horror comics were a secular American Jewish response to Auschwitz."[22]

Then came the underground comics of the '60s, with their explicit sex, drugs, and rock-and-roll preoccupations. Spiegelman speculates that "perhaps the whole taboo-smashing ethos of the underground comix scene did allow me to stir up the buried connections to the unspeakable that my mother's book shelf [of early Holocaust historical pamphlets] opened up."[23]

In addition to all the commentary and materials related to *Maus* itself and the prehistory of the work, Spiegelman also discusses some consequences of the success of *Maus*. For obvious reasons, the German reception is of particular interest. Spiegelman relates that:

> The initial response to the book in Germany in 1987 was intense. I was at the Frankfurt Book Fair when it came out, and was aggressively barked at by a reporter: "Don't you think that a comic book about Auschwitz is in bad taste?" I liked my response. I said, "No, I thought Auschwitz was in bad taste."[24]

In light of this, it seems worth noting that the German translation of the title of volume 1 was strikingly different than the original English. "My Father Bleeds History" became "My Father Vomits History" ("*Mein Vater Kotzt Geschichte Aus*").

I will end this chapter with the oddest, most ironic story about the fate of *Maus* Spiegelman tells:

> I insisted that foreign editions use the same cover as the Pantheon book, but my German editor, Michael Naumann, explained that they had a problem since it's against German law to show a swastika, except in works of serious historical research. He got permission from the German government to use my cover! But in the wacky world of unintended consequences, a few years later I saw a documentary about skinheads in Germany and one of them had a *Maus* bookstore poster in his bedroom—it was the only swastika he could get, poor fella![25]

9

FROM THE NEW WORLD
BACK TO THE OLD

Jewish Comics Abroad

T hroughout this book we have followed the story of how American Jews created the modern comic book. This chapter turns toward the rest of the world and looks at a number of important foreign comics artists in both Europe and Israel. Like Art Spiegelman, these contemporary artists stand on the shoulders of the groundbreaking generations who had to code the Jewish characteristics in their early work and moved on to more overtly Jewish themes only in their later graphic novels. For many of the new generation, Jewish identity and themes are central and explicit.

Many boundaries are being crossed when a graphic novel about Algerian Jews of the 1930s is serially published in France in the first years of the twenty-first century. Such genre-bending seems to be part of the life mission of Joann Sfar, a remarkably imaginative and immensely popular graphic novelist, who is a leading figure of the new wave of Franco-Belgian comics artists. His vast output, with his name on more than two hundred books as writer and/or artist, includes a sprawling story that's a comic take on the sword-and-sorcery action genre, comic tales of vampires that feature some of the liveliest dead characters you'll ever meet, biographies mixing real and fictional characters (Chagall meets

Tevye), and, most significantly for our purposes, a unique blending of Ashkenazi and Sephardic Jewish traditions in art and story. For Sfar is also the most strongly Jewish-identified of this new European wave of comics creators. He has a large and devoted following elsewhere in the world, but he is nowhere near as well known in the U.S. as he should be. If this chapter can help rectify this glaring blind spot of American popular culture, I'll be only too happy to introduce more people to his delightful inventiveness and creativity.

When most Americans think of Judaism, they think of the Ashkenazi Judaism of northern Europe with which they are most familiar, although in fact prior to the large waves of immigration beginning in the nineteenth century, first from Germany and then from Eastern Europe, most American Jews shared the heritage of Sephardic Jewry, descended from the Jews of Spain and Portugal. In both his person and his work Sfar consciously embodies a synthesis of these traditions. He was born in 1971 in the French city of Nice to Jewish parents, a Sephardic father who was a lawyer and an Ashkenazi mother who was a singer. He's working with the same creative tension between a rational intellectualism associated with northern European culture and a sensualist passion associated with the culture of southern Europe and the Mediterranean that Thomas Mann explored in a non-Jewish context a century earlier in his novella "Tonio Kröger," in which the title character struggles as an artist to reconcile within himself what he identifies as the two inherited poles of his personality, his father's German and his mother's Italian temperaments.

Sfar draws in different styles. The cleaner lines of *Dungeon* and the *Vampire* series draw on the Francophone Franco-Belgian *ligne claire* ("clear line") style of the *bande dessinée* ("drawn strip", i.e., comics or graphic novels) tradition associated with a strip such as *Tintin* (whose protagonist shows up to be mocked in *The Rabbi's Cat 2*). The ornate flowing style of *The Rabbi's Cat*, on the other hand, is more at home on Sephardic soil, where illustrative and decorative arts were never viewed with the suspicion attached to them as idolatrous that one found in Ashkenazi culture, and whose art and literature are suffused with the more ornamental and flowery styles of the Islamic culture in whose midst they flourished. The more elaborately drawn panels are packed with elaborately styled objects and additional people or creatures in the background. His monsters may have any number of additional arms, legs (or better yet, tentacles), eyes (perhaps bobbing from additional appendages), and even heads (occasionally removable). His ghosts sometimes have amorphous bodies that seem not so much to end as to trail off. Were Sfar not also a filmmaker himself, one would say that the only director capable of ever bringing this to the screen would be Guillermo del Toro (*Pan's Labyrinth*, *Hellboy*), who arrives at a similarly playful aesthetic of the monstrously macabre from a very different, but perhaps analogous, source, his Mexican Catholicism. The stories, too, fluctuate between a more linear, straight-ahead mode, as in his historically based biography of Chagall, and a more rambling, circular narrative flow in his expansive *Dungeon* series.

Sfar is best known in the U.S. for *The Rabbi's Cat*, made into a 2011 animated film codirected by Sfar, and its sequel, *The Rabbi's Cat 2*.[1] These stories allow us entry into the world of Algerian Jewry of the 1930s, seen through the eyes of the loyal cat in the household of the rabbi, a congenial dispenser of profound folk wisdom, and the rabbi's daughter Zlabya. The skinny cat's self-centered conniving cynicism plays off the rotund rabbi's generous gregarious optimism. The cat understands both human and animal speech, and acquired the power of human speech by eating a parrot. (Not even a talking parrot, mind you, just a noisy, annoying one, which is why the cat eats him.)

Upon acquiring speech the cat wants a bar mitzvah, believing he is already knowledgeable enough, because he learned to read when the rabbi had taught his daughter. (No one knew it at the time because he hadn't yet eaten the parrot!) This leads to a contentious Talmudic dispute between the cat and the rabbi. The cat narrates the rabbi's teachings in a sequence in which text and image provide point and counterpoint: "He tells me Jewish teaching works by analogy." (This is the caption of a panel in which the cat watches the rabbi pour a cup of a hot drink for each of them.) "He tells me I'm refusing to enter into it because my sight is clouded by Western thought. . . . [B]y the time you've finished naming a thing, it has already changed, and the name you gave it no longer defines it exactly, so you end up with empty words in your mouth." (Now the cat is *really* puzzled, so much so that there's a large exclamation point in the panel because the cat has come so close in peering into the cup, examining his own reflection, that his nose has broken the surface of the liquid, sending disruptive waves through the image.) "Westerners want to resolve the world. Turn multiplicity into oneness. That's a delusion, says the rabbi." (Now we've backed up and see the back of the rabbi's head, with the rest of his face blocked by the word balloon, and liquid is dripping from the cat's nose as he looks up at the rabbi.) . . . The rabbi continues: "Western thought works by thesis, antithesis, synthesis, while Judaism goes thesis, antithesis, antithesis, antithesis. . . ." By this time the cat has ceased contemplating his own reflection in the cup and begun drinking, so his only response now is "Slurp! Slurp!"[2]

The scene is brilliantly constructed, with a complex and profoundly effective interplay between text and image. From the cat's point of view, his interactions with the cup in each new panel are a stream of action that is entirely independent of what the rabbi is saying. He's clearly taking it all in, but he's double-tasking. For the reader, his silent actions illustrate the rabbi's words in simultaneously amusing and enlightening ways. The cat is contemplating and closing in on his reflection as the rabbi goes deeper into his explanation of how Western philosophy attempts to see the world as a reflection of its own categories, and he disrupts his reflection by reaching too far into the liquid just as the rabbi is explaining why the world eludes the grasp of Western thought. The crowning irony Sfar presents in the sequence is that precisely when the rabbi delivers his final verdict that Western philosophy is a delusion, we're faced with the only seemingly ill-placed word balloon in the book, which actually hides the central action.

For most readers this contrast of Jewish versus Western thought will seem quite strange, because for most of us Judaism very much belongs to the West. But Sfar is reaching back to an older ethnic geography, in which, from a typical Western view, Jews were a Semitic, therefore Eastern, even Asiatic people. As we'll see shortly, this is part of his larger vision of reconciling Ashkenazi and Sephardic Judaisms, the Judaism of northern Europe versus that of the Mediterranean, and thereby even helping to bridge the gap between Jews and Arabs in the Middle East.

In the second volume the cat is at first the only one able to converse with a Russian Jewish painter. He has arrived in a packing crate of books in which he sealed himself, thinking it was the best way for him to get to Ethiopia, where he mistakenly thought the crate was going, and where he believes he can find the lost mythical Jerusalem inhabited by the descendants of King Solomon and the Queen of Sheba living in peace and glory. The eventual expedition to find the lost city includes the Russian Jew, the rabbi, the cat, and a sensualist Russian exile. They are joined en route by the painter's new love, a black African woman, and the rabbi's cousin, a musician and collector of songs, Sheikh Mohamad Sfar. The sheikh and the rabbi meet annually en route to the grave of their common ancestor, Messaoud Sfar, about whom the cat and the sheikh's donkey argue, one claiming him as a great rabbi and the other as a Sufi saint. Their argument comes to involve the origins of the Sfar name itself. The cat insists, "Sfar comes from 'Sofar,' which means 'to write' in Hebrew. Sfar is a Jewish name." The donkey counters, "You ass, Sfar comes from 'yellow' in Arabic. It evokes the sulfur flower used by coppersmiths. Sfar's Arab through and through." One infers that Joann Sfar's deeper point is that once upon a fabled time in the troubled Middle East, Jews and Arabs shared a common culture in which both of these claims could have been harmoniously true. It helps that Sfar's name itself points back to this earlier time. The Jews of the Middle East are referred to as Sephardim, and the *sf* sound in *Sfar* brings us back to the Hebrew pronunciation of Sephardim, which doesn't separate the *s* and *f* sounds with any intervening vowel as we do in English.

While *The Rabbi's Cat* draws on his father's Sephardic heritage, Sfar turns to his mother's Eastern European roots for a series on klezmer musicians and their itinerant travels during roughly the same time period, the first of which is translated in English as *Klezmer, Book One: Tales of the Wild East*.[3] In the reflective "Notes for *Klezmer*, Volume 1," Sfar explains what being a Jew means to him, and how it explains much of his oeuvre. After rejecting both secularism and blind faith, he declares his favored way of being a Jew:

Saying that you've been in mourning since the destruction of the Temple and that life doesn't last long and it's sad but that perhaps one day the Messiah will come, and all the while implying that he won't but that you should still await him expectantly, that's more to my liking.

And watching over the dead. I'd want to take the Jews from my village and bring them to safety inside my paintings, Chagall used to say.[4]

Sfar's invoking this saying of Chagall's in the context of honoring the dead means that he's interpreting this not to mean that art can somehow save or protect living people but that it can protect and preserve the legacy of the departed. The allusion to watching over the dead means more than just honoring one's ancestors, though this is indeed central to Judaism—the most solemn parts of many services are memorial commemorations. It's also an important component of Jewish community. The community burial society, or *Chevra Kadisha* ("Holy" or "Sacred Society"), who care for the dead between death and burial, traditionally played a central and essential part of organized Jewish life. In *The Rabbi's Cat* we first get to know the rabbi's future son-in-law as he arrives to supervise such rituals. Sfar's concern with the dead plays an important role in his work, as his stories abound with all sorts of denizens of worlds after death: vampires, mummies, ghosts, and others. He deals with these figures in a unique and compelling fashion. While many writers, Kafka being a key example, make the normal strange, Sfar's worlds make the fantastical normal, through both the story and art.

One of Sfar's lead characters in several books is Ferdinand, endearingly introduced as "a vampire who bites his victims with only one tooth in order to pass as a mosquito." A cover illustration shows two formally attired figures looming above an image of an ocean liner, with the book's title, *Vampire Loves,* written above. One of the figures, the man, simply looks like a bewildered partygoer holding a glass of wine, but then you look closer and notice those pointed ears, and realize that may not be red wine in the glass after all. Once you get into the story you realize that the woman whose arms are draped around his shoulders is quite literally draped there: This is Sigh, whose long, slender body is shaped like a shawl so she can wrap herself around people.[5]

One needs to enter into Sfar's world in order to appreciate the playful charm of his work. In *Little Vampire Goes to School,* Little Vampire misses not having other kids to play with, so with the permission of the adult ghosts who run the old haunted mansion where he "lives" he flies off to school accompanied by his bright-red flying dog, Phantomat.* Little Vampire is terribly disappointed to find the school empty because it's night. The Captain of the Dead, a skeleton in pirate garb, has a solution: All the ghosts will also go to the school at night. He asks the ghosts to "bring their own school supplies so they wouldn't write in any of the daytime students' notebooks. Because ghosts shouldn't be noticed by mortals."[6] But Little Vampire writes in a notebook anyway, and the next day pupil Michael Duffin is astonished to find "there in his notebook, a miracle: His homework was done, and there were no mistakes!" Little Vampire reveals his identity to Michael in an exchange of notes in Michael's notebook.

When a ghost snitches on Little Vampire to the Captain, the Captain declares this a grave offense (my pun, not Sfar's) and directs Little Vampire to bring Michael to the mansion to make sure he doesn't tell anyone. Sfar seamlessly integrates Jewish allusions into his broader agenda of entertaining his audience. When the Captain tells Michael he can go home, they have the following dialogue, the Captain seated in his high-backed chair in full pirate regalia and little Michael standing in front of him barefoot in his pajamas:

---

*The name would resonate satirically with the French audience; Fantômas was an enormously popular character in books, films, and comics, looking like the character being played by the actor in the opening movie-with-a-movie scene in the recent almost-silent film *The Artist.* In fact, the cover of *Vampire Loves* bears some resemblance to the famous cover of the first *Fantômas* volume from 1911.

Michael: You're not going to torture me? How do you know I won't tell everyone that you live here.

Captain: I can see it in your eyes.

Michael: I was kinda hoping you'd make me swear on a skull or something.

Captain: You want to swear a pirate's oath? All right.

Michael: I swear to devote my life to protecting the dead and keeping their memory. And if I break my word, may a thousand curses befall me.

Captain: Now do the sign of the cross.

Michael: No. I can't do that.

Captain: It would give more strength to your oath.

Michael: But I'm Jewish, Captain. The cross doesn't mean much to me.

Captain: Do the sign of the star in that case.

Michael: We don't do that either. (*Pause*) And I don't believe much in God. (*Pause*) 'Cause my parents are dead.

Captain: You're a bit young to believe in nothing.

Michael: Well, maybe he exists, Captain, but after what he did to me, I don't feel like I owe him anything.

Captain: You should think about all that some more. Sad times often open miraculous doorways.

As for the sequel, *Little Vampire Does Kung Fu!*, well, when someone writes a better summary than you can, the thing to do is appreciatively give thanks and then shamelessly quote, so here, with all due gratitude, are the opening paragraphs of Campbell Robertson's review:

If Rabelais had written a children's book, it probably would have looked something like LITTLE VAMPIRE DOES KUNG

FU! . . . The boisterous tale begins when a young boy named Michael asks his grandfather the eternal question: how can I get back at the bully who has been humiliating me at school? Grandfather urges a policy of restraint, which, of course, leaves Michael unsatisfied. Enter the Little Vampire, who takes Michael to see Rabbi Solomon, kung fu master.

Yes, you read that correctly. It is just a taste of Little Vampire's bizarre world, where Michael meets sorcerers, fakirs, Cossack goblins, Siamese dragons, and even Albert Einstein. When not quarreling among themselves, all of the characters are bombarding Michael with advice, though it is clear that Michael and his vampire friend are far wiser than the supposed sages.[7]

Other Little Vampire tales have yet to be translated into English, as is altogether much too much of Sfar's work. Among those in which Jewish themes are most central are *Les Olives Noires* (*The Black Olives*), a tale of an adventurous young Jewish boy in ancient Israel trying to survive under the occupying Romans after the loss of his parents, during a time when many Jews believe their messiah has come amidst circulating tales of a certain wandering rabbi; *Chagall en Russie* (*Chagall in Russia*), in which the young Chagall meets Tevye the milkman and is attracted to his daughter; *Pascin*, a fictionalized biography of the early-twentieth-century Jewish modernist painter as known for his bohemian lifestyle as for his portrayals of Parisian prostitutes[8]; and *Le Petit Monde du Golem* (*The Little World of the Golem*), in which some of what have become his stable of characters are introduced. The same character of Little Vampire but here an adult named Desmodus pines for the tree-woman grown from a mandrake root of a tree from which Desmodus attempts to hang himself, and who is sold to Jewish painter Chaim Soutine in Vilna as the ideal model because she's alive but stands perfectly still. Both musicians and painters consistently appear as characters in Sfar's work. His thesis as a university student was on "the relationship that Jewish painters have with the human body, with a particular emphasis on Chagall, Soutine, Kokoschka, and Pascin."[9]

Sfar moves easily and constantly from amusing puns to philosophical musings, having studied philosophy at the École des Beaux-Arts (School of Fine Arts) in Paris. As an example of the former, in the opening page of *Little Vampire Goes to School,* as the skeletons rise from their graves for their nightly revelry "dressed in their Sunday best," one of them asks a couple, "Would you give me your daughter's hand?" and receives the reply, "We lost it. Still got her foot if ya want." In much of Sfar's world the plots serve as "skeletons," so to speak, on which to hang the verbal and visual fun of it all. As for the directions in which his philosophical leanings take him, one might glean something from considering which two classic works of Western philosophy he's chosen to illustrate: Plato's *Symposium,* a discussion of the nature of love at a party fueled by much drinking, and Voltaire's *Candide,* the picaresque tale that is simultaneously an example and a mocking critique of philosophical thought.

This ability shared by Voltaire and Sfar to participate in a genre while also mocking it is much in evidence in the sprawling multivolume story of the world of *Dungeon,* the major opus of Sfar and his collaborator Lewis Trondheim, one of the leading and most prolific comics creators in the European and specifically French scene. This double vision of both having your cake and eating it too not only exemplifies what we identified earlier as the ironic, satiric stance typical of Jewish humor, but more specifically for Sfar it also embodies what he declares to be his favorite way of being a Jew (quoted above): saying that you believe in the coming of the Messiah even while implying that you don't. The whole enterprise is projected to eventually encompass hundreds of volumes, with Sfar and Trondheim joined by other contributors. It's a spoof of the sword-and-sorcery genre, a fantasy adventure genre that Jews see as primarily Christian, as discussed in the second chapter of this book.

The series begins with the Keeper of the dungeon, Hyacinthe de Cavallere, who was initially an idealistic adventurous youth in love with a sexually adventurous female assassin. Disillusioned, he has turned the family castle he inherited into an enormous cavernous dungeon from which he profits by luring adventurers to their dooms delivered by the monsters down below. To guard the dungeon he employs Marvin, a dragon who can breathe fire—accompanied by a fiery shout of "Tong Deum!"—but only after a full vegetarian meal, and whose religion forbids him from killing anyone after they've insulted him, and eventually Herbert the duck, master of the Sword of Destiny, which mostly assists but sometimes also argues with him. One of the dramatic turns in the series is when planet Terra Amata explodes, but instead of being destroyed it turns into a series of floating islands, which orbit around the remaining center of gravity. The inhabitants of Terra Amata become a diasporic people, their lives continuing to revolve around the center of their world even after that center no longer exists, and continuing to be involved in humorous stories even when in those stories their own survival is imperiled. Terra Amatans come to seem like wandering Jews.

The grand plot isn't really the point of it all, though. It's really about all the surprising twists and turns along the way, the countless enjoyable little side jokes and stories that simply have to be read to be appreciated in their astonishing inventiveness.

While *Dungeon* seems to be a series of somewhat aimless, albeit highly enjoyable, comic adventure stories, it also exemplifies how Sfar situates himself within the Jewish textual tradition. In a 2007 interview conducted in conjunction with the exhibit "From Superman to the Rabbi's Cat"* at the Museum of the Art and History of Judaism in Paris,** Sfar responds to a question about how Jewish literature has influenced his style of storytelling with an answer that that harks back to the rabbi's exposition in *The Rabbi's Cat.* "A text, a commentary, a commentary on the commentary . . . I work a little like that," he says. "What fascinates me is the desire to never finish the story."[10]

Sfar is on solid orthodox ground when he declares that in Judaism the story never ends. The central work of biblical commentary, the Talmud, is always printed in a standardized format. In the center of the page lies the biblical passage, which is surrounded by commentary, with a wide margin left at the edges, to visually convey to readers the message that they should supply their own new layer of commentary on the

---

* *"De Superman au Chat du Rabbin."*
** Musée d'art et d'histoire du Judaïsme.

commentary. No interpretation or interpretations can be exhaustive of the text, and all valid interpretations, as determined by the rabbis, are declared to have been part of the original meaning. It's an important precedent not just for Sfar but for the roots of comic books in Jewish tradition, that the meaning of the text is partially conveyed by its graphic layout.

This Talmudic graphic style of core text surrounded by commentary is visually embodied in comic form in *Testament,* a series written by Doug Rushkoff and illustrated by Liam Sharp that ran from 2006 to 2008, published by DC's "mature" Vertigo line. On many pages the biblically inspired stories at its core are surrounded in the margins by divinities of various ancient religions commenting on the action—beings such as Krishna, Yahweh, Astarte, Moloch, and Atum-Ra arguing with each other. Rushkoff is an innovative media theorist concerned with cyberculture as well as with the revitalization of Judaism, and part of his view is that biblical tales should not be understood as having happened long ago and far away but as living stories that are always with us in eternal recurrences of archetypal characters. *Testament* dramatizes this view, as the story of Abraham's sacrificial binding of Isaac is interspersed with a futuristic science fiction tale of a father's sacrifice of his son to a higher cause, and the tale of the punishment of the loss of a universal language inflicted on humanity following the fall of the Tower of Babel accompanies a story arc about attempts to defeat a plot to accomplish global authoritarian control by imposing a universal monetary currency via a chip implanted under everyone's skin.

This tradition of ever-expanding commentary surrounding a textual core is what underlies the remarkably leisurely, non-goal-directed nature of Sfar's spinning-out of tales, in which one feels no rush whatsoever to get to the end of the story, which instead of driving to its goal, like the standard adventure quest, keeps circling around in the way Jewish texts unfold around the worship of an ineffable God in layer after layer, just as the parts of Terra Amata keep revolving around its center. Readers of the *Dungeon* series know well how pleasurable it can be to be first told a story, and then a story of how we got to that story, and then a side story of the same characters, on and on, apparently ad infinitum. More than anyone else producing graphic novels today, Sfar invites us to share in the sheer pleasure of storytelling. Both story and art pleasingly meander through their twists and turns, and we are happy to go along for the joy of the ride.

As of this writing, Sfar's latest work to be translated into English is his graphic novel adaptation of Antoine de Saint-Exupéry's beloved *The Little Prince*, the classic illustrated book for all ages, whose combination of playfully endearing charm and deeply humanist philosophy is perfectly suited to Sfar's sensibilities.[11] The Little Prince retains the look given to him by Saint-Exupéry, but Sfar fittingly draws this story of a European stuck in the desert in a style midway between his Ashkenazi and Sephardic modes, so that one regularly encounters well-delineated characters set within swirling backgrounds.

Sfar and Trondheim are leading figures in the new wave of comics coming out of France and Belgium. They represent what is referred to as the *nouvelle bande dessinée* movement, said to have "the ambition of reconceptualizing and reworking aspects of BD in order to liberate it and authenticate it as a medium of artistic expression."[12] In European culture graphic novels were taken more seriously much earlier than in the U.S., with greater literary expectations for plot and character, as well as greater expectations that the art draw on fine arts traditions. Among the more ambitious Jewish-themed projects, those of the Italian master Vittorio Giardino stand out as finely drawn realistic fiction, telling tales of espionage in 1930's Europe in the Max Fridman series,[13] and telling the coming-of-age tale of Jewish teen Jonas Fink in the 1950s in the multivolume *A Jew in Communist Prague*. Another example is a series of graphic novels from the Anne Frank House aimed primarily at young audiences, one being a biography of Anne Frank herself, as well as two works of Eric Heuvel, *A Family Secret* and *The Search*, which both deal with the Nazi occupation of the Netherlands, though these books are not by Jews.[14]

We have seen that Sfar integrates Ashkenazi and Sephardic Jewish elements in his work. Sephardic Jewish culture has traveled a long way, from its medieval origins in Spain to modern Israel at the other end of the Mediterranean, to combine again with Ashkenazi culture. One result has been the emergence of a thriving Jewish graphic novel scene in Israel. In both Sfar's work and Israeli graphic novels, we find the heroic narrative tradition associated with graphic novels turned on its head. Sfar pursues this inversion largely to comic effect, but in Israel it is used for dramatic purposes. Especially noteworthy is how Israeli graphic novelists have used the medium to develop a critique of their society, accomplished through their striking ways of approaching issues of war and violence.

The single greatest creative force driving the flourishing of English language graphic novels in Israel has been the Actus Tragicus comics publishing collective, founded in 1995 by principals Rutu Modan and Yirmi Pinkus, along with Batia Kolton, Itzik Rennert, and Mira Friedmann. Rutu Modan has emerged as the leading figure in the genre, with her work serialized in the *New York Times* in 2007 and 2008 and her most celebrated work, *Exit Wounds*, receiving significant awards and distinctions.

Not all of this work can neatly fit into a single characterization, but there are general tones and common themes. One major concern is to reexamine the roots and meaning of Jewish violence. This impetus arises from the ongoing Israel-Palestinian conflict, in which a new generation of Israelis has grown up as occupiers, contradicting the specific post–World War II legacy, as well as a much longer history of anti-Semitism, in which Jews saw themselves as victims rather than perpetrators of violence. The "graphicness" of graphic novels and their roots in superhero comics make graphic novels a particularly appropriate medium in which to explore violence. This theme of violence, coupled with an interest in the supernatural that emerges from historically marginalized but recently rediscovered strains of Jewish mysticism, produces in the Israeli graphic novel genre a sort of magical realist or quasi-surrealist treatment of violence. Characters in these works often inhabit a kind of shadow or dream world, finding themselves radically questioning what they thought they knew to be reality. The mundane flatness of the visual world portrayed in the art often clashes with the nightmarish nature of the narrative being told. While the aesthetic in mainstream American comics gravitates toward attempting to create a near-seamless integration of words and pictures, the Israeli aesthetic in contrast plays them off against each other, producing a disorienting effect that brings the reader into the world of an Israeli society neither quite at war nor quite at peace, but rather always unsettled and disquieted. Here the lingering emotional residue of the history of war and violence is a more pervasive presence than the violence itself.

This complex interplay of story and art is strikingly effective in Modan's *Exit Wounds,* the most celebrated graphic novel to come out of Israel to date.[15] If one were to thumb through the book to gain a quick visual impression, one would come away with a sense of having been exposed to a series of fairly large blocks of monotone colors, mostly earth tones and grays, much of it fairly drab, and none of it especially striking. Above all, there would be a sense of flatness. Flat. Too flat. So flat, in fact, that there must be some hidden depth if there's any story here at all, and that's precisely what the characters in the story repeatedly discover: that people they thought they knew turn out to have hidden dimensions of greater depth. The reader's experience of delving into the art mirrors the reader's and characters' experiences of delving deeper into the Israeli psyche, where all is not as calm as it appears to be on the surface.

The story starts when a young female from the army asks to speak to a young male cab driver. She tells him an unidentified victim of a recent street bombing was probably his father, from whom he's long been estranged. When they go to the morgue to obtain a DNA sample from the body to match against the son's DNA for identification, the authorities inform them that they have already buried the body, in the non-Jewish section because they didn't know his identity, and they can't even exhume the body because there's a cemetery workers strike.

In the meantime, secrets emerge. The woman was involved with the father, so her coming to the cab driver was personal, not official, business. She thinks the victim was his father because she recognized a striped scarf she made for him in TV footage from the scene. Nobody's heard from him since before the attack. It's not just that the father himself is elusive; it's that even figuring out who he was proves elusive to the son. The way his father is described by others just doesn't match his own sketchy recollections of the parent with whom he hasn't communicated in years. The woman and the son attempt to track down witnesses but get nowhere until they find an older woman who was at the scene. It turns out she was involved with the father too, having rekindled a romance from forty-five years earlier when they remet at an army reunion.

All this leads to the original woman and the son becoming involved, but their lovemaking ends when she remarks, "Like father like son." Her apologetic, "I was just kidding. . . . I thought it would make you laugh" doesn't fix the situation. "You were wrong," he replies, and stalks off angrily.

Some time later a TV report reveals that the unidentified victim wasn't his father after all. After more time passes, he receives a considerable sum of money from a law firm, constituting his proceeds from the sale of his father's home, in the form of a check signed by his father. He obtains his father's new address from the contract for the sale, and goes to that apartment. He finds his father has remarried, to a very religiously observant woman, who tells him to his great surprise that his father is at the synagogue. He waits, but gives up and leaves before the father returns. Through it all, the characters' muted emotions find expression in the muted artistic style.

In a society where bombings and disappearances are commonplace, one learns to stifle one's emotional responses to survive each day. The result is a disconnect between how people live their daily lives and the larger historical realities in which those lives are embedded. Many Israelis have families and circles of friends in which while one member is under the sun on the beach at Tel Aviv another is under the gun on patrol at the border. This is the Israeli society captured in *Exit Wounds*. The interaction and counterpoint between the subdued artwork and the tragedies told give the tale great poignancy. These people inhabit a world in which no one can retain the original cause of the problems between estranged family members, and people numb themselves to the persistent pain of their wounds. People only retain conscious engagement with their state of affairs when someone from the outside arrives to disrupt the status quo. The contrast between the one-dimensionality of how people look and speak versus the depth of the pain underneath is a critical portrait of an Israeli society in denial of its condition. The breakdown of the family and loss of identity in *Exit Wounds* is a metaphor for the breakdown of the Middle East and its psychic toll on Israelis.

The book's conclusion suggests that it will require a leap of faith to resolve the problem. The young man is stuck up in a tree because the branch he had used to climb up there broke under his weight. His only way down is to jump. The woman, standing below, says she'll catch him. But he's dubious, even though she's taller than he is and has undergone military conditioning. He doubts not just her ability but also her intention to catch him, because they've had a falling-out. The last panel shows him taking the plunge into empty space, but she is out of the frame, and we never find out whether she caught him or not, or even made the attempt.

The themes of the self-delusional and wishful thinking that Modan seems to think characterize Israeli society also strongly emerge in her story "The Homecoming," which appeared in both the 2002 Actus anthology *Happy End* and the 2008 collection of her work, *Jamilti and Other Stories*.[16] In Modan's typical subdued coloring, a lone plane is shown circling the beach of a kibbutz. On the radio is a report that the plane is on a terrorist bombing run from Lebanon, but a father has convinced himself that it's really his son, Gadi, whose plane was shot down over Lebanon eight years ago and is presumed dead by everyone else. He's sure Gadi has now escaped and is flying himself home in this plane. Then the Israeli Air Force arrives to blow up the plane. The wreckage lands on the beach. The father is now overjoyed that it wasn't his son after all, but others don't see how he can tell, because the body has been decapitated.

Other Israeli comics switch from subdued understatement to colorful exaggeration to mount similar social criticisms. Instead of submerging what's underneath, they bring it out in surreal ways. These tales turn toward the grotesque, in both art and plot. Typical are Tomer Hanuka's *The Placebo Man*, in which he offers strange tales of the estranged, and

Koren Shadmi's collection of graphic short tales *In the Flesh*, which has a violent macabre sensibility.[17] This tone also permeates the five stories by popular Israeli writer Etgar Keret that were turned into comics stories in the Actus collection *Jetlag*, where the art is exaggerated to play off the tone of the stories.[18] Keret is one of the most popular and respected of the current Israeli writers, and has collaborated with members of the Actus group, especially Modan, on a number of projects. In a review of a collection of his short stories, Todd McEwen writes, "Keret's locale is . . . stasis. His narrator is trapped in . . . disconnection from the world's real possibilities and pleasures."[19]

In the lead story in the *Jetlag* collection, illustrated by Batia Kolton, the magician performing at a kids' party grabs the interest of the jaded kids when he performs his rabbit-out-of-the-hat trick and finds himself holding, by the ears, a rabbit's severed head. He never finds the rest of the rabbit's body, and stops performing after the next time he tries the trick, when he ends up holding by the neck not a rabbit, but the body of a dead baby. The title tale involves an airplane that the crew is going to gently crash on purpose as they do every year or two so that after one or two kids die "people will take the whole flight safety issue more seriously." A man is saved by the flight attendant who's fallen in love with him in flight, so she gets him off the plane with a parachute before the crash. Itzik Rennert's art here looks like what you might end up with if the satiric sketches of German artists George Grosz or Otto Dix were more explicitly pornographized, Technicolorized, and muralized by the Mexican muralists. In the final tale a travel agent falls in love with an acrobat he sees perform at a traveling Romanian circus, even though he can't understand a word she says. Her words are there on the page in what looks like Romanian, but certainly for most of us who knows what they mean? At the end he's left waiting where he *thinks* she said to meet him, but he's not sure. He ends up inheriting her monkey, who's now paralyzed and in a tiny wheelchair because he broke his spine trying to save her when she fell in her tightrope act. Here Modan's lines and coloring emphasize the way the man takes the bizarreness of it all in stride, including the last panel where the new stride he's trying out is walking atop a railing by the beach as would a tightrope walker.

Keret also collaborated with popular artist Asaf Hanuka on the graphic novel *Pizzeria Kamikaze*.[20] The story is based on Keret's short story "Kneller's Happy Campers," which was also adapted into the feature film *Wristcutters: A Love Story*. Here the title alone signals that this is going to be the scene of a violent collision between the mundane and the extraordinary, an impression reinforced by the striking cover image of a man apparently losing consciousness and falling backwards from a bathroom sink, dropping from his hand the glass of water to be used while taking the bottle of pills he was reaching for on the shelf with his other hand. The cover accentuates the contrast and abrupt transition from the ordinary to the unexpected: The white bathroom takes up about a third of the space at the left, while the larger space into which he's falling is stark black, the two spaces separated by the title running top to bottom framed and in a kind of lettering that evokes a flashing neon sign. Inside the book, the first line confirms the expectation of the unexpected: "I think she cried at my funeral." Then the opening lines of the first main chapter are even more disconcerting: "Two days after I killed myself I found a job at some pizza joint called 'Kamikaze.' My shift manager was cool and helped me find a place to live." You quickly discover that everyone in town has killed themselves: "On some of them you could tell straight off how they did it. With the scars on their wrists and everything."

Mordy, our main character, quickly makes a friend of Uzi, a young man whose whole family is there—his parents killed themselves about five years ago, and his little brother just arrived. He explains, "Shot himself too. In the middle of basic training. Maybe I shouldn't say this, but we were so stoked when he got here we coulda died. You shoulda seen my dad—grabbed the kid and cried like a baby." Most of the book is taken up by a road trip the two guys undertake to find Mordy's girlfriend, after an old roommate informs him that she has killed herself too. It's all a disconcerting world in which people have lost their moorings and are forced to take the bizarre for a new normal, and in which one's fate can turn on a dime. Very much an allegory for life in the Middle East.

There have been some attempts to create American-style superhero comics for Israelis, but they never really caught on, probably because of the radically different ways in which Americans and Israelis do and don't experience violence and the threat of violence as part of their daily lives. Sabraman, created by fifteen-year-old Uri Fink, who went on to become a major figure in mainstream Israeli comics, appeared for a while starting in 1978. *Sabra* is modern Hebrew for "a native Israeli," and you can imagine what image those Israelis wanted to project when you realize that before it acquired this new meaning the word referred to a native desert cactus.

As opposed to American comic violence, which explodes in your face, most Israeli comic violence creeps up on you, even taking place off the page. In *Exit Wounds,* the one news photograph we see of the bombing at the heart of the story is not of the victims, but a close-up of what's left on the sidewalk in its wake: one shoe, an unclothed doll with one leg missing, blood splotches. The concern is with the real-life aftereffects of violence, not the violence itself. On the one hand U.S. comics art seems more realistic in its portrayal of violence, in that it is more direct and graphic. But it generally neglects the real aftereffects of violence, the psychological effects on those involved, and reduces violence to cartoonish caricature. The art of these Israeli comics, on the other hand, is more stylized, with violence portrayed in a comics art form that does not pretend to be realistic. Their treatment of the psychological effects of violence however makes their treatment more realistic, and more poignant. This is a violence that lingers deeply long after it has been committed.

The fruits of this Israeli creativity emerged on the stage of global cinema in 2008. The film *Waltz with Bashir* examines the 1982 war in Lebanon through a veteran's attempts to regain his memory of what he did by talking to other veterans who might have been there with him. Described as the first full-length "animated documentary," the film uses new animation techniques to probe the impact on Israeli soldiers of their participation in the war, exploring issues of individual and collective memory and responsibility. The dreamlike treatment of violence, the way it is shown more through its aftermath than when it's committed, the contrast between the controlled formalism of the art (was there ever a more formalized musical form than a waltz?) and the chaos that lies underneath, the counterpoint between the horrors being described and the muted storytelling style that seems on the surface to downplay the drama but actually heightens it, all work to great dramatic effect once it all sinks in, and it's all typical of Israeli graphic novels. The powerful result is what *Los Angeles Times* film critic Kenneth Turan called "a seamless mixing of the real and the surreal, the personal and the political, animation and live action."[21] At the 2009 Oscar ceremonies, noted actor Liam Neeson's expression when he opened the envelope to announce the Academy Award for Best Foreign Film mirrored the surprise of many in the audience when the Israeli film did not receive the award.[22] It did win the Best Foreign Film awards at the Golden Globes and from the National Society of Film Critics, as well as the Best Animated Film Award from the Los Angeles Film Critics Association.

Maybe there's something about the land and language of Israel itself at work in the way these works achieve so much of their power through a style of muted understatement. Walk in a bamboo forest and observe how the light pierces through in long thin rays, and you'll gain a greater appreciation for Chinese calligraphy. Watch the colors of the sunset in the New Mexico sky, and you'll discover the colors of the palette of the art of the Southwest. Experience the monotone flatness of the desert and the old worn stones of Jerusalem, and you'll see sources of Israeli art. As America's heroes speed through its cities, Israel's walk through its deserts.

Maybe there's an influence of the Hebrew language, too. Hebrew is a no-frills language, with prepositions tacked on to other words, verbs sometimes dispensed with, vowels eliminated in its written form. Israelis are known for a directness of speech, which can come across to others as blunt to the point of harshness. I wonder whether this underlies how the dialogue in these works sometimes seems clipped.

This new generation of Israeli comics artists has found a creative way to subvert the traditional comics genre into a critique that subverts their society's view of itself. They show us a society that has purchased a surface calm at the cost of repressing historical memory. For a people who collectively define themselves precisely by their historical memory, this is a profoundly deep wound. These artists fulfill one of the crucial functions of art in any society, that of holding up a mirror in which that society may see itself reflected, if it will but look. Their reflections also reveal the looming return of the repressed that lurks just beneath the calm surface, which in this case threatens to return with a violent vengeance. Having become inured to and anesthetized against the violence in which Israeli citizens are embedded, the Israeli psyche now mirrors the stories and art in these graphic novels—life goes on as before, says the story, but the art tells a different tale, and bespeaks one or the other extremes of a flattened emotional palette versus a frantic explosion of color.

These artists are of a generation that has come of age in a new situation that has been profoundly disturbing to the Jewish psyche, one in which they have been forced to confront their roles as perpetrators and not just as victims of violence. They have produced work that confounds the associations with childish violence of the comics genre with which they all grew up to produce a sophisticated critique of violence. Theirs is a graphic and novel contribution to the language and message of graphic novels.

10

THE AMAZING ADVENTURES OF
MICHAEL CHABON

Kavalier & Clay

Michael Chabon's novel *The Amazing Adventures of Kavalier & Clay* is a brilliant fictional account of the birth of the comics industry, and in fact covers much of the history treated in the early chapters of this book. It deftly demonstrated that the great American comic book was a suitable subject for a great American novel, and for me personally, it validated my idea that the Jewish dimension was absolutely central to that story. It received the Pulitzer Prize for literature in 2001, making it a striking bookend to the decade that began with the other Jewish "comic book" Pulitzer winner, Spiegelman's *Maus*.

Like *Maus, Kavalier & Clay* reflects the artistic coming-of-age of the post-Holocaust generation of American Jews. Also like *Maus,* it met with great popular success in addition to critical acclaim, unlike many winners of such prestigious prizes. The popularity of both has a lot to do with their audiences: The baby boomers who used to buy comics for dimes and quarters from racks at the corner store now peruse shelves of much more expensive graphic novels at major bookstores. Reading these books provides two satisfactions for the price of one: the serious pleasures of adult literature, and the guilty pleasures of revisiting the distinctive entertainment medium of one's youth. Nesting one inside the other provides pleasures of both discovery and rediscovery.

Chabon is recognized as one of his generation's major literary voices.[1] His combination of soaring creativity and linguistic precision gives us irresistible flights of imagination that are still firmly grounded. His interest in comics is partly inherited—his grandfather worked as a typographer at one of the New York plants that printed comics and he would bring them home to his son. Chabon's father later continued the tradition, bringing comics home for his children.*

After *Kavalier & Clay*, Chabon published *The Final Solution,* in which an eighty-nine-year-old man, whom one deduces to be Sherlock Holmes, confronts not just his final case but the Nazis'"Final Solution." Another detective novel is *The Yiddish Policeman's Union,* an alternative history in which the Jews settle in Alaska instead of Israel after the Holocaust, and which reads like a one-man attempt to infuse Yiddish language and culture into the American literary mainstream. On the first page we're introduced to principal character Detective Meyer Landsman (Yiddish for "someone from the same country"—that is, the Old Country back in Europe) and his investigation into a murder on Max Nordau Street (Nordau was a doctor and Zionist leader, and the principal figure associated with an early-twentieth-century movement emphasizing physical fitness training and mental discipline to create a "muscular Judaism").[2] Chabon explains his attraction to detective stories by saying it's a way of "producing the sense of mystery with a capital 'M'. This allows us to talk about things that cannot be explained. In that sense, one of the great insoluble Mysteries of the human race is the Holocaust."[3]

There's a curious aspect to the some of the critical literature about *Kavalier & Clay.* Some seem to think that because it's "serious" literature, it can't actually be about comic books, just as like-minded people rush to rescue classic books such as *Frankenstein* or *Brave New World* from consignment to the science-fiction category because they're rec-

---

* Interestingly, Spiegelman tells a similar story of his father bringing home comic books for him which he'd received from a business connection.

ognized as serious literature. The comic book aspect of *Kavalier & Clay* tends to be treated like a Hitchcockian MacGuffin. (The MacGuffin was what Hitchcock called the thing in the film that all the characters were frantically chasing after, but the audience couldn't care less about, so it could just as well have been one thing or another without making the least bit of difference to the film: diamonds, uranium, secret plans, a Maltese falcon, whatever.) Some scholarly critics treat the comic book aspect of *Kavalier & Clay* as no more than the peg on which Chabon hung his serious literary concerns, implying that any number of other pegs could equally have allowed the author to explore his themes. There are indeed some works for which this is true. Think of certain films involving sports. Sometimes which sport the film is about is basically irrelevant and the story is really only about the characters; for example when *Here Comes Mr. Jordan* was remade as *Heaven Can Wait*, it didn't make one bit of difference that the protagonist's sport changed from boxing to football. But sometimes the work demands that it be about the specific sport because it's about the interactions of these characters with precisely this sport. *Chariots of Fire* or *Personal Best* couldn't possibly have been about anything other than running track.

In the case of *Kavalier & Clay*, separating the comics part from its supposedly more "serious" ambitions does a real disservice to the work. The book is very much about the birth of comic book superheroes, and it's precisely because of this that Chabon is able to also deal with his other themes. I'm going to attempt to correct this critical error here by overcompensating in the opposite direction. I'm going to discuss it as primarily a book about the Jewish origins of comic book superheroes, which means I'm going to consciously not do justice to much of the book.

The novel begins in 1939 New York, where seventeen-year-old Jewish Brooklynite Sammy Klayman is working as a clerk in the offices of a manufacturer of cheap novelties who is also starting to publish comic books. This businessman is specifically searching for a moneymaker of a character to rival Superman. Sammy is a budding artist enamored with the pulps, and he begins to pursue an idea he has had for some time. Meanwhile, his Czech cousin Josef Kavalier arrives as a refugee from Prague. Sammy soon discovers that his cousin is a far better artist than he is. The boys get themselves hired to come up with new comics characters, Sammy taking the professional name of Sam Clay and making his cousin, the newly Americanized Joe Kavalier, swear not to tell his mother he's changed his name. As they're walking around Lower Manhattan, brainstorming about what powers their new superhero should have, Sam explains his realization that cuts to the heart of the matter. Their conversation about how they might seize the moment reveals the real reason for the birth of the superheroes, their raison d'être:

> Every little skinny guy like me in New York who believes there's life on Alpha Centauri and got the shit kicked out of him in school and can smell a dollar is out there right this minute trying to jump onto it, walking around with a pencil in his shirt pocket, saying "He's like a falcon, no, he's like a tornado, no, he's like a goddamned wiener dog," Okay?[4]

Agreeing that coming up with their character's specific powers is not the key question they have to answer, Sammy continues his train of thought, explaining why their hero must have something more distinctive about him than just being a super crime fighter who dresses strangely. There must be some animating motivation behind his actions that captures the reader's imagination. As they begin to develop their own character, Sam starts to narrate to Joe, in a radio announcer voice:

> "To all those who toil in the bonds of slavery and, uh, the, the shackles of oppression, he offers the hope of liberation and the promise of freedom!" His delivery grew more assured now. "Armed with superb physical and mental training, a crack team of assistants, and ancient wisdom, he roams the globe, performing amazing feats and coming to the aid of those who languish in tyranny's chains! He is"—he paused and threw Joe a helpless, gleeful glance, on the point of vanishing completely into his own story now—"the Escapist!"

"'The Escapist.'" Joe tried it out. It sounded magnificent to his unschooled ear—someone trustworthy and useful and strong. "He is an escape artist in a costume. Who fights crime."

"He doesn't just fight it. He frees the world of it. He frees people, see? He comes in the darkest hour. He watches from the shadows. Guided only by the light from—the light from—"

"His Golden Key."

"That's great."[5]

To think of superheroes as they were originally conceived as fundamentally being costumed crimefighters or supercops, then, is to mistake means for ends. Yes, they fight the bad guys, but not just to preserve the law and order of the status quo. They are liberators, watchfully waiting in the shadows until they emerge in the darkest hour to enable the oppressed to escape the shackles of tyranny. They are the fantasy creations of the little guys, the kids who got beat up in the neighborhood, and they fight not just for them but for their people, who are also unable to protect themselves against overpowering forces. And as we've seen in this book, over and over again, those little guys were the Jews, individually and collectively. They or their parents had come to this country like Joe Kavalier, as one of the "huddled masses yearning to breathe free," to borrow a phrase from the "The New Colossus," the famous poem inscribed at the base of the Statue of Liberty, written by Emma Lazarus, who was a New York Jew known in her lifetime principally for her efforts to combat anti-Semitism. The allusion fits well here because it's hard to imagine a more coming-to-America name than the Escapist's secret identity: Tom Mayflower.

The thing is, escape turns out to be a tricky business, not accomplished in a single bound. As we repeatedly learn in *Kavalier & Clay*, it's difficult enough to escape from life-threatening danger. But the greater and longer-lasting challenge is to escape from the escape. Chabon's characters consistently get burned as they escape from the frying pan into the fire. Arrangements are made for Joe's younger brother to escape from Prague and the Holocaust and come to America, but the ship he's on is attacked by the Germans and sunk crossing the Atlantic. Sam temporarily escapes persecution for his homosexuality by entering into a heterosexual marriage but then yearns to escape this unfulfilling relationship. Joe hides out to escape detection but then can't emerge back into the world from the prison he's created for himself. Over and over again, the solution to a problem then itself becomes a new problem.

Similarly in *Maus* Spiegelman presents a story in which his life task is to escape from an escape. In his case he needs to escape from the pall cast over his own life by what his father had to go through to escape the death trap of the Holocaust. As we've seen, as Spiegelman struggles to come to terms with his father in *Maus* he even suggests at one point that he is perhaps the real survivor in the story, or at least that he should also be accorded the status of being a survivor, the one who survived his father's survival.

This all adds up to a very Jewish warning against thinking you've ever really got it fully made, against feeling too much safety, pride, or joy. This tradition can be seen throughout Jewish ritual, even when this particular meaning doesn't stem from any formal religious doctrine. For instance, the Jewish wedding ceremony ends with the groom stomping on a glass to break it. Yes, it's a joyful noise that signals the beginning of the celebration, and the couple's married life together. But it's also said by some to be a reminder of the destruction of the ancient Temple in Jerusalem, and by others of a more mystical bent as a noise to ward off demons, because humans are said to be especially vulnerable to malevolent supernatural intervention at such times of transition (birth, marriage, death). Another example: There is a point in the Passover seder when one ritually dips a finger into a cup of wine ten times in order to spill ten drops onto his or her dinner plate. The official reason is as a commemoration of the ten plagues. But it's also said to be a reminder that even when celebrating the liberation from slavery you should be sure that your cup doesn't run over.

This sense that within every escape or liberation lies a new danger creates ongoing apprehension, resulting in an anxiety-ridden living of life at a distance once removed from one's own direct experiences, because one feels that one always needs to keep a watchful eye out to avoid being caught with one's guard down. In a sense, one ends up living even one's own life vicariously, through a glass darkly, as it were. *Maus* and *Kavalier & Clay* embody that sensibility and attempt to bring their readers to experience it as well, sharing structural similarities that at times situate their readers at points once removed from the stories they tell. Both use a story-within-a-story format for this purpose, more centrally so in the case of *Maus*, with Vladek's story embedded within Art's, but it's there in *Kavalier & Clay* too, as we get to read the adventures of the characters created by Chabon's characters. For the children of Holocaust survivors there's often a sense that it's their parents whose lives were really meaningful, that the parents' experiences define not just the survivors' generation but their children's too, whose comfortable American lives seem to them to be just a pale reflection, once removed from authentic Jewish experience. As we see here it shows up in their storytelling, with one story embedded in another or told in intermittent flashbacks.

Looking at *Kavalier & Clay* from the perspective of comic book history, one can't help but be amazed at how closely it tracks the actual history of the origins and growth of comic book superheroes. The key turning points are all here: the Lower Manhattan streets filled with the vibrant energies of the scrappy New York Jewish immigrant environment that gave birth to it all, the creators being deprived of their just financial rewards, the Kefauver Committee hearings, the ongoing lawsuits, and the early glimmer that the form could develop into something much more important than it was at the time.

Central above all else was a single cover image of Hitler sent reeling by a sock on the jaw, as Joe Kavalier's cover of the first appearance of the Escapist stands in for Jack Kirby's cover of *Captain America* #1. Chabon has altered some of the particulars, but he distills the essence of that cover and its significance. As he writes, there were "the two principals, the Escapist and Hitler," with the Escapist delivering "an immortal haymaker" that sends Hitler flying backward:

> The violence of the image was startling, beautiful, strange. It
> stirred mysterious feelings in the viewer, of hatred gratified, of

cringing fear transmuted into smashing retribution, which few artists working in America, in 1939, could have tapped so easily and effectively as Josef Kavalier.[6]

A blowup of the center of that imagined image, featuring fist explosively pounding jaw, was the design on the original hardcover publication of *The Amazing Adventures of Kavalier & Clay*. Here, in literary form, Chabon pays tribute to Jack Kirby, with Joe (originally Josef) Kavalier standing in for Kirby (originally Jacob Kurtzberg), wielding his pencil on the pulse of America on the eve of World War II. More than any other single image, that cover captures the Jewish fantasy that the comics realized.[*]

Two other legendary Jewish figures, one real and one mythical, consistently appear, disappear, and reappear throughout *Kavalier & Clay*. The first is Houdini.

The book tells us that "Houdini was a hero to little men, city boys, and Jews; Samuel Louis Klayman was all three."[7] Later, in one of the book's very few footnotes, Chabon explains:

> The still-fresh memory of Harry Houdini in the American mind thirteen years after his death—of his myth, his mysterious abilities, his physique, his feats, his dedicated hunting down of frauds and cheats—is a neglected source of the superhero idea in general; an argument in its favor, as it were.[8]

Houdini was born Erik Weisz, a rabbi's son, in Budapest in 1874 and died in 1926. While of course mostly known for his live escapes, Houdini also starred in several silent adventure films made between 1919 and 1926. Chabon is right that Houdini is a figure floating in the Jewish collective unconscious. Houdini symbolized the little man (he was indeed quite short) triumphing over looming entrapment by a newly technologized world. No contraption and especially no indus-

---

[*] Quentin Tarantino's 2009 film *Inglourious Basterds* does a good job exploring similar territory!

trialized steel could hold him—no chains, safes, handcuffs, or prison bars. He was more than a man of steel; he was a man who triumphed over steel. The image Houdini projected was an updated and immigrant version of the older American story of John Henry battling the steam engine. His most celebrated stunts were performed outdoors, where his audiences could be the working-class immigrants who embraced him as their own. He keeps showing up in the Jewish imagination. When Jack Kirby inaugurated his "Fourth World" of a new superhero mythology, most of his new heroes appeared as members of teams, and his only solo new creation was Mr. Miracle, an escape artist whose real name was Scott Free. Houdini is also a recurring figure in Jewish writer E. L. Doctorow's popular and influential novel *Ragtime*, a groundbreaking precursor of *Kavalier & Clay* in its style of telling a fictional story in which real-life characters appear. When DC was running its *Elseworlds* series of graphic novels, putting its heroes in alternative settings, one story pairing Batman and Houdini was written by Jewish comics artist and writer Howard Chaykin, who in his distinctive visual style had also created comics heroes identified as Jewish, Dominic Fortune and American (Reuben) Flagg. (The story, narrated by Houdini, has him teaching Batman a thing or two about escapes.)[9] Houdini's latest comics incarnation is as the subject of the graphic novel biography *Houdini: The Handcuff King* by Jason Lutes and Nick Bertozzi. Houdini also appears as the object of a Jewish boy's admiration in Lutes's major work, *Berlin*, an ambitious graphic novel of life in the city during the years of the Nazis' rise to power.[10] And as I write this one can visit an exhibit on "Houdini: Art and Magic" at the Jewish Museum in New York.

The other major figure of Jewish legend in *Kavalier & Clay* is the golem, who bookends the story by playing a central role at both its beginning and end. The way Josef Kavalier had escaped from the Nazis in Prague was by being hidden in the casket in which the golem was smuggled out of Prague for safety, a task assigned by the Jewish community's leaders to Josef Kavalier's instructor. Skilled in escape artistry, Bernard Kornblum was originally "from Vilna, the holy city of Jewish Europe, a place known, in spite of its reputation for hardheadedness, to harbor men who took a cordial and sympathetic view of golems."[11] The

crate mysteriously appears in New York at the end of the book, contain-
ing what had been the golem when it left Prague but is now only dirt
because he has journeyed too far from his point of origin by the banks
of the Moldau River. Once more in *Kavalier & Clay*, for all his power
even the golem couldn't escape from his escape.

In an interview, Chabon recounted an enlightening conversation he
had with Will Eisner:

I asked him why so many of the young men in the business in
the late '30s and '40s were Jews. And he gave, I guess, the standard answer—that the opportunity was just there. That if you
were a young Jewish kid who wanted to be an artist, the more
respectable forms of commercial art, illustration, advertising
art—all those fields were closed to you at the time. But comics
would take you.

But then he stopped and he said, 'But I do think there's something in the Jewish storytelling tradition that's exemplified by
the golem, this idea of an imaginary champion that is going to
come along and right all wrongs for an oppressed people.' And
that totally astonished me, because I had already written the
golem into the book, even though I had only written 70 or 80
pages. I intuitively knew there was going to be some connection
between the golem and the superhero. And to hear this pioneering creator articulate this same idea was a magic moment.[12]

Early in the novel, Joe's first attempt at creating a comic book superhero had been the golem but he didn't get to use it. In later years, he
has the original idea of a novel-length comic book, one about the golem,
that he spends years working on. When Sammy raises his concern that
it's "awfully Jewish," with not just the golem but also angels and all, Joe
responds with the most quoted line in the book: "They're all Jewish,
superheroes. Superman, you don't think he's Jewish? Coming over from
the old country, changing his name like that. Clark Kent, only a Jew
would pick a name like that for himself."[13]

In pondering why he's so attracted to the golem, Joe rejects the

Frankensteinian interpretations of the creature's nature as a monster out of control and the Faustian interpretations of its creator's overreaching ambitions. Rather, for him the creation of the golem is an attempt by human beings to join God in God's imperfect creation of life. This is a way of understanding the nature of the Creation that in acknowledging God's imperfection as well as making a place for human beings in the ongoing Creation of the world is more aligned with traditional Jewish than Christian theologies:

> The shaping of a golem, to him, was a gesture of hope, offered against hope, in a time of desperation. It was the expression of a yearning that a few magic words and an artful hand might produce something—one poor, dumb, powerless thing—exempt from the crushing strictures, from the ills, cruelties, and inevitable failures of the greater Creation. It was the voicing of a silent wish, when you get down to it, to escape.[14]

So there you have it, the secret origin of comic book superheroes revealed at last, in Joe Kavalier's interpretation of the meaning of the golem: "hope, in a time of desperation. . . . a yearning that a few magic words and an artful hand might produce . . . escape."

Throughout this book we've talked about the past of comic books. I'd like to end with a few brief thoughts about the present position of comics in our culture and my hopes for the future. Comics are a perfect embodiment of our current media moment. We are at the height of a transition from print to electronic media, from a verbal to a visual culture. The comics medium exists right at the point of synthesis of these verbal and visual modes, so it's no wonder that comics characters so thoroughly permeate popular culture. The comics form uniquely speaks to our time. With its combination of words and pictures, there's nothing that looks more like the immediate ancestor of the modern web page than the comics page. "The Internet era is friendlier to the visual story," summarizes Yirmi Pinkus, Israeli comics artist and one of the founders of the Actus collective. "The importance of the text decreases and that of the visual image increases. It is the visualization of the culture. Today everything comes with a picture, an image—and comics seep into this reality very naturally."[15] To use Stan Mack's words from his introduction to his graphic novel *The Story of the Jews: A 4,000-Year Adventure*, comics may be seen as standing "between ancient illuminated manuscripts and a modern web site."[16]

As to my hopes for the potential impact of this book, as far as I'm concerned we'll know we've made progress in reclaiming this important part of the Jewish contributions to our common cultural heritage when I can open books with titles like *Jewish Art in America* or *Jewish-American Literature* and flip to the index in the back in full confidence that I will find included there entries on comic books and graphic novels, and names like Will Eisner, Jack Kirby, Joe Kubert, and Superman.

In this book we began by exploring how Superman, an alien immigrant from another planet, got all wrapped up in the American flag, whitewashed of his ethnic origins, and eventually transformed into a contemporary icon of Christian virtue. To do so, we went behind the origin stories of the superheroes, to get at the stories behind those stories, the true-life adventures of generations of Jewish men and the super worlds they created in their comic book pages, influenced by Jewish history and traditions of the Old Country, and looking toward the future in the new world. It's a story that showed how comic book superheroes transcended their ragged origins to become major symbols of mainstream American culture, how the Jewishness of the medium came out of the closet, and how the medium of comic books and graphic novels spread its influence further in new forms of Jewish creativity.

Look! Up in the sky! It's a champion of the oppressed! It's a messianic liberator! Yes, it's the Jewish imagination in flight.

ACKNOWLEDGMENTS

My thanks to Ben Yalom for his indispensable vision and guidance in bringing this book to completion. My daughter, Artemis Brod, did the research on which part of the section on the golem in chapter 2 is based. The entire manuscript benefited from being read and commented on by Karen Mitchell and Johnanna Ganz. Comments by audience members at venues at which I presented earlier versions of parts of this book helped me clarify my ideas and convinced me there might be interest in what I had to say here. I thank these audiences and the many persons who invited me to speak and organized these events, as well as the institutions at which they were held: University of Osnabrück, Germany; University of Paderborn, Germany; Universities of Nebraska, Southern California, and Northern Iowa; Freie Universität Berlin; Humboldt University, German-American Institute of Nuremberg; Augustana College; Judaica Center, European University at St. Petersburg, Russia; Spiro Ark (Jewish Cultural Centre), London; "Kabbalah Right Now" Conference, Skidmore College; "Understanding Superheroes" Conference, University of Oregon; Jewish Museum of Florida; Reconstructionist Rabbinical College; Congregation Kehillat Israel, Pacific Palisades, California; Temple Sholom, New Milford, Connecticut; Agudas Achim Congregation, Iowa City; Ottumwa Area Arts Council, Iowa; Bettendorf Iowa Public Library; Saint John's University, Minnesota; Center for Jewish Studies, University of Minnesota; American Academy of Religion; Midwest Jewish Studies Association; Northeast Modern Language Association. Part of the research for this book was conducted during a summer fellowship and a professional development assignment granted by the University of Northern Iowa. I wish to thank my agents Sandra Dijkstra and Jill Marsal and my editors Martie Beiser and Leah Miller for their essential support and assistance. I thank Joe Kubert, Rose Kushner, and Varda Burstyn for enlightening and enjoyable conversations, and Michael Kaufman for connecting me to the latter. I thank Scott Morschhauser for his collection of Jewish comic books. Steve Bergson played an important early role in introducing me (and others) to a broader world of discourse about Jews in comics.

NOTES

INTRODUCTION

1 Jules Feiffer, *The Great Comic Book Heroes* (New York: Dial Press, 1965).
2 Stanislav Andreski, *Social Sciences as Sorcery* (London: Andrei Deutsch, 1972).
3 David Huxley and Joan Ormrod, "Editorial," *Journal of Graphic Novels and Comics* 1, no. 1 (June 2010): 1.
4 Pete Seeger, "Foreword: So Long, Woody, It's Been Good To Know Ya" in Woody Guthrie, *Bound for Glory: The Hard-Driving, Truth-Telling Autobiography of America's Great Poet-Folk Singer* (Boston: E. P. Dutton, 1943; New York: Plume/Penguin), viii. Citations refer to the Plume/Penguin edition.
1 Jack Dann, ed., *Wandering Stars: An Anthology of Jewish Fantasy & Science Fiction*, (New York: Pocket Books/Simon & Schuster, 1974); Jack Dann, ed., *More Wandering Stars: An Anthology of Outstanding Stories of Jewish Fantasy and Science Fiction* (Woodstock, VT: Jewish Lights Publishing, 1999). See also Clifford Lawrence Meth and Ricia Mainhardt, eds., *Strange Kaddish: Tales You Won't Hear from Bubbie* (Morristown, NJ: Aardwolf Publishing, 1996).
2 William Tenn, "On Venus, Have We Got a Rabbi," in Dann, *Wandering Stars*, 21–54.
3 Simcha Weinstein, *Up, Up and Oy Vey: How Jewish History, Culture, and Values Shaped the Comic Book Superhero* (Baltimore: Leviathan Press, 2006). Disclosure: I don't disagree with most of what his book says about Superman—how could I, since part of it quotes from an essay in which I presented an earlier version of the case I make in this book?
4 George Ross, *"Death of a Salesman* in the Original," in *Death of a Salesman: Text and Criticism*, ed. Gerald Weales (New York: Viking. 1967; New York: Penguin, 1977), 259–64 (page citations are to the Penguin edition).
5 Ibid., 259.
6 Ibid., 261–62.
7 Ibid., 261.
8 Arthur Miller, "Responses to an Audience Question & Answer Session," *Michigan Quarterly Review: A Special Issue on Arthur Miller*, Fall 1988, XXXVII:4, Laurence Goldstein, ed. (Ann Arbor: University of Michigan), 817–827, 821.
9 Barbara Breitman, "Lifting up the Shadow of Anti-Semitism: Jewish Masculinity in a New Light," in Harry Brod, ed., *A Mensch Among Men: Explorations in Jewish Masculinity* (Freedom, CA: Crossing Press, 1988), 107.

CHAPTER 1

1 Jerry Siegel and Joe Shuster, *Superman Archives*, vol. 1 (New York: DC Comics, 1989), 10. Previously published as *Superman* 1 (New York: DC Comics, 1939). DC Comics later engaged in historical revisionism to the extent of actually falsify-

ing the original story. When the story was reprinted in *Giant Superman Annual* 2 in 1960, the line "nothing less than a bursting shell could penetrate his skin" was changed to "not even a bursting shell could penetrate his skin." See Ted White, "The Spawn of M. C. Gaines" in *All in Color for a Dime*, ed. Dick Lupoff and Don Thompson, (New York: Ace Books, 1970), 24.

2 The story is wonderfully told by Gerard Jones in *Men of Tomorrow: Geeks, Gangsters and the Birth of the Comic Book* (New York: Basic Books, 2004), to which I am greatly indebted.

3 Arie Kaplan, "Kings of Comics: How Jews Created the Comic Book Industry, Part I: The Golden Age (1933–1955)," *Reform Judaism* 32, no. 1 (Fall 2003): 17. This article is one of a three part series that Kaplan later expanded into *From Krakow to Krypton: Jews and Comic Books* (Philadelphia: Jewish Publication Society, 2008).

4 Jay Schwartz, "Jews and the Invention of the American Comic Books," *JWeekly*, October 21, 2005, http://www.jweekly.com/article/full/27413/cover-story-jews-and-the-invention-of-the-american-comic-book/.

5 Andrew R. Heinze, *Adapting to Abundance: Jewish Immigrants, Mass Consumption, and the Search for American Identity* (New York: Columbia University Press, 1990), 207.

6 Neal Gabler, *An Empire of Their Own: How the Jews Invented Hollywood* (New York: Crown Publishers, 1988).

7 For all except Dr. Mystic see Jim Steranko, introduction to Siegel and Shuster, *Superman Archives*, vol. 6. The latter is in Greg Sadowski, ed., *Supermen: The First Wave of Comic Book Heroes 1936–1941* (Seattle: Fantagraphics Books, 2009), 12–13.

8 This background to Superman's creation came to light only in recent years. Gerard Jones reported it in *Men of Tomorrow*, and it circulated further when Brad Meltzer made it central to the plot of his novel *The Book of Lies* (New York: Grand Central Publishing, 2009), in which he provides the factual account in an author's note at the end of the book (335–336).

9 Jones, *Men of Tomorrow*, 122.

10 Sadowski, *Supermen: The First Wave of Comic Book Heroes*, 186.

11 Greg S. McCue with Clive Bloom, *Dark Knights: The New Comics in Context* (London: Pluto Press, 1993) 20–21. Quoted from Ron Goulart, *Ron Goulart's Great History of Comic Books* (New York: Harmony Books, 1976), 84.

12 Feiffer, *The Great Comic Book Heroes*, 18–21. This introduction was reprinted as a separate paperback by Fantagraphics in 2003, described as a "seminal essay of comics criticism . . . widely acknowledged to be the first book to analyze the juvenile medium of superhero comics in a critical manner, but without denying the iconic hold such works have over readers of all ages."

13 Feiffer's comic graphic novelette *Tantrum* (New York: Alfred A. Knopf, 1979) charmingly tells the story of a man who literally regresses back to childhood. His Oscar-winning short animated film *Munro* also delightfully plays with the same theme of the difficulties many people have in telling the men from the boys— Munro is a four-year-old boy mistakenly drafted into the army who struggles mightily and painfully to convince people he doesn't really belong there.

14 Jules Feiffer, "The Minsk Theory of Krypton," *New York Times Magazine*, December 29, 1996, 15.

15 Zeddy Lawrence, "Web Master," *Totally Jewish—Lifestyle Channel*, July 8, 2004, http://www.totallyjewish.com/lifestyle/features/?disp_feature=jHOskA (site discontinued).

16 Henry Louis Gates Jr., "A Big Brother from Another Planet," *New York Times*, September 12, 1993, H:51.

17 *Superman: The Sunday Classics, Strips 1-183, 1939–1943* (New York: DC Comics; Northampton, MA: Kitchen Sink Press, 1998), 2.
18 Kaplan, "Kings of Comics," 16.
19 Mark Stuart Gill, "Crisis Management," *Premiere*, April 1995, 74.
20 Paul Breines, *Tough Jews: Political Fantasies and the Moral Dilemmas of American Jewry* (New York: Basic Books, 1990), 141.
21 Daniel Boyarin, *Unheroic Conduct: The Rise of Heterosexuality and the Invention of the Jewish Man* (Berkeley, University of California Press, 1997), 2–4.
22 Feiffer, *Great Comic Book Superheroes*, 27.
23 *Superman: The Sunday Classics*, 3.
24 Frank Miller, interviewed in *Comic Book Superheroes Unmasked*, dir. Steve Kroopnick, 2003 (first aired on The History Channel, June 23, 2003).
25 "De-Jewification" is a term used by Donna Perlmutter to describe the loss of ethnicity when works such as Neil Simon's *Brighton Beach Memoirs* and Nora Ephron's *Heartburn* went from stage to screen in the '80s. See her "Jewishness Goes Back in the Closet on the Screen," *Los Angeles Times*, April 12, 1987, Calendar: 20–24.
26 *The Kents* 1–4 (New York: DC Comics, 1997). John Ostrander, Timothy Truman, Michael Bair.
27 Robert Pinsky, *The Life of David* (New York: Nextbook/Schocken, 2005).
28 Jerry Siegel and Joe Shuster, *The Superman Chronicles*, vol. 1 (New York: DC Comics, 2006), 4.
29 E. Nelson Bridwell, ed., *Superman: From the Thirties to the Seventies* (New York: Crown, 1971), 13.
30 Jim Harmon, *The Great Radio Heroes* (New York: Ace Books, 1967), 90.
31 Alan Kistler, "10 Things You Might Not Know About Superman," *Newsarama* (blog), June 22, 2010, http://www.newsarama.com/comics/superman-facts-history-100622.html.
32 Tom De Haven, *Our Hero: Superman on Earth* (New Haven, CT: Yale University Press, 2010), 24.
33 Bob Joy, ed., *The Adventures of Superboy* (New York: DC Comics, 2010).
34 Thomas Andrae and Mel Gordon, *Siegel and Shuster's Funnyman: The First Jewish Superhero, from the Creators of Superman* (Port Townsend, WA: Feral House, 2010).
35 Craig Yoe, *Secret Identity: The Fetish Art of Superman's Co-Creator Joe Shuster* (New York: Harry N. Abrams, 2009).
36 De Haven. *Our Hero*, 57.

CHAPTER 2

1 John Dominic Crossan, *The Historical Jesus: The Life of a Mediterranean Jewish Peasant* (San Francisco: HarperCollins, 1991).
2 My thanks to Betty DeBerg for emphasizing this to me.
3 Raul Hilberg, *The Destruction of the European Jews* (New York: Harper & Row, 1979), 1–4.
4 Murray Zimiles, *Gilded Lions and Jeweled Horses: The Synagogue to the Carousel* (Waltham, MA: Brandeis University Press, 2007).
5 Zimiles, *Gilded Lions*.
6 Aleksandra Shatskik, *Vitebsk: The Life of Art*, trans. Katherine Foshko Tsan (New Haven, CT: Yale University Press, 2007), inside front jacket.

NOTES

7 Shatskikh, 3.
8 James Sturm, *Market Day* (Montreal: Drawn & Quarterly, 2010).
9 Jeri Zeder, "Chagall's Political Art: The Lesser-Known Works," *Forward*, February 20, 2009, 16.
10 Zeder, "Chagall's Political Art," 28.
11 After the translation in *One Little Goat—Had Gadya*, lettered and illustrated by Betsy Platkin Teutsch (Northvale, NJ: Jason Aronson, 1990).
12 Nancy Perloff, introduction to *Had Gadya—The Only Kid: facsimile of El Lissitzky's edition of 1919*, ed. Arnold J. Band (Los Angeles: The Getty Research Institute, 2004), iv. I have based my remarks on Lissitzky's *Had Gadya* on the images in this volume.
13 Perloff, *Had Gadya*, vi.
14 Kenneth B. Moss, *Jewish Renaissance in the Russian Revolution*, (Cambridge, MA: Harvard University Press, 2009).
15 A recent elaborate and sophisticated graphic novel version is J. T. Waldman, *Megillat Esther* (Philadelphia: Jewish Publication Society, 2005).
16 Alon Raab, "Ben Gurion's Golem and Jewish Lesbians: Subverting Hegemonic History in Two Israeli Graphic Novels" in *The Jewish Graphic Novel: Critical Approaches*, eds. Samantha Baskind and Ranen Omer-Sherman (New Brunswick, NJ: Rutgers University Press, 2008), 216.
17 Ben Zion Bokser, *The Maharal: The Mystical Philosophy of Rabbi Judah Loew of Prague* (Northvale, NJ: Jason Aronson, 1994), 57.
18 Arnold L. Goldsmith, *The Golem Remembered, 1909-1980: Variations of a Jewish Legend* (Detroit: Wayne State University Press, 1981), 38.
19 Joachim Neugroschel, *The Golem: A New Translation of the Classic Play and Selected Short Stories* (New York: W. W. Norton & Company, 2006), 72.
20 Neugroschel, *The Golem*, 17 et passim.
21 Elie Wiesel, *The Golem: The Story of a Legend* (New York: Summit Books, 1983), 31.
22 Neugroschel, *The Golem*, 51.
23 Ibid., x–xi.
24 *Superman* 248 (New York: DC Comics, February 1972), 3.
25 *Superman* 258 (New York: DC Comics, November 1972), 16.
26 *Superman: The Man of Steel* 82 (New York: DC Comics, August 1988). Jon Bogdanove, Louise Simonson.
27 Eric J. Greenberg, "Is Superman 'Judenrein?'," *The Jewish Week*, June 26, 1998, http://www.thejewishweek.com/features/superman_%E2%80%98judenrein%E2%80%99.
28 James Sturm, *The Golem's Mighty Swing* (Montreal: Drawn & Quarterly, 2001).
29 Alfred North Whitehead, *Process and Reality* (New York: Free Press, 1979), 39.
30 Abraham Joshua Herschel, *The Sabbath: Its Meaning for Modern Man* (New York: Farrar, Straus and Giroux, 1951), 7.
31 See Michael Weingrad, "Why There Is No Jewish Narnia," *Jewish Review of Books* vol. 1, no. 1, (Spring 2010): 16-20.
32 Weingrad, "Why There Is No Jewish Narnia," 16.
33 Stephen D. Korshak, ed., *Frank R. Paul: Father of Science Fiction Art* (New York: Castle Books, 2010).
34 See the excellent account of the specifically Jewish aspect of this lineage, in both Yiddish and English language publications, in the early pages of Paul Buhle, ed., *Jews and American Comics: An Illustrated History of an American Art Form* (New York: New Press, 2008).
35 *Superman: The Dailies, 1939-1942* (New York: Sterling Publishing, 2006), 22.

36 This is the plot of a novel said to have influenced Siegel and Shuster, Philip Wy-
    lie's *Gladiator* (New York: Alfred A. Knopf, 1930; Lincoln: University of Nebraska
    Press, 2004).
37 Isaac Asimov, "Introduction: Why Me?", *Wandering Stars*, 17.

CHAPTER 3

1   Ted Cohen, *Jokes: Philosophical Thoughts on Joking Matters* (Chicago: University of
    Chicago, 2001), 60.
2   W. E. Burghardt Du Bois, *The Souls of Black Folk* (New York: Fawcett, 1961), 16.
3   Eddy Portnoy, "It's a Mad Mad Mad World: The Story of Mad Magazine Founder,
    Al Jaffee's Life and Ongoing Juvenilia," review of *Al Jaffee's Mad Life*, by Mary-Lou
    Weisman, *Forward*, October 1, 2010, 15.
4   Shimon Dzigan and Israel Schumacher, *The Complete Works of Dzigan and Shu-
    macher, 1935-1958*, Israel Music, 2004, three compact discs, disc 2, track 1, "Ein-
    stein, Weinstein." My translation.
5   *The Mad Archives*, vol. 1. (New York: DC Comics, 2002), 14. Previously published
    as *Mad* 1, no. 1 (New York: Educational Comics, October–November 1951).
6   Menachem Wecker, "Levine, an Artist Who Drew in Yiddish," *Forward*, January 15,
    2010, 3.
7   Gloria Steinem, *Mad Archives*, back jacket.
8   Art Spiegelman, *MetaMaus* (New York: Pantheon Books, 2011), 189.
9   Spiegelman, *MetaMaus*, 191.
10 *Mad Archives*, 109.
11 Kaplan, "Kings of Comics," 22. See Amy Kiste Nyberg, *Seal of Approval: The His-
    tory of the Comics Code* (Jackson, MS: University Press of Mississippi, 1998).
12 Harvey Kurtzman and Wallace Wood, "Superduperman," *Mad Archives*, 117–124.
13 Siano, Brian, "Tales from the Crypt—Comic Books and Censorship—The Skep-
    tical Eye," *Humanist*, March–April 1994, *http://findarticles.com/p/articles/mi_
    m1374/is_n2_v54/ai_15216386/*. Cited in "Mad (magazine)," *Wikipedia*, retrieved
    March 12, 2012, *http://en.wikipedia.org/wiki/Mad_(magazine)*.
14 Kaplan, "Kings of Comics," 21.
15 David Hajdu. *The Ten-Cent Plague: The Great Comic-Book Scare and How it
    Changed America* (New York: Farrar, Straus and Giroux, 2008), 217.
16 Stan Lee, "Stan's Soapbox By the Numbers" in *Stan's Soapbox: The Collection*, ed.
    Brian Cunningham (New York: Marvel, 2009), 137.

CHAPTER 4

1   All of these can be found in comic historian Ron Goulart's *Comic Book Culture: An
    Illustrated History* (Portland, OR: Collectors Press, 2007), 159–179.
2   Bradford W. Wright, *Comic Book Nation: The Transformation of Youth Culture in
    America* (Baltimore: The Johns Hopkins University Press, 2001), 31.
3   Brian Walker, *The Comics Before 1945* (1943; repr. New York: Harry N. Abrams,
    2004), 307. Citations refer to the 2004 edition.
4   Richard Koszarski, *Hollywood on the Hudson: Film and Television in New York from
    Griffith to Sarnoff* (New Brunswick, NJ: Rutgers University Press, 2008), 332.
5   Koszarski, *Hollywood on the Hudson*, 326.
6   Jack Burnley, Stan Kaye, Wayne Boring, Joe Shuster, John Sikela, Ed Dobrotka,
    and staff, covers of *Action Comics* 94–99, March–August 1946, reprinted in *Su-
    perman in Action Comics: Featuring the Complete Covers of the First 25 Years* (New
    York: Abbeville Press, 1993), n.p.

7 *From Superman to Spider-Man: Adventures of the Superheroes*, directed by Michel Viotte (Strasbourg, France: Kalamazoo International, ARTE France, 2002), DVD.

8 Hajdu, *The Ten-Cent Plague*, 266.

9 Wright, *Comic Book Nation*, 168–169.

10 Mark Evanier, *Wertham Was Right!* (Raleigh, NC: TwoMorrows Publishing, 2003), 176.

11 I use this story to make a slightly different point in my contribution to the "Concealed/Revealed: Goyim" section of *Jewish Currents* 64, no. 4 (Summer 2010), 66.

12 Nyberg, *Seal of Approval*, 166–169.

CHAPTER 5

1 Will Eisner, *Expressive Anatomy for Comics and Narrative: Principles and Practices from the Legendary Cartoonist* (New York: W. W. Norton, 2008), 126–131.

2 Mark Evanier, *Kirby: King of Comics* (New York: Harry N. Abrams, 2008), 22.

3 Evanier, *Kirby*, 44.

4 Jim Simon, "The 1950's Fighting Americans" in *The Simon and Kirby Superheroes*. (London: Titan Books, 2010), 176.

5 Stan Lee and Jack Kirby, *Marvel Masterworks: The Fantastic Four* (New York: Marvel Comics, 2003), 10-14. Previously printed in *The Fantastic Four* 1 (New York: Marvel Comics, 1961)

6 *Fantastic Four* 3, no. 56 (New York: Marvel Comics, August 2002). Karl Kesel and Stuart Immonen.

7 Roberto Aguirre-Sacasa and Duncan Rouleau, "The True Meaning Of . . ." in *Marvel Holiday Special 2004* (New York: Marvel Comics, January 2005).

8 *Fantastic Four* 538 (New York: Marvel Comics, August 2006).

9 Leonard Pitts, "Comic Book Character Tells Us It's OK to Be Who We Are," *Waterloo Courier*, July 1, 2002. The description as a "comic book freak" is from an August 31, 2009, radio interview on NPR's *Talk of the Nation* with Neal Conan, retrieved November 6, 2010, *http://www.npr.org/templates/story/story.php?storyId=112410699*.

10 Pitts, *Courier*, 61.

11 Evanier, *Kirby*, 122.

12 Stan Lee and George Mair, *Excelsior!: The Amazing Life of Stan Lee* (New York, Fireside, 2002), 26.

13 "5 Questions for Danny Fingeroth," *Forward*, March 9, 2012, 2.

14 Evanier, *Kirby*, 58.

15 Kathy Shaidle, posting to *jews-in-comics* (message board), October 7, 2002, http://groups.yahoo.com/group/jewishcomics/message/120.

16 Jordan Raphael and Tom Spurgeon, *Stan Lee and the Rise and Fall of the American Comic Book* (Chicago: Chicago Review Press, 2003). See also Ronin Ro, *Tales to Astonish: Stan Lee, Jack Kirby and the American Comic Book Revolution* (New York: Bloomsbury, 2004).

17 Ro, 99.

18 *The Uncanny X-Men* 199 (New York: Marvel Comics, 1985).

19 Peter Sanderson, *Ultimate X-Men* (London: Dorling Kindersley Publishing), 2000.

20 *X-Men Unlimited* 38 (New York: Marvel Comics, 2002).

21 Judith Dinowitz, posting to *jews-in-comics* (message board), June 1, 2004, http://groups.yahoo.com/group/jewishcomics/message/520.

22 Stan Lee and Steve Ditko, *Marvel Masterworks: The Amazing Spider-Man*, vol. 1 (New York, Marvel Comics, 1987), 1–14.

23 Ibid., 13.
24 Peter Sanderson, *Marvel Universe* (New York: Harry N. Abrams, 1996), 75.
25 Stan Lee, "Foreword" in Tom DeFalco, *Spider-Man: The Ultimate Guide* (London: Dorling Kindersley Publishing, 2001), 1.
26 Nacha Cattan, "Kavalier and Clay's Escapist Adventure," *Forward*, December 19, 2003, 10.
27 For those wanting a more erudite explanation, there's this (my italics): "A *shlemiel*, according to some language students, is derived from the Hebrew and means 'someone who is not from God,' while a *shlimazel*, these same self-appointed experts insist, means a person without *mazel*, or luck." Note how in the first case there's that 'El' syllable again, one of the ancient names for God, as in Kal-El, so that a schlemiel might be seen as someone lacking grace, i.e., clumsy. Some will recognize the word *mazel* from the phrase *mazel tov*, used to mean "congratulations" but literally wishing someone "good luck." David C. Gross, *Yiddish Practical Dictionary, Romanized Expanded Edition* (New York, Hippocrene Books, 1995), 120.
28 "Born Under a Bad Sign," Booker T. Jones and William Bell, 1967, *http://www.elyrics.net/read/a/albert-king-lyrics/born-under-a-bad-sign-lyrics.html*, retrieved May 10, 2012..
29 My thanks to Alexi Brod for verifying this to me in a personal conversation, July 20, 2004 in Cedar Falls, IA.
30 Thomas Winter, *Making Men, Making Class: The YMCA and Workingmen, 1877–1920* (Chicago: University of Chicago Press, 2002, 11.

CHAPTER 6

1 Mike Benton, *Masters of Imagination: The Comic Book Artists Hall of Fame* (Dallas: Taylor Publishing Company, 1994), 13.
2 Will Eisner, *Comics and Sequential Art* (Tamarac, FL: Poorhouse Press, 1985) and *Graphic Storytelling and Visual Narrative* (New York: W. W. Norton, 2008).
3 Will Eisner, *Expressive Anatomy*.
4 Thomas Andrae, *Creators of the Superheroes* (Neshannock, PA: Hermes Press, 2011), 163–165.
5 Jerry Bock and Sheldon Harnick, *Fiddler on the Roof*, book by Joseph Stein (New York: Crown, 1964), 3.
6 Andrae, *Creators*, 171–173.
7 Bob Andelman, *Will Eisner: A Spirited Life* (Milwaukee: M Press, 2005), 36.
8 Will Eisner, *The Dreamer* (New York: DC Comics, 1986), 21.
9 Eisner, *Dreamer*, 26.
10 *Will Eisner's The Spirit: A Pop-Up Graphic Novel*, Adapted by Bruce Foster (San Rafael, CA: Insight Editions, 2008).
11 Jim Steranko, *The Steranko History of Comics*, vol. 2 (Reading, PA: Supergraphics, 1972), 113.
12 Steranko, *The Steranko History*, 115.
13 Hajdu, *The Ten-Cent Plague*, 49.
14 Steranko, *The Steranko History*, 116.
15 Hajdu, *The Ten-Cent Plague*, 50.
16 Will Eisner, *A Contract with God and Other Tenement Stories* (New York: Baronet Publishing Company, 1978).
17 Eisner, *Contract*, n.p.
18 Jules Feiffer, *Tantrum* (New York: Alfred A. Knopf, 1979).

19 Max Allan Collins, "On the Road Again: Another Shamelessly Autobiographical Introduction" in *Road to Perdition 2: On the Road* (New York: Paradox Press, 2004), n.p.
20 Tim Follos, "Graphic Art: Art Spiegelman," *Express Night Out*, May 4, 2009, http://www.expressnightout.com/content/2009/05/art_spiegelman.php.
21 Elif Batuman, "Into the Eisenshpritz," *London Review of Books*, April 10, 2008, retrieved September 14, 2010, *http://www.lrb.co.uk/v30/n07/elif-batuman/into-the-eisenshpritz*. Moore's view being cited here can be found in a 2000 interview with Barry Kavanagh at http://www.blather.net/articles/amoore/northampton.html.
22 Will Eisner, *Invisible People* (New York: DC Comics, 2000).
23 Will Eisner, *A Life Force* (Princeton: Kitchen Sink Press, 1988) and *Dropsie Avenue: The Neighborhood* (New York: DC Comics, 2000).
24 Will Eisner, *Invisible People* (New York: DC Comics, 2000).
25 Will Eisner, *Fagin the Jew* (New York: Doubleday, 2003), 4.
26 Jean-Paul Sartre, *Saint Genet: Actor and Martyr* (New York: George Braziller, 1963), 59. Sartre declared, "Perhaps the book where I have best explained what I mean by freedom is, in fact, *Saint Genet*." "An Interview (1970)" in *Phenomenology and Existentialism*, ed. Robert C. Solomon (New York: Harper & Row, 1972), 513.
27 Eisner, afterword to *Fagin*, n.p.
28 Search conducted on August 1, 2010. The site promotes "Bible Believers," part of the "Believers Church," and tracks back to Cloverdale Bibleway.
29 Will Eisner, *The Plot: The Secret Story of the Protocols of the Elders of Zion* (New York: W. W. Norton, 2005).
30 Steranko, *The Steranko History*, 116.
31 Michael Chabon, introduction to *Michael Chabon Presents the Amazing Adventures of the Escapist* 1 (Milwaukie, OR: Dark Horse Comics, 2005), n.p.
32 Will Eisner, "The Escapist and the Spirit" in Chabon, *Michael Chabon Presents the Amazing Adventures of the Escapist* 6. (Milwaukie, OR: Dark Horse Comics, 2005), n.p.

CHAPTER 7

1 Trina Robbins, *From Girls to Grrlz: A History of {{female symbol}} Comics from Teens to Zines* (San Francisco: Chronicle Books, 1999), 91.
2 Miss Lasko-Gross, *Escape from "Special"* and *A Mess of Everything* (Seattle: Fantagraphics Books, 2006 and 2009).
3 Sarah Glidden, *How to Understand Israel in 60 Days or Less* (New York: DC Comics, 2010).
4 Miriam Libicki, "Jewish Memoir Goes Pow! Zap! Oy!" in Baskind and Omer-Sherman, *The Jewish Graphic Novel*, 253–273.
5 Herbert Marcuse, *Eros and Civilization: A Philosophical Inquiry into Freud* (Boston: Beacon, 1955; New York: Vintage, 1962), xvii. Citations refer to the Vintage edition.
6 Harvey Pekar and Dean Haspiel, *The Quitter* (New York: DC Comics, 2005); Harvey Pekar and JT Waldman, *Not the Israel My Parents Promised Me* (New York: Hill and Wang, 2012).
7 Harvey Pekar and Paul Buhle with Hershl Hartman, eds., *Yiddishkeit: Jewish Vernacular and the New Land* (New York: Abrams Comicarts, 2011).
8 Joe Kubert, in interview with author, Dover, NJ, August 14, 2008.
9 Bill Schelly, *Man of Rock: A Biography of Joe Kubert* (Seattle: Fantagraphics Books, 2008), 184.
10 Kubert, interview.
11 Joe Kubert *The Prophecy, Part One* (New York: DC Comics, 2006), 5.

12 Schelly, *Man of Rock*, 174.
13 Ibid., 173.
14 Joe Kubert, e-mail message to author, December 7, 2010.
15 *Ragman* 1, no. 3 (New York: National Periodical Publications, December–January 1976–1977).
16 *Ragman* 3 (New York: DC Comics, December 1991), 4. Plot and breakdowns by Keith Giffen, script by Robert Loren Fleming, art by Pat Broderick.
17 Joe Kubert, *The Adventures of Jaakov and Isaac* (Jerusalem: Mahrwood Press, 2004).
18 Joe Kubert, *Fax from Sarajevo: A Story of Survival* (Milwaukie, OR: Dark Horse Press, 1996), 29.
19 Kubert, *Fax*, 80.
20 Joe Kubert, *Jew Gangster* (New York: ibooks, 2005), 28, 79. The book is often cited with the subtitle *A Father's Admonition*, but this doesn't appear in the book itself.
21 *Brownsville*, written by Neil Kleid and drawn by Jake Allen (New York: NBM, 2006).
22 *Caper*, nos. 1–12, written by Judd Winick, illustrated by Farel Dalrymple, John Severin and Tom Fowler (New York: DC, 2003–2004).
23 Rich Cohen, *Tough Jews: Fathers, Sons and Gangster Dreams* (New York: Simon & Schuster, 1998); Rachel Rubin, *Jewish Gangsters of Modern Literature* (Champaign: University of Illinois Press, 2000); Warren Rosenberg, *Legacy of Rage: Jewish Masculinity, Violence, and Culture* (Amherst: University of Massachusetts Press, 2001); Elliott Horowitz, *Reckless Rites: Purim and the Legacy of Jewish Violence* (Princeton: Princeton University Press, 2006).
24 Joe Kubert, *Yossel: April 19, 1943. A Story of the Warsaw Ghetto Uprising* (New York: ibooks, 2003).
25 Kubert, *Yossel*, 23.
26 Ibid., 24.
27 Ibid.
28 Kubert, interview.
29 Kubert, *Yossel*, 118.
30 Ibid., 119.
31 "The Stroop Report: The Warsaw Ghetto Is No More," teletype message of May 8, 1943, Jewish Virtual Library, retrieved December 5, 2010, *http://www.jewishvirtuallibrary.org/jsource/Holocaust/nowarsaw.html*.
32 Kubert, introduction to *Yossel*, 3.
33 Pascal Croci, *Auschwitz* (New York: Harry N. Abrams, 2003).
34 George Gene Gustines, "Comic-Book Idols Rally to Aid a Holocaust Artist," *New York Times*, August 9, 2008, A17, 23.
35 Neal Adams, "Will Eisner: An Appreciation" in Andelman, 23.

CHAPTER 8

1 Art Spiegelman, letter to the editor, *New York Times Book Review*, December 29, 1991, 4. Cited in James E. Young, "The Holocaust as Vicarious Past: Art Spiegelman's 'Maus' and the Afterimages of History," *Critical Inquiry* 24, no. 3 (Spring 1998): 697, retrieved December 19, 2010, http://www.jstor.org/stable/1344086.
2 Spiegelman, *MetaMaus*, 208.
3 Ibid., 73.
4 Adrienne Rich, "Split at the Root: An Essay on Jewish Identity" in *Blood, Bread and Poetry: Selected Prose 1979–1985* (New York: W. W. Norton, 1986), 100.

5   Art Spiegelman, *Maus: A Survivor's Tale*, vol. 1, *My Father Bleeds History* (New York: Pantheon Books, 1986), 110.
6   Art Spiegelman, *Maus: A Survivor's Tale*, vol. 2, *And Here My Troubles Began*, (New York: Pantheon Books, 1991), 46.
7   I have written of this in my life in "The Lasting Legacy of Temporary Survival" in *Second Thoughts: Critical Thinking from a Multicultural Perspective*, ed. Wanda Teays (Mountain View, CA: Mayfield, 1996), 336–340.
8   Spiegelman, *Maus*, vol. 1, 100.
9   Ibid., 109.
10 Ibid., 159.
11 Spiegelman, *Maus*, vol. 2, 136.
12 Ibid., 42.
13 Ibid., 43.
14 Spiegelman, *Maus*, vol. 1, 5.
15 Arthur Miller, *Death of a Salesman* (New York: Viking, 1949; New York: Penguin, 1976), 107. Citations refer to the Penguin edition.
16 Spieglman, *MetaMaus*, 165.
17 Art Spiegelman, "Maus" in *Breakdowns: Portrait of the Artist as a Young %@&*!* (New York: Pantheon, 2008), n.p.
18 Art Spiegelman, *In the Shadow of No Towers* (New York: Pantheon, 2004), 3.
19 Spiegelman, *MetaMaus*.
20 Ibid., 6.
21 Ibid., 37.
22 Ibid., 200.
23 Ibid., 49.
24 Ibid., 155.
25 Ibid., 155, 159.

CHAPTER 9

1   Joann Sfar, *The Rabbi's Cat* and *The Rabbi's Cat 2* (New York: Pantheon, 2005 and 2008).
2   Sfar, *The Rabbi's Cat*, 24–25.
3   Joann Sfar, *Klezmer Book One: Tales of the Wild East* (New York: First Second, 2006).
4   Sfar, notes in *Klezmer*, V.
5   Joann Sfar, *Vampire Loves*, trans. Alexis Siegel (New York: First Second, 2006), 99.
6   Joann Sfar, *Little Vampire Goes to School* (New York: Simon & Schuster, 2003), n.p.
7   Campbell Robertson, "Children's Books; with Rabbi Solomon, Kung Fu Master." *New York Times*, October 19, 2003, retrieved October 24, 2010, http://www.nytimes.com/2003/10/19/books/children-s-books-with-rabbi-solomon-kung-fu-master.html.
8   Ann Miller, *Reading Bande Dessinée: Critical Approaches to French-language Comic Strip* (Chicago: Intellect Books/University of Chicago Press, 2007), 63.
9   Bart Beaty, *Unpopular Culture: Transforming the European Comic Book in the 1990s* (Toronto: University of Toronto Press, 2007), 188.
10 "Interview: Joann Sfar, Prolific Author," retrieved October 29, 2010, http://www.pacome.be/wordpress. My translations from the French.
11 Joann Sfar, *The Little Prince: Adapted from the book by Antoine de Saint-Exupéry* (Boston: Houghton Mifflin Harcourt, 2010).
12 Michael D. Picone, "Teaching Franco-Belgian *Bande Dessinée*" in *Teaching the*

Graphic Novel, ed. Stephen E. Tabachnick (New York: The Modern Language Association of America, 2009), 310.

13 Vittorio Giardino, *A Jew in Community Prague*, vol. 1, *Loss of Innocence* (trans. Jacinthe Leclerc), vol. 2, *Adolescence* (trans. Jacinthe Leclerc and Joe Johnson), vol. 3, *Rebellion* (trans. Joe Johnson) (New York: NBM, 1997, 1997, 1998.)

14 Sid Jacobson and Ernie Colón, *Anne Frank: The Anne Frank House Authorized Graphic Biography* (New York: Hill and Wang, 2010). Eric Heuvel, *A Family Secret*, trans. Lorraine T. Miller (Zaandam, the Netherlands: Anne Frank House/Resistance Museum Friesland, 2005). Eric Heuvel, Ruud van der Rol, Lies Schippers, *The Search*. trans. Lorraine T. Miller (New York: Farrar Strauss Giroux, 2009).

15 Rutu Modan, *Exit Wounds* (Montreal: Drawn & Quarterly, 2007).

16 Batia Kolton, Itzik Rennert, Rutu Modan, Anke Feuchtenberger, Mira Friedmann, Yirmi Pinkus, *Happy End: Graphic Novellas*, trans. Jesse Mishory (Tel-Aviv: Actus Independent Comics, 2002). Rutu Modan, *Jamilti and Other Stories* (Montreal: Drawn & Quarterly, 2008).

17 Tomer Hanuka, *The Placebo Man* (Gainesville, FL: Alternative Comics, 2006). Koren Shadmi, *In the Flesh* (New York: Villard, 2009).

18 Etgar Keret and Actus Comics, *Jetlag: 5 Graphic Novellas*, trans. Dan Ofri (New Milford, CT: The Toby Press, 1998).

19 Todd McEwen, "Plastic People," review of *Missing Kissinger*, by Etgar Keret, *The Guardian*, March 24, 2007, retrieved November 20, 2010, *http://www.guardian. co.uk/books/2007/mar/24/featuresreviews.guardianreview21*.

20 Etgar Keret and Asaf Hanuka, *Pizzeria Kamikaze*, trans. Miriam Shlesinger (Gainesville, FL: Alternative Comics, 2006).

21 Kenneth Turan, quoted on *Waltz with Bashir*, directed by Ari Folman (Strasbourg, France: Bridgit Folman Film Gang, Les Films D'ici, Razor Film Produktion, Arte France and Noga Communications—Channel 8, 2008; Sony Pictures Classics, 2009), DVD, back cover of box.

22 Folman, *Waltz with Bashir*.

CHAPTER 10

1 Helene Meyers, *Reading Michael Chabon* (Santa Barbara, CA: Greenwood/ABC-CLIO, 2010), 1.

2 Michael Chabon, *The Yiddish Policeman's Union* (New York: HarperCollins, 2007).

3 From a post on *SugarBombs* (blog) retrieved December 26, 2010, http://www.sugarbombs.com/kavalier/?page_id=4. The article originally appeared in *Stuff* (Australia), April 2005.

4 Michael Chabon, *The Amazing Adventures of Kavalier & Clay* (New York: Random House, 2000), 94.

5 Chabon, *Kavalier & Clay*, 121.

6 Ibid., 150.

7 Chabon, *Kavalier & Clay*, 3.

8 Ibid., 120.

9 *Batman/Houdini: The Devil's Workshop* (New York: DC Comics, 1993), written by Howard Chaykin and John Francis Moore, art by Mark Chiarello.

10 Jason Lutes and Nick Bertozzi, *Houdini: The Handcuff King* (New York: Hyperion, 2007).

11 Chabon, *Kavalier & Clay*, 15.

12   From a post on *SugarBombs*, retrieved December 26, 2010, *http://www.sugarbombs.com/kavalier/?page_id=13.* The article originally appeared in *Publisher's Weekly*, August 2000.
13   Chabon, *Kavalier & Clay*, 585.
14   Ibid., 582.
15   Nirit Anderman, "Getting Into the Picture," *Haaretz*, December 8, 2008, retrieved December 30, 2010, *http://www.haaretz.com/culture/arts-leisure/getting-into-the-picture-1.251570.*
16   Stan Mack, *The Story of the Jews: A 4,000-Year Adventure* (Woodstock, VT: Jewish Lights Publishing, 2001), xiv.

ABOUT THE AUTHOR

DR. HARRY BROD is professor of sociology and humanities at the University of Northern Iowa. He lectures extensively at many colleges and universities, regularly consults for media and other institutions, and serves on the editorial boards of several journals. Dr. Brod served as director of the Iowa Regent Universities Men's Gender Violence Prevention Institute, and on the board of directors of Humanities Iowa. He received the Harry Cannon Award for Exemplary and Sustained Contributions to the Field of Men's Studies from the American College Personnel Association's Standing Committee for Men, as well as the Leadership and Service Award from the Men's Center of Saint John's University (Minnesota), and held a fellowship in law and philosophy at Harvard Law School. He has appeared on *CNN, Today, Geraldo,* and other TV and radio programs, been interviewed in *Newsweek, Rolling Stone, The Wall Street Journal, The New York Times, Los Angeles Times, The Chronicle of Higher Education,* and other publications, and his articles have been published in many journals and popular magazines. His previous books are *A Mensch Among Men: Explorations in Jewish Masculinity, Brother Keepers: New Perspectives on Jewish Masculinity, The Making of Masculinities: The New Men's Studies, Theorizing Masculinities, White Men Challenging Racism: 35 Personal Stories, The Legacy of the Holocaust: Children and the Holocaust,* and *Hegel's Philosophy of Politics: Idealism, Identity, and Modernity.* A DVD of his lecture "Asking for It: The Ethics and Erotics of Sexual Consent" is distributed by Media Education Foundation. He is the father of two children.